Southern West Cameroon Revisited (1950-1972)
Volume One
Unveiling Inescapable Traps

Anthony Ndi

Langaa Research & Publishing CIG
Mankon, Bamenda

Publisher:
Langaa RPCIG
Langaa Research & Publishing Common Initiative Group
P.O. Box 902 Mankon
Bamenda
North West Region
Cameroon
Langaagrp@gmail.com
www.langaa-rpcig.net

Distributed in and outside N. America by African Books Collective
orders@africanbookscollective.com
www.africanbookcollective.com

ISBN: 9956-791-44-X

© Anthony Ndi 2014

DISCLAIMER

All views expressed in this publication are those of the author and do not necessarily reflect the views of Langaa RPCIG.

To the unsung patriots and heroes, whose names are enshrined in these pages, that the eternal ideals for which they burnt out their lives may remain radiant beacons for Cameroon posterity.

About this Book

This book contributes to discussions on the topical issue of "Fifty Years after the independence of the Southern Cameroons", by taking a critical look at the process that lead up to Southern Cameroons' 'reunification' with *la République du Cameroun*. This was the period spanning from 1951 to 1961, and possibly up to 1972. This immediately conjures two overriding factors; first, the British colonial policy in Southern Cameroons, which dominated political life in the period leading up to: the Plebiscite, the Buea Tripartite Conference, the Bamenda All Party Conference, the Foumban Constitutional Conference and the Yaounde Tripartite Conference during the phase, 1959-1961. This constituted one huge hoax, whilst that from 1961-1972 and, beyond was dominated by the enigmatic figure of President Ahrnadou Ahidjo. At the heart of the first, are the declassified British secret papers which have uncovered the ugly undercurrents that characterised British colonial policy, while on the other hand, is President Ahmadou Ahidjo, who practically personalized the administration of the Federal Republic of Cameroon. His domination of the entire existence of the Federal Republic of Cameroon, (1961-1972) was overshadowed by the fact that he could not brood sharing power with any individual or institution. Simply put, he was allergic to democratic principles-or any form of opposition to his authority. As well, he was a matchless dictator especially in his ambivalent dealings with Southern West Cameroon. Apparently, it was the "destiny" of Southern Cameroons 'that up to 1961, it was harnessed to the tenterhooks of Great Britain and from 1961-1972, transferred to those of the Ahidjo Regime; neither of which wished its people well.

Praise for this Book

"In his new work, Anthony Ndi bombards us with exciting new revelations about the events leading up to the reunification of Cameroon and beyond. What counts for many still today as a tragic historical memory, is given substance and cause in his careful analysis of the sources available, now reinforced by new materials released since 2012 from the archives of the UK Foreign Commonwealth Office. Ndi's focus on the personalities of the major players leading to the breaking of the promise made by the British to support independence for Southern Cameroons and the subsequent plebiscite decision to re-join La République du Cameroun, enriches our understanding of the mixture of shrewd tactics by and naive blunders of the many that actually shaped events. As a case study in the realities of how decisions were made and later regretted in a period of quite shameful indiscretion, we are given a salutary account of how a history that hitherto had been written from the standpoint of the victor, needed to be and here is rewritten from that of the vanquished."

Michael Rowlands, Emeritus Professor of Anthropology and Material Culture, University College London

"A monumental treatise with startling revelation on Cameroons' national history, written with superb confidence suitable in the circumstance of celebrations marking the Golden Jubilee of Southern Cameroons independence- mature times enough for the inescapable traps of its history to be unveiled and unleashed for posterity."

Professor Tafah Edokat Oki Edward, Vice Chancellor, University of Bamenda

"Writing a foreword to a book written by a luminous historiographer like Anthony Ndi can be exciting and challenging. Exciting because it gives on the opportunity to discover new facts and appreciate new techniques in the state of the art of historiography. In the same instance, presenting a foreword to a study of this calibre is challenging.

Challenging because the historical plot espoused by the author resides in a setting of controversies where the tension between the force of argument and the argument of force seem to be conspicuously evident and where rhetoric and reality stand astride"

Mathew Basung Gwanfogbe, PhD, Associate Professor of History, University of Bamenda.

"This book by Anthony Ndi argues forcefully and convincingly that Ahidjo's 'bad faith' and determination to introduce a centralized personal authoritarian rule largely explains the failure of the Federal Republic of Cameroon… without a fair trial period"

Professor Tazoacha Asonganyi, University of Yaounde I

About the Author

Anthony Ndi pursued Bed(Hons) History at the University of Ibadan, Nigeria, and proceeded to the School of Oriental and African Studies (SOAS), University of London for the MA and PhD in African History, He was the Registrar and Head of the History Department at the Bamenda University of Science and Technology (BUST) for eight years and currently is the Deputy Vice Chancellor for Research and Cooperation and Head of the History Department in the Catholic University of Cameroon (CATUC), Bamenda. He is Visiting Lecturer at the Universities of Buea and Bamenda. Anthony Ndi is Associate Professor of History and has published numerous articles and books. He belongs to several professional history and related associations and currently is Associate Editor of *Pan-Tikar Journal of History* of the University of Bamenda. He has a passion for historical research.

Table of Contents

Acknowledgements xi
Foreword xiii
Preface xv
Abbreviations xxiii
Introduction xxxiii
List of Photographs xxxv

Chapter 1: Independence And Reunification: An Analysis Of Basic Issues 1
A Historical Panorama 1
Double British Standards 3
A Broad Analysis of the Issues 6
The Paradox 8
Southern Cameroons Refused Independence 8
Nature, Reason and Shape of Reaction 12
Milne's Revelations Revolutionize Cameroon History 15

Chapter 2: Reunification Account: Setting Basic Records Straight 23
Golden Jubilee Celebrations Whet Appetites 23
Distinction of the Summit Magazine interview 25
The Response: Inherent Limitations 27
Reunification: Certainly, Not a "Gamble"! 29
Best Decision Everything Being Equal 31
Forging a Unique Identity 33
Southern Cameroons: Political Maturity 34
 Special UNTC Status and Privileges 35
A Case of Sheer 'Bad Faith' 37
Two Critical Omissions and a Flawed Target 40
Victims, Predators and Oppressors 41
The "Royal Presidency of Alhadji Ahmadou Ahidjo" 44

Chapter 3: Southern Cameroons: Political Maturity 49
An Evolved Political Culture 49

Qualifications and Political Leadership..52
A Distinct Southern Cameroons Political Culture.............................57
Peaceful, Harmonious Transfer of Power in 1959...........................58
The Sagacity of Traditional Rulers..59
High Calibre Political Leaders: Products of their Time....................61
"Maquizzards", Rebels, Nationalists, or Freedom Fighters..............65
'Jocular' Not Bloody Fights... 70
Political Leaders: Past, Present and Global.. 71
Visionary Leaders: Simple, Austere, Honest and Realistic................73
Malcolm Milne Pays Glowing Tribute to Foncha Cabinet.............. 74
A Unique Southern Cameroons Civil Service......................................75
Cameroonisation...77

Chapter Four: The Plebiscite: Litmus Test Of Political Maturity.. 81
Origins of the Plebiscite... 84
The Mamfe Plebiscite Conference 10-11 August 1959..................... 85
Role of Kamerun Students Unions..87
Plebiscite: Basic Irreconcilable Positions..89
The UN Debate: A Catch 22 Scenario..90
Plebiscite Questions: Reasons and Genesis..95
The Plebiscite in Context: Statistical Analysis......................................99
 Invisible Hand of British Colonial Administration..........................100
Consistent Voting Patterns in Favour of Secession..........................101
British Support: Remarkable Suggestive Trends............................... 103
Best Solution Obstructed by Britain..107
Conclusion.. 111

Chapter 5: The Constitutional Marathon, From Bamenda to Foumban.. 115
The Bamenda All Party Conference: 26-28 June 1961......................115
Endeley Refrained from Attending Bamenda Conference............... 118
Ndeh Ntumazah: Opponent and Critic... 118
"Unanimous Endorsement at Bamenda"..120
Foumban Constitutional Conference: 16-21 July 1961..................... 121
Representation at the Conference..123
Reception at Foumban.. 125

President Ahidjo Opens the Conference..................................126
Foncha Speaks for Southern Cameroons Delegation..................130
Endeley for Reconciliation..132
Fuelling Conspiracy Theories: "Endeley Exclusions"................. 133
Time Extended for Anglophone Delegates............................... 136
Thoroughness and Harmony...137
Closing Remarks..139
"Foumban Conference in Complete Agreement"...................... 140
Fonlon Facilitates Serene Procedure.. 141

Chapter 6: Foumban: Beyond The Constitutional Conference..143
Contemporary Observations on Foumban Accord...................143
Mukong: Critical of Britain and the UN.................................. 143
President Ahidjo's Magnanimity.. 144
Equality Clause: Reunification a Political Decision...................145
Devolution in Point of Law..145
Pertinent, Sober Reflections with Hindsight............................147
Albert Mukong: Pertinent View.. 148
Nerius N Mbile Favours Centralisation................................... 149
Emmanuel Egbe: Reflections on Foumban............................... 151
Foncha: Star of Foumban, Awards and Decorations................. 152
Foncha: Civil and Municipal Decorations................................ 154
The Setting: Significance.. 155
Other Awards, Tributes and Decorations................................. 156
Penultimate Conclusion..157
Beyond the "Glitter and Glamour of Foumban........................158
Doubts Cast about Security.. 158
Choice of Foumban: A Contrary View.................................... 160
Alleged massive 'Corruption' and Deceit................................. 161
Anglophones Delegates Opportunely Undeceived!...................163
A ramified conclusion.. 168

Chapter 7: Foncha's Waterloo: "Secret Deals and Hidden Constitution"..171
Smear Campaigns and Conspiracy theories..............................171
KNDP-UC joint committee.. 174

Concerted determination to teach Foncha a lesson......................... 175
The so-called 'Secret Deal': Sources... 177
Buea Tripartite Conference: Proceedings and Impact.....................182
Embarrassing disagreements...186
Open collusion between British and the Republic of Cameroon Delegations.. 191
Buea Tripartite Conference: Lamentable Future.............................194
Conclusion... 197

Chapter 8: Indictments: Foncha Opposed Southern Cameroons... 199
Brash unsubstantiated accusations..199
'Independence' Foncha's Passion.. 201
KNDP Ideology: "Independence before Reunification"..................206
Double British standards...208
Towards provoking Civil Strife... 212
John Ngu Foncha: Sketch biography.. 217
The Professional Teacher...218
Launching into Political Life...218
Member of Parliament and Party Leader..219
Socio-Cultural and Spiritual Life: House Arrest, Trapped!.............220
Foncha as observed in his Nkwen home town.................................223
Conclusion... 225

Chapter 9: Malcolm Milne or "Dr.Jerkyll and Mr.Hyde"   227
The 'Nadir': Malcolm Milne Awful disclosures............................... 227
Dread of Destitution..230
Harold Macmillan: "Wind of Change Address".............................231
Malcolm and Field innately idiosyncratic..233
Malcolm Milne pays generous tributes to civil servants..................235
Remorse and Regret... 237
Phillipson's Appointment: Seals Fate of Southern Cameroons....... 239
Independence Excluded as Plebiscite Option.................................. 242
Phillipson: Constitutional and Economic adviser............................ 243
Open support for KNC/KPP alliance...244
Deadly Traps:Withdrawal of British Troops....................................246
Milne and Foncha: "No Love Lost"..249

Malcolm Milne takes seriously ill..252
Wrapping up..253
Malcolm Millne sets final seal on Conspiracy Theories.....................254
Milne and Ahidjo: Accomplices over Southern Cameroons............256

Postscript..259
Epilogue... 265
Appendices (I-IV)..283
Bibliography..315
Index..321

Acknowledgments

This book has been realized with noteworthy contributions from several institutions and individuals. Among these, are public archives including: the National Archives, Buea (NAB), the Regional Archives, Bamenda (RAB) and the Saint Thomas Aquinas Major Seminary (STAMS) Archives and Library, Bambui. Further to these, I was privileged to be granted access to the rare private archives of the Foncha Family, Nicholas Ade Ngwa's scrap book, and the personal papers of Francis Nkwatoh, John Mofor Ndi (Late), Hon Joseph Kwi, Nelson Ngayinkfu and, a priceless collection of papers from Professor Verkijika G. Fanso. In addition to these contributions I also had in-depth discussions with many of these people and dozens of others acknowledged in the text. Primus Forgwe and his assistants went to great lengths in rendering me inestimable assistance at the National Archives in Buea.

Above all, this work has greatly been enriched by the individual and collective, open, critical observations and discussions with the entire faculty of the Department of History, Higher Teachers' Training College (HTTC) of The University of Bamenda (UBa) from among whom mention may be made of Professors Mathew B. Gwanfogbe and Simon N. Tata; Doctors Canute Ngwa, Nixon K. Takor, Michael K. Lang and Kingsley A. Ollong. Equally, I make special mention of my colleagues, Professor Charles Alobwed'Epie and Rev. Professor Anthony Yilaka of the Catholic University of Cameroon (CATUC), Bamenda, who did an x-ray of the manuscript, while Professor Tozoacha Asongnyi of the University of Yaoundé I has significantly enhanced the argument by his insightful contribution in the preface.

Dr. Emmanuel Y. Sobseh of the Department of History, HTTC, UBa besides repeatedly and critically reading through the manuscript was part of the production process, while Dr. Walter G. Nkwi of the Department of History, University of Buea shadowed me throughout the process from conception to conclusion. I have taken the liberty to exclude persons whose names are already cited in the text.

Research assistance and secretarial processing was amply provided by a diligent team comprising: Mado Kichuisi, Henry Yombo, Marina

Titu Nfor, Lilian Biih and Manuela Kamga. An exceptional spouse, over this exercise Mrs. Patience L. Ndi further distinguished her talents as a keen and critical proof reader. I cannot find appropriate words to express my profound indebtedness to these dedicated and selfless folks without whose individual and collective contributions this book would hardly have seen the light of day. However, finally, alone, I take full responsibility for its final realisation.

Foreword

Writing a foreword to a book written by a luminous historiographer like Anthony Ndi can be exciting and challenging. Exciting because it gives one the opportunity to discover new facts and appreciate new techniques in the state of the art of historiography. In the same instance, presenting a foreword to a study of this calibre is also challenging. Challenging because the historical plot espoused by the author resides in a setting of controversies where the tension between the force of argument and the argument of force seem to be conspicuously evident and where rhetoric and reality stand astride. The study is premised in a context of disdain and suspicion on apologetic historical axioms where poles of adherence share opinions and shades facts. This makes the author to think that "political action in society oscillates between lived experience, reflection on lived experience and conception". In whatever case, it is in his judgment that the architect of historical construction is very powerful, indomitable, and is capable of achieving any aim he sets for himself". It is with this objective that the author re-visits central debates in Cameroon's political history especially those pegged around the events prior to, during and after the reunification between British Southern Cameroons and the Republic of Cameroon.

Interestingly, the author has drawn evidence from the same sources used by other historians to bring in fresh insights to what he terms "the persistent stigmatization of Dr. John Ngu Foncha", a key factor and actor in Cameroon's political history. A case in time is the "Alleged Secret Deals and hidden documents saga between Foncha and Ahidjo in Cameroon history where extensive references are made to Malcom Milne's No Telephone to Heaven... but where thorough investigations produce divergent results.

Here comes a historical muse that gives an incisive flash back of events in pre-independence Cameroon and chains up with developments leading to the birth and death of the federal and unitary states in Cameroon. In length and breadth, the author has quarried most of what constitute useful data to provide and reorient the sense of interpretation of what remains in living history as "the inescapable traps of the reunification tale". The book, Revisiting Southern Cameroons 1951-1972: Unveiling Inescapable Traps is a new rendition of Cameroon history where facts, clear and unbridled as they are, straight and uncheckered as they appear, bring new evidences to hitherto uncharted investigations. The author responds with lucidity and precision to what runs in shady or anti-scientific opinions in extra-academic circles and what can be termed uncritical or tangential reasoning in scholarly circles.

The author with very untainted insight places his investigation within the ambit of controversies, ambivalences, ambiguities as well as emotional and apologetic historiography surrounding the process of reunification in Cameroon. It is an abysmal investigation where individual interests are discarded for the sake of historical objectivity. The book undoubtedly deepens appreciation in Cameroon's national history as it canvasses the centrality of the process of reunification with the aim of giving it a sense of purpose and relevance. This book coming at a time when the nation is celebrating its Golden Jubilee is valued for its distinctive artistic style which is simple and eloquent and for its contents which is original and critical in shaping truncated facts.

The actor-oriented approach used by the author, in most parts, where the voices of the key players of the reunification process are brought to the fore, understood in their context and analysed to dispel contravening circumstances is perhaps the yardstick that makes this authoritative source of historical writing, a must read stuff. In very unequivocal sense, this book is a cornerstone in the era of historiographical renaissance in Cameroon. At the same time, it is going to provoke much more insightful research.

Mathew Basung Gwanfogbe, PhD,
Associate Professor of History,

Preface

Let me start this preface with a quote from "God's Little Devotional Book for Graduates."

> When Honorius was Emperor of Rome, the great Coliseum was often filled to overflowing with spectators who came from far and wide to watch the state-sponsored games. Part of the sport venue consisted of human beings doing battle with wild beasts or with one another, to the point where one was killed. The assembled multitude made holiday of such sport and found the greatest delight when a human being died. On just such a day, a Syrian monk named Telemachus was part of the vast crowd in the arena. Telemachus was cut to the core of his heart by the utter disregard he saw for the value of human life. He leaped from the spectator stands into the arena during a gladiatorial show and cried out, "This thing is not right! This thing must stop!" Because he had interfered, the authorities commanded that Telemachus should be run through with a sword, which was done. He died, but not in vain. His cry kindled a small flame in the nearly burnt out conscience of the people and within a matter of months the gladiatorial combats came to an end. The greater the wrong, the louder we must cry out against it. The finer the cause, the louder we must applaud.[1]

Following the reunification/unification of the two Cameroons on October 1, 1961, and the derailment of the intended purpose of the project, Fonlon, Foncha, Jua, Gorji Dinka, Mukong, and many others kept shouting from the public arena: "This thing is not right! This thing must stop!" Some of them explained with anger, passion and persuasion that what was being done to erase the history of Southern Cameroons from the bosom of the new country of October 1, 1961 would inevitably affect the endurance of the unification mission. They said that the reunification agenda would crumble from the weight of

---

[1] "God's Little Devotional Book For Graduates."

the apparent ignorance and conceit of nationalists of "Republic of Cameroon." In response, those who were in charge sent some of them to jail; others like Foncha were just pushed aside with arrogance and disdain.

Number 16 of Summit Magazine (April- June 2011) carried an interview with Professor Victor Julius Ngoh, the Deputy Vice Chancellor for Research and Cooperation, University of Buea on the subject, "Reunification Fifty Years After." The interview seemed to tell Southern Cameroonians in a veiled manner that it is their fault that they are suffering the fate they are suffering in the united Cameroon today, since they are the ones who put the rope around their own neck and handed the end to those they are complaining about today! This book by Anthony Ndi is a mark of the seriousness with which the academic community has taken his comments. The book titled "Southern Cameroons Revisited, 1950-1972: Unveiling Inescapable Traps," presents the facts of the matter from an "insider" perspective. Indeed, the book can be said to be another shout from the open arena: "This thing is not right! This thing must stop!"

In one of the themes in the book, Anthony Ndi discusses "Methodology: the nature of history." A science can only consider itself a science if its tenets are universally applicable. History is usually said to be the province of selfless servants of the truth. Truth is universal, and is unchanged by the fact of being known by one, many or none. Diversity cannot be applied to the truth, since there can be no multiple or diverse truths. There could be many possible interpretations of the truth, but some things are simply not true. A lie is a lie, no matter how loudly it is argued or how persuasively it is phrased. In historical and scientific discussions it is possible to overemphasize the achievement of some people, and downplay those of others; most historians write with some amount of bias – that is why history must always be rewritten. Although not all bias amounts to distortion, it is clear that the approach of the Summit Magazine interview results in a serious distortion of the truth about Foncha's achievements as a leader of the Southern Cameroons struggle. In history, it is important and necessary to support with facts and evidence, texts or formulae, what one says about a subject. The purpose such rigour, at least in academe, is to ensure that history does not become a vehicle for indoctrination and manipulation of public opinion.

Hindsight usually enjoys more knowledge than is available at decision point. Memory is usually known to play many tricks on some historians and actors. So from the vantage point of hindsight many journalists and historians usually construct their theories using paper-thin foundations of interviews and sources to allow them to revise their initial wisdom long discredited by unfolding events. For the same reasons, many details in personal memoirs are usually not even slips of memory but self-serving fiction. The scientific method requires that such "sources" be treated with caution.

It usually takes only one commanding personality per generation to change a city, a state, a nation. Such personalities rise above the flow of events only when thrust up by forces under the surface. A rare personality like Foncha that was thrust up by the urge for independence of Southern Cameroons and its reunification with the Republic of Cameroon definitely altered the direction of many forces in society at that time. He succeeded to steer events towards the course he wanted. He changed the course of events, meaning that his personality had a vitality that moved history. Like many such personalities in history, he was carried up or borne down by forces outside himself. It is known that every human being has both a weak and needy part of their soul, and a part of their soul that is strong and filled with resolve. To treat Foncha as if he lacked this duality, and was only weak and needy is unfair. This work by Anthony Ndi allows not only the academic world but also every interested party to crosscheck some "facts" about Foncha and reach more valid conclusions than has been possible before now.

History usually unfolds as humans live their lives in the melee called politics. Politics is a domain where the interaction of individual wills in various domains leads to the creation of a common will.

Neither the interviewer nor the interviewee of the Summit Magazine interview is a political virgin. They are both living in the present in Cameroon. Unfortunately, they did not seem to have proceeded from the cognitive dissonance that this is supposed to induce. The Cameroon we are living in today is the product of the interaction of individual wills during a period that extends from the

Foncha times to today. To treat the individual will of Foncha as if it was played out in a vacuum is obviously a most unscientific exercise. A historian should always maintain a lively intellectual curiosity and an interest in everything "historical," in what other people think and why they think the way they think, because everything really is related to everything else.

The political is the way in which a society and its members come to understand themselves as this society rather than some society of accidental coexistence willed on them by some outside forces. The political is a process by which a society expresses its autonomy, giving itself its own mode of existence. The political is the condition of the possibility of politics. The distinction between the political and politics creates the space within which democracy becomes possible. The creation and preservation of that space in society is a daunting political task which demands the avoidance of the always-present temptation which Ahidjo fell prey to, either to reduce the political to politics, or to overcome their distinction in a higher unity that eliminates divisions within the body politics of society.

A wrong impression is given in the Summit Magazine interview that the unification agenda failed because of the weaknesses of Foncha, or because it was a "gamble," or because "Foncha and Muna were not well educated" and "KNDP lacked sufficient qualified personnel, therefore their negotiations were weak." This book by Anthony Ndi argues forcefully and convincingly that "Ahidjo's 'bad faith' and determination to introduce centralized personal authoritarian rule largely explains the failure of the Federal Republic of Cameroon barely within a decade of its creation without a fair trial period." Indeed, the obstacles on the unification road were effectively the abolition by Ahidjo of the space in which democracy was possible. He did this by "unifying" society into a higher synthesis that human nature makes impossible: he signed his Ordinances of exception, and created a one-party state!

Justice Nyo'Wakai, a legal luminary in his book The Law and My Times questions why although Cameroon has known no crisis since independence that put parliament out of service, the Chief Executive – Ahidjo - "tended to request the legislative arm to surrender to him (to sign ordinances) and they too seem to do so with relish..."² Immediately following unification on 1October 1961, Ordinance No. 062/OF/18 of 19 March 1962 on subversion was signed instituting tight restraints on freedom of expression and association, and allowing the security forces to arrest, torture and send citizens who voiced dissent to prison with abysmal prison conditions - all of which served to intimidate them. The Ordinance established new offences termed "subversion" or "rebellion" which all prohibited free expression of opinion, making it a crime for anyone to oppose or criticize any government action. Thus, barely five months after unification on October 1, 1961, people like Albert Mukong, Gorji Dinka and others who dared to shout from the public arena that "This thing is not right! This thing must stop!" were bundled up and sent to jail, or intimidated to submission. Indeed, we are told by the author that because of the effect of the Ordinances and one party rule, the claim that "all the parties voluntarily surrendered their individuality to form a unique party for the purpose of national unity and development" is false because "the historical facts do not match this assumption." He further states that: "The entire life of the Federal Republic of Cameroon, (1961-1972) and beyond, on the other hand, was dominated by the unnerving intrigues of President Alhadji Ahmadou Ahidjo, who could not brood any form of opposition to his authority.

If "fate" can be accepted as part of a people's history, then these were the determinants that got factored into the developments that have shaped the destiny of Southern and subsequently former West Cameroonians so far..."³ One-party rule was tantamount to totalitarianism and violated human rights, human dignity, and communal autonomy. Ahidjo's one party regime was a totalitarian attempt to overcome opposition between the democratic individual and the community of which he or she was a member. It removed the space in which individuals would have engaged in the travails of nation building through autonomous self-interpretation or critical reflection. As is always the case, it came about either because there was a hidden agenda (to wipe out the identity of Southern Cameroons), or because

---

² Justice Nyo'Wakai, Under The Broken Scale of Justice: The Law And My Times (Langaa Research and Publishing CIG, Mankon, Bamenda 2009), p. x.
³ Albert Mukong, What's To Be Done? (Bamenda, July 1985), p. 4.

he felt that the tension between the likes of Foncha, Mukong, Dinka, Fonlon, and others, and himself following the achievements of the Foumban Conference would not be managed by him democratically. As a result, a synthesis was sought, the result of which was the loss of both freedom and communal autonomy, the eradication of the culture of democracy, and the expansion of one-man or group power. A political culture was created in which those who questioned the justice of the action of the regime looked like mentally deranged people.

Ahidjo's power was expanded not by force but by corrupting a self-interested, easily beguiled, and sometimes irresponsible citizenry in exchange for material reward or social honours. We are informed that "Jua preponderantly won repeatedly in the party's conventions at Kumba and Bamenda and even in parliament; Muna assured of Ahidjo's support, was adamant that only the President of the Federal Republic of Cameroon (FRC) had the right and authority to appoint the Prime Minister of West Cameroon and not the party's conventions and parliamentary majorities, norms totally anathema to the British parliamentary system which obtained in West Cameroon. ...Ahidjo then had Jua despite his parliamentary majority as expected replaced by Muna, who was not even a Member of the West Cameroon House of Assembly in 1968. After this the West Cameroon Westminster parliamentary system was thrown to the winds and chaos set in as what obtained thereafter was neither the presidential or parliamentary system but simply the politics of patronage and sycophancy...."[4]

Thus, Ahidjo's totalitarian adventure was a well thought-out strategy, not an accident, an historical aberration, an irrational folly or some childhood illness! It was not imposed on a unanimously resistant people, since it was supported from within by Muna and others. As put by Dr. Ndi, "The newly created Cameroons United Congress [CUC] of ST Muna became the bane for the destruction of the KNDP... the Cameroon United Congress (CUC), the West Cameroon version of Ahidjo's UC party ... undercut and weakened the KNDP and especially its leadership. This was the first step in the destruction of West Cameroon's Anglo-Saxon, Westminster parliamentary system. With Muna under his heel, Ahidjo created a huge crevice through which the seeds of discord were sown for West Cameroon to be shattered

---

[4] Idem.

because what ensued soon afterwards was an administration which was neither of the Westminster parliamentary pedigree nor of the typical French and American presidential systems..." To gain favours a new breed of people not known in Southern Cameroons until then, came on stage: selfish, cowardly people raising flattery and lies into authorized currency of the time. It can be said that German Kamerun created a sort of "common sense" in both French and English-ruled Cameroons. Reason why there was a plethora of political parties, all bearing the letter "K" [Kamerun]: KNDP, KNC, KPP, OK, KUP, etc. But the existence of a shared or common sense does not exclude the autonomy of the individual or groups, which is in fact the premise of the common sense. The essence of a common sense is to create a political bond based on mutual recognition by autonomous individuals and groups; to create a solidarity based on responsibility towards other autonomous individuals and groups, as a pre-condition for confronting the fundamental critical questions facing society.

Political action in society is usually divided into periods, described as "lived experience", "reflection" on lived experience, and "conception" of new action or new beginnings. The "new" action always constitutes the first stage of the next political "period." The human spirit is very powerful, indomitable, and is capable of achieving any aim it sets itself, including challenging any odd that props up on the road of its evolution. This is why in human history new beginnings are always possible. Unfortunately, Ahidjo seemed to believe that empirical political choices are caused by empirical considerations. This was in ignorance of this normative sense in which the political binds rights- bearing individuals into an autonomous "reflective" community that endures, evolves over time and generates responses to new challenges that arise in their society. History shows that individual conception of the nation may at any time become political when the conditions of the possibility of their self-affirmation challenge the previously assumed definition of politics that surrounded the concept. This could create tension between the political and politics –as is already the case in Cameroon in relation to unification/reunification - and open up the public space in which society (and its members) can reflect on what it is and what it wants to be.

The Ordinances and one-party state may have acted like a vast refrigerator that reduced the reunification zeal into a condition of stupor. There was no doubt that the refrigerator would breakdown with time. Apparently, to prepare for such an eventuality, the problematic gift Ahidjo deposited on the seat of power as his parting gift, "set out at dawn" as Wole Soyinka would put it. Biya went as far as possible to legalise Ahidjo's turpitudes with his problematic and provocative change of name of the country back to "Republic of Cameroon" using law N° 84-1 of February 4, 1984! Now the debate on the wisdom of the acts is right in the public domain, and it is robust and wide-open. It has to be dealt with very seriously, at the risk of compromising the whole unification agenda. It is always good to have more than one side of a story. Anthony Ndi's multifaceted association with Foncha give him insight into the man; Professor Ngoh's academic forays with the history of Cameroon give him an outsider's perspective of the man. Each of them has painted a picture of the man John Ngu Foncha. It is left to the academic world, and the public at large to draw their conclusions. As for me, I can state unequivocally that I am happy I read the work of Anthony Ndi, because of the way previous writings I had read had influenced my thinking about Foncha. I can now state with confidence that I am convinced the man did his best about the course he set himself.

Introduction

The Landscape

> "Not to know what took place before you were born is to remain forever a child" (Marcus Tulius Cicero).

The title of this book derives from a topic appropriately selected to kick-start discussions in the year of celebrations marking the Golden Jubilee of the Independence (and Reunification) of Southern Cameroons.[5] The subtitle, interestingly, is taken from the autobiography of Malcolm Milne, the Deputy Commissioner of Southern Cameroons, while the rest is deduced from sorting out, analysing and classifying an assortment of historical data on the theme. At first sight the title is likely to sound preposterous and exaggerated, but such a feeling is sure to dissipate on appropriate confrontation with the details. It is therefore essential to throw in some light right at the beginning to illuminate the background issues.

These concentrated around two focal points: the insurmountable hurdles calculated to frustrate the quest by the Southern Cameroonian political leadership and people in their struggle towards autonomy, strangely enough by their British Colonial Master in collusion with France and the United Nations during the crucial years, 1958-1961. This was compounded by the prevailing Cold War politics in which every single international issue was seen through tainted glasses and interpreted in terms of either favouring Capitalist Western Europe under the hegemony of the United States of America or Communist Eastern Europe led by the Soviet Union. Meanwhile, the Afro-Asian bloc, which claimed veiled neutrality at the United Nations, vacillated in between them. Thus situated, the terms "conspiracy" and "treachery" become the mildest euphemisms the reality of the saga of the "snares" that the "nice, gentle, little people" of the Southern

---

[5] 1 Epilogue, the Editorial Board of the Summit Magazine in its issue, Number 16 of April-June 2011.

Cameroons faced at the hands of the British[6] and then at independence and reunification, treacherously thrust into the coy arms of the Ahidjo Regime. This was characterised by his sly but unbridled pursuit of power and authority that was astutely and steadily unleashed through 1961-1972.[7] Thus it is evident that during the crucial years from 1958-1961, Southern Cameroons was placed on the tenterhooks of Great Britain, while, from 1961-1972 these were hurriedly replaced by those of the administration of President Ahmadou Ahidjo. Combined, they constitute the series of "inescapable traps", as Malcolm Milne describes it, with which Southern Cameroons was beset. Chilling revelations of British deeds and misdeeds in connection with their unbending determination to obstruct autonomy for Southern Cameroons only recently came to light with the publication of the declassified British secret papers, further amplified by Malcolm Milne's spontaneous confessions.[8]

---

[6] Malcolm Milne, No Telephone to Heaven From Apex To Nadir - Colonial Service in Nigeria, Aden, The Cameroons and The Gold Coast 1938-1961 (Meon Hill Press1999), pp.424-428.

[7] PRO CO.554/2412 XC3343, "Ahidjo rejects defence responsibility for Southern Cameroons", Secret and Personal CC.74/69., JO Field of 8 October 1960 to Rt. Hon. Iain Macleod MP.

[8] As Deputy Commissioner for Southern Cameroons Milne was one of the major executors of British Colonial policy in the Territory. Martin Njeuma, "Reunification and Political Opportunism in The Making of Cameroons Independence http:// lucy. ukc.ac.uk/Chilver/Paideuma/paideuma-REUNIFI.html. 9/9/13

Malcolm Milne

Deputy Commissioner, Southern Cameroons

On the side of the Ahidjo Regime, the saga of the sordid traps neatly laid out against the Southern Cameroons delegates to the historic Foumban Constitutional Conference explode from another confessional source, the octogenarian retired Divisional Officer, (Sous Prefect) of Foumban Municipality at the time, Mr. Emmanuel Njoya. That these plots were carefully timed and unleashed on the occasion of the very first encounter by the two former Trust Territories to formulate terms for reunification is of inestimable significance especially as the Anglophone delegates approached the conference with child-like confidence and trust in 'meeting their brothers' for the very first time. Equally unearthed, are verbatim accounts of the alleged "secret deals" between Foncha and Ahidjo dug out from reports and correspondence in the declassified British secret papers. These reveal by far, vastly dissimilar versions from those so far paraded as gospel truth.

Open collusion between the British, French and Republic of Cameroon delegates against an "enfeebled and besieged Foncha Government" was abundantly dramatized during the disastrous discussions at the Buea Tripartite Conference in May 1961,[9] happening just before the Bamenda All Party and the Foumban Conferences. Between this botched meeting and the Foumban Constitutional Conference, the British Colonial Administration placed every conceivable stumbling block in their power to isolate, discredit, destabilise and frustrate the Foncha regime; employing some of the most incredibly sordid, perfidious and sinister strategies imaginable. As will be seen, this is the source of the "conspiracy theories" that have bedevilled Southern Cameroons History with reference to Foncha: "hiding the draft of the highly centralised Federal Constitution," which he got from President Ahmadou Ahidjo and the "secret deals" he and Muna are supposed to have struck with him over the distribution of political spoils in the envisaged Federal Administration.

Chilling Revelations

The worst of British blackmail, however, was the provocative and sudden withdrawal of their defence forces from the territory at the most vulnerable point in its history, faced as it was with fratricidal maquizzards (terrorist) attacks raging across the Francophone border. To ensure that the declaration had maximum devastating effect, the announcement was carefully timed to coincide with the assembling of delegates at the Bamenda All Party Conference in late June 1961, with the openly declared objective of sparking disaffection and unrest within the KNDP, and against the Foncha Government. There are those who postulate, and with good reason, that the British actually prepared the ground for, and expected a civil war to break out, the reason why Commissioner JO Field "abandoned" the highly exalted ceremony of handing over Southern Cameroons to President Ahidjo on 1 October, 1961 and sought solace on a British Man O' War Ship at Victoria Harbour.[10]

In perspective and with the privilege of hindsight, this is easily one of the worst examples of British double-dealing and perfidy in the

---

[9] PRO CO.554/2249 XC 3406, .In Addition, Foncha was considered 'leftist,' Patrick Johnston.

[10] Ibid p.434, "Trap set for Foncha"; also, Mr. Omer BB Sendze, "Reflections on the Role of Mr. Foncha in Cameroon Politics"p.7. Dec. 2009.

territory, when they plainly disavowed Foncha and the people of Southern Cameroons, withdrew British defence forces and openly took sides with the Ahidjo Government against the Foncha cabinet. That this happened when Ahidjo arrogantly declared that he was not ready to handle defence or offer any form of economic assistance to Southern Cameroons, adds hue to this disgusting picture.[11] Nevertheless, though betrayed and prostrate the Foncha cabinet was adamant against any entry of the "uncouth" Republic of Cameroun forces into Southern Cameroons territory without permission, What they desired of Great Britain was the immediate return home of Southern Cameroonian soldiers serving in the Nigerian army to lay the nucleus of their own defence system. Put in context, this virtually amounted to the British administration handing over Southern Cameroons to President Ahidjo on a platter of gold tacitly meaning that he should complete the emasculating process they had so well begun.[12]

This was the pinnacle of the "inescapable traps" which as Malcolm Milne later disclosed, were meticulously designed and laid out to ensnare Foncha and by extension, the entire Southern Cameroons by the British Colonial Administration. In Malcolm Milne's words:

> They made Foncha's task extremely difficult. He was in effect, being driven into a tunnel with steadily converging sides as the hunters of Nkambe tackled groups of the red forest hog. What he seemed oblivious of was the fact that at the convergence of the sides a pit had been dug from which there was no escape.[13]

As this incredible tale unfolds, it comes out that the British actually masterminded, coordinated and executed this plot to the desired end since they succeeded in ensuring that Southern Cameroons was finally transferred not to Foncha or an agreed "federal body" as stipulated by the United Nations but directly into the firm grips of the Ahidjo regime, which eliminated all fantasies and chances of autonomy. Actually, as of late May 1961, after the failed Buea Tripartite

---

[11] Ibid., Patrick Johnston.
[12] PRO CO.5542247/2247 XC 3343, Milne to Geoffrey of 1 July 1962.
[13] Milne, No Telephone, p.434. my emphasis

Conference, the Southern Cameroons leadership had been thoroughly humiliated, emasculated and literally shackled under Ahidjo's tentacles without any chance of freeing themselves. This is the precise sense in which it could be said that the Southern Cameroons delegates proceeded to the Foumban Constitutional Conference like lambs being led to the slaughter. This enormously gratified the British desire for vengeance since they saw it as a well-measured punishment for Southern Cameroonians in their stubborn determination to vote for reunification with the Republic of Cameroon as demonstrated in the plebiscite results, instead of integration with Nigeria.[14]

Independence Option Blocked

Worst of all, Britain tactfully blocked every chance of the inhabitants during the plebiscite of voting for independence, the one option they relished. This happened, thanks to the appointment of Sir Sydney Phillipson as "expert" economic adviser to the Southern Cameroons Government, whose carefully choreographed reports tabled before the UN painted a pathetic picture of the territory as an economic millstone, which could only survive by leaning either on the Federation of Nigeria or Republic of Cameroon but not on her own to attain independence. It was in accordance with this plot that Sir Sydney Phillipson recklessly steered the Mamfe All Party Conference of 10-11 August 1959 to the rocks such that it concluded as a tower of Babel without agreement.

Southern Cameroons thus weakened, it was President Ahidjo's turn to unleash his own ploys, which he did with consummate diplomacy beginning right at the Foumban Constitutional Conference. The second part of the "tale" in the hands of Ahidjo though subtle and covert was ultimately no less ruthless in effect. This is vividly recalled by Mr. Emmanuel Njoya who as "Sous Prefect" was the second in command in the organisation of the "deceptive" reception for the Southern Cameroonian delegates at the Foumban Constitutional Conference. Almost fifty years later, Njoya relived this bizarre episode vividly and unequivocally. He recounts his experience in the manner of a solemn confessional statement:

---

[14] Ibid., p.434

> As l must speak the truth, we cajoled, lured and enticed the Anglophones by our way of welcoming them; we were given so many things to prepare for the conference – with all these things at our disposal we lured the Anglophones. …we were given special instructions to blindfold them: so each delegate had a refrigerator in his room, which was always full of champagnes and other assorted drinks; each big one among them had two refrigerators in his room, had a well-made bed with the most beautiful and expensive mattress and bedding.[15]

Yet, for the intended purpose of rendering the delegates wholly unproductive during the impending discussions this was still not good enough. Consequently, even the moral, ethical and emotional endurance of the Anglophone delegates was tested to the uttermost limit. Njoya explains the snares that were further put in place:

> There were two beautiful girls who were assigned to permanently take care of him. These are things which normally should not be told - these girls were instructed to permanently take care of our guest – that was real corruption- corruption has always existed- it has not started today… but at that time, it was not corruption for selfish interests as it is today … at the time it was good corruption to build the country.[16]

Their instructions were clear, to ensure that the Anglophone delegates to that important first contact as "brothers" were thoroughly incapacitated through an excess of "inverted kindness and hospitality".[17] Finally, it is the odd combination of these British colonial and Republic of Cameroun vices inflicted on Anglophone Cameroonians over the past half century that resulted in cries that still echo and re-echo of: marginalisation, assimilation and second class status in the Republic of Cameroon. [18]

---

[15] Frontier Telegraph, Vol. II No. 0007 of Jan. 16, 2008, p.4. My emphasis

[16] Ibid, My emphasis

[17] This is simply to make the point as disclosed by Malcolm Milne in the British context that Foncha [Southern Cameroons5] was totally emasculated and rendered intellectually impotent.

[18] PRO CO.554/2252 XC 4478 of 2 May 1961, para., 6.

What is paradoxical is that this tragic story of "woes" and regrets of Southern Cameroons originates from the duplicity perpetrated by Great Britain, its colonial master, which in 1946 had undertaken the solemn pledge to faithfully execute Article 76 (b) of the United Nations Trusteeship Council. By this, it undertook to guide Southern Cameroons, part of the former German Colony of Kamerun, safely through all the stages of socio-cultural, economic and political development to the port of self-government and ultimately "independence." In this capacity, as the colonial lord and master, Great Britain was looked up to as the guardian, shepherd and protector of the Trust Territory of Southern of Southern Cameroons.[19] Apparently, all worked well until 1958, when the goal of independence became perceptible. It was at this point that Great Britain the shepherd and guardian swerved round from "protector" to become "predator" and started laying out obstacles against Southern Cameroons so that the alternative to integration with Nigeria was not independence but joining Republic of Cameroon.

Blatant British Disloyalty to the Foncha Government

Since the KNDP leadership rejected integration with Nigeria and chose "negotiated reunification with Republic of Cameroun after extended trusteeship and independence," the British Colonial Administration set out to clip their wings. The British had administered British Southern and Northern Cameroons from 1922-1961 as integral parts of Nigeria, certain that the destiny of these two parts of the Trust Territories lay indisputably in integration with their Nigeria colony. One of those painful confessions stick out when Malcolm Milne, without any qualms, openly states in his autobiography that there arrived a point where the British expatriates found it difficult to remain loyal to the Foncha Administration as they were obliged to because of his rejection of integration with Nigeria. In fact, this alone,

---

[19] 15 The Cameroons Under the United Kingdom Administration Report by Her Majesty's Government in the United Kingdom of Great Britain and Northern Ireland to the General Assembly of the United Nations for the Year 1959, 1960, p.104., also, Anthony Ndi, National Integration and Nation Building in Cameroon: The Golden Age of Southern (West) Cameroon, (Gospel7Press, Bamenda, 2005), pp. 26-28.

epitomises brazen British blackmail and backing for the CPNC opposition, while mounting every conceivable obstacle against the KNDP of Foncha. It is a strange coincidence that at this point Foncha without knowing these facts instinctively asked for Malcolm Milne to be relieved of his functions since he had become an obstacle to unification.[20] Interestingly and finally, after his conversion, Malcolm Milne described this attitude of the British as a betrayal of the confidence of the nice people of Southern Cameroons for which reason they could not justify their mission in the Trust Territory.[21]

That the Republic of Cameroon under President Ahidjo into whose "care" Southern Cameroons was safely delivered by Great Britain continued the craft of preying began unfolding during the very first encounter of the representatives of the two states as "brothers" at the Foumban Constitutional Conference qualifies this work to be read and understood in the sense of a series of traps. However, the question is whether these are necessarily "inescapable" traps. Malcolm Milne the "convert" eventually does not think so. He instead maintains that the British obligatorily should make amends for the grave injustices they meted to the "nice little people of Southern Cameroons". At the end of his autobiography the question Malcolm Milne poses for Southern Cameroonian researchers is as fresh as ever: "What goals did the British set out to accomplish for the Trust Territory of Southern Cameroons?" It remains the challenge for Southern Cameroon intellectuals, especially historians, political analysts and social scientists to tackle.[22]

Critically examined in perspective with the wisdom provided by hindsight, the image that emerges of Southern Cameroons Fifty Years after Independence and the role played by its leadership clearly is the exact opposite of that paraded in political and historical circles to the public. Emasculated and transfixed, actually crushed between two predators – Great Britain and the Republic of Cameroun under President Ahidjo – Southern Cameroons by all definitions was reduced to a "victim" of international conspiracy by default. Unfortunately, this picture is easily missed when historical facts are examined superficially

---

[20] Milne, *No Telephone*, p.434
[21] Ibid., p. 414; "Betrayal of Support and Security" by JO Field in Malcolm
[22] Ibid., No Telephone, pp. 424-447.

or merely taken at face value without in-depth analysis. In which case, the Southern Cameroonian leadership, the "victims", are cursorily projected and made to answer for woes that were clearly externally inflicted on them. The two predators who exercised covert and overt agendas for its total capitulation, subjugation and near annihilation like in the example of 18th Century Poland are let off the hook. This is the tragic story that needs careful revisiting. Considering the conventional adage that "Every generation rewrites its own history," in the light of new ideas, new developments, new research data and new methodology for the interpretation of such information, the history of "Southern Cameroons Fifty Years after Independence," at the centre of which are the Golden Jubilee celebrations declared by President Paul Biya on 17 May 2010 is the most propitious moment for this exercise to be undertaken in all its ramifications for posterity.[23]

---

[23] Cameroon Tribune Hors Serie Octobre 2011 "Reunification One Cameroon, A Dynamic Story." pp. 131-134.

Abbreviations

ANLK	Armée Liberation National Kamerun
CAM	Cameroon Anglophone Movement
CNF	Cameroon National Federation
CNU	Cameroon National Union
CUC	Cameroons United Congress
CO	Colonial Office
CPDM	Cameroon People's Democratic Movement
CPNC	Cameroons Peoples National Congress
CWA	Catholic Women's Association
CWU	Cameroon Welfare Union
CYL	Cameroon Youth League
DO	Divisional Officer
EO	Executive Officer
FASAF	Father Samson's Foundation for Underprivileged Children
FRC	Federal Republic of Cameroon
GCE	General Certificate of Education
GCEB	General Certificate of Education, Board
KNDP	Kamerun National Democratic Party
KNC	Kamerun National Congress
KPP	Kamerun People's Party
KUC	Kamerun United Congress
KUNC	Kamerun United National Congress
LGB	Leader of Government Business
NA	Native Administration / Native Authority
NAB	National Archives, Buea
NCBWA	National Congress of British West Africa
NCNC	National Council of Nigeria and Cameroons
NYL	Nigerian Youth League
OK	One Kamerun (party)
PRO	Public Records Office
PT	Pupil Teacher / Probationary Teacher
RC	Republic of Cameroun
SCHA	Southern Cameroons House of Assembly

SDO	Senior Divisional Officer
STAMS	Saint Thomas Aquinas Major Seminary (Bambui
UC	Union Camerounaise
UNTC	United Nations Trusteeship Council
UNVM	United Nations Visiting Mission
UPC	Unions des Populations du Cameroun
USSR	Union of Soviet Socialist Republics
UNTC	United Nations Trusteeship Council

List of Photographs

1. Malcolm Milne.. xxv
2. Paul Biya and Ni John Fru Ndi.. xxxvii
3. Christian Cardinal Tumi... 11
4. Johnson O Field.. 15
5. Northern Cameroons Peoples Democratic Party 1959............ 48
6. The Endeley KNC/KPP Government 1958.............................. 54
7. Dr. and Mrs. Endeley Congratulate Mr. JN Foncha in 1959...... 58
8. Achirimbi II (Fon of Bafut)... 60
9. Peter Ndembo Motomby Woleta... 62
10. Individual UPC Leaders.. 66
11. UPC Leaders – Group Picture... 68
12. Muammar Ghadaffi.. 72
13. The Foncha KNDP Government 1959.................................. 73
14. Voters at the Polls on 11 February 1961............................. 93
15. Counting the votes... 93
16. Press Conference by the PM (Foncha)................................ 94
17. Plebiscite Results... 99
18. Foncha Addressing Crowd at Tiko..................................... 109
19. Phases of the Bamenda All Party Conference..................... 112
20. Ndeh Ntumazah.. 119
21. Dr. and Mrs. Endeley and Mbile at Tiko Airport.................. 122
22. Anglophone Delegates on Arrival at Koutaba..................... 123
23. Foumban Conference in Pictures....................................... 125
24. Albert Womah Mukong.. 129
25. Foncha Addressing Conference at Foumban....................... 130
26. Emmanuel Tabi Egbe.. 131
27. Sultan Seidou Njoya Njmoulouh, Foncha and Assale........... 151
28. Mme Njoya née Nyimbe Jeanne... 154
29. Some Anglophone Delegates at Foumban.......................... 164
30. Fon SA Angwafo III of Mankon... 167
31. Foumban Group Photograph 168
32. Foncha and team at Ebubu Massacre................................. 215
33. Omer BB Sendze.. 216
34. Harold MacMillan British PM.. 232

35. Foncha KNDP Government... 235
36. Bamenda Corps in Pictures... 237
37. Nkrumah Visit, 1959.. 240
38. Malcolm Milne Receives President Ahidjo........................... 255
39. The Milnes and the Munas 1980.. 258

President Paul Biya, Head of State (Right) and Ni John Fru Ndi (Left) Leader of the SDF Opposition

President Paul Biya: through the 1990 Liberty Laws, reintroduced Multiparty Politics and authorised Celebrations marking the Golden Jubilee or the Fiftieth Anniversary of Southern Cameroons Independence and Reunification

Logo: Golden Jubilee Celebrations 1961 - 2011

Note the National Monument in the Background

Federal Republic of Cameroon

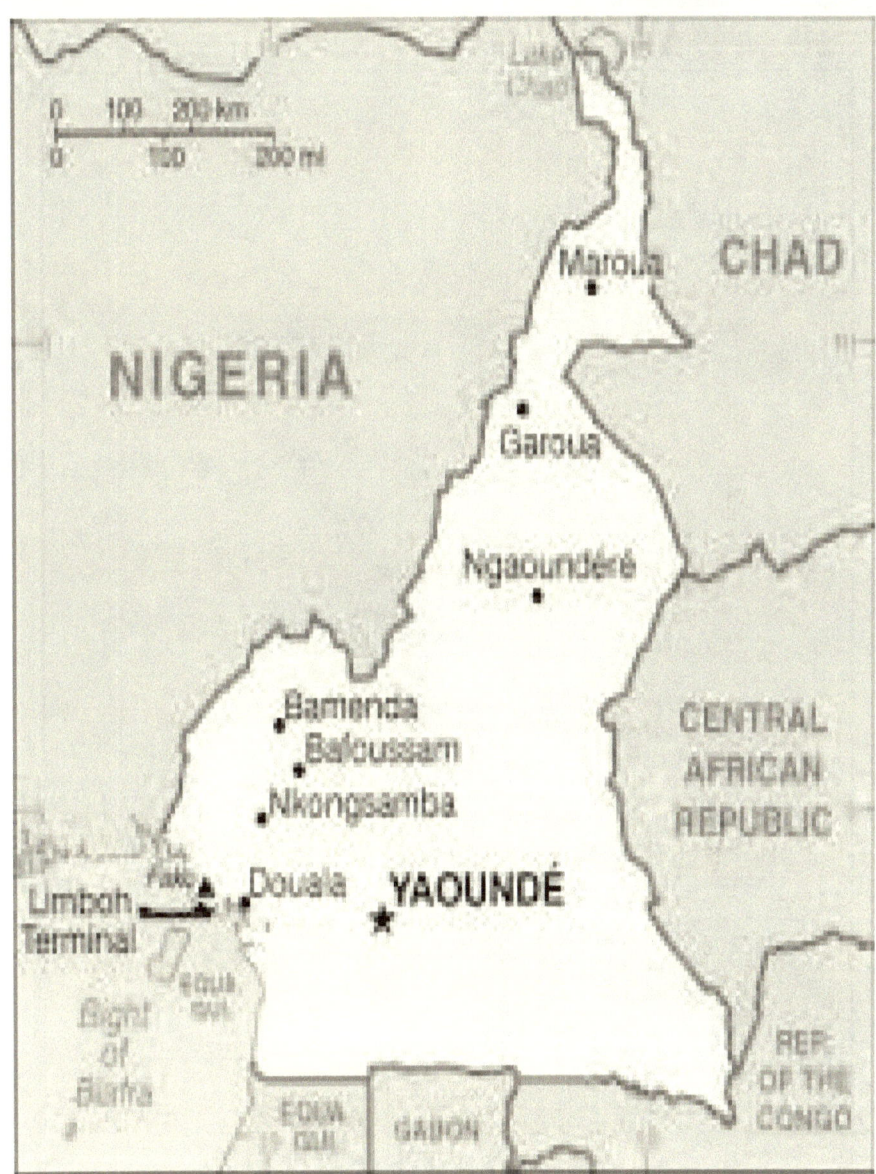

Southern Cameroons Ethnic Groups 1950 -1961
(Southern Cameroons had some 200 ethnic groups)

Chapter 1

Independence and Reunification: An Analysis of Basic Issues

A Historical Panorama

This book is the product of a triple mandate: which started from a presentation at a Regional Symposium in Bamenda and concluded at a conference convened by the Minister of Arts and Culture in Yaoundé on 28 June 2011 in connection with celebrations marking the Golden Jubilee of the "Independence and Reunification of Southern Cameroons". It was in this context that the author took up the assignment to immortalize this unique occasion by critically re-examining some of the crucial issues in the history of Southern Cameroons. Coincidentally, these meetings happened at about the same time that the Summit Magazine in its issue of 6 April-May 2010 granted a classic interview to Dr. Victor Julius Ngoh, Professor of History and Deputy Vice-Chancellor in Charge of Research, University of Buea.[1] By all counts it was a remarkable interview of epic proportions as it turned out to be wide ranging and all – embracing: challenging and raising several controversial issues of historical interest, many of which had already been expressed in his earlier historical works that need re-examination. As a result, it generated comments among all categories of the public: the man in the street, politicians, lawyers and above all, intellectuals, serious political analysts and historians.

Since then several reputable journals have spontaneously on their own, taken the cue greatly enriching and enhancing the historical debate. However, it is as a rejoinder to the Summit Magazine interview and, as part of the enduring debate on the issue of the "Golden Jubilee" celebrations marking the independence and reunification of Southern Cameroons and the Republic of Cameroun, that this modest contribution is being made and, strictly from a historical and

---

[1] For further details on the issue of publication, see the Epilogue

intellectual perspective. As far as possible, the entire account focuses exclusively on principles; and individuals are only referred to, where they impinge on the historical nexus.

Finally, as a matter of course and principle in historiography, every generation faces the eternal challenge to rewrite its own history in the light of: new interpretations of its past; or, the emergence of new information; new inventions and discoveries that question lopsided prevailing concepts; new evidence erupting from research and archaeological findings, as well as fresh technologies for translating extant historical knowledge. In this light, the Golden Jubilee approximates close to two generations, thus qualifying for a tall critical retrospective look at Cameroon History in all its ramifications. This is feasible using the penetrating rear mirror of history with the advantage of time, the unfailing catalyst; which allows the dust of controversies to settle, permitting sober reflections to supervene over hasty emotional and temperamental conclusions of the past to mellow in favour of impartial judgment.

The research resulting in this book has largely, but not exclusively been triggered by vital questions raised in the Summit Magazine interview and a broad spectrum of other deliberations. Positively, in the first place, the interview provided fresh historical information to the public arena but, because of the miasmic nature of the issues raised, it equally exposed substantial areas of commission, omission or of default that this piece of work seeks to redress. Thus, despite the fact that the British left indelible, nostalgic Anglo-Saxon legacies and footprints worthy of emulation in the areas of: good governance, human rights, quality education, self- actualization and ethics, there were as well lamentable lapses of a profound nature that totally elude rationalization. These lapses were glaring in the spheres of economic development and, above all the culture of graciously letting go of Southern Cameroons with the approach of independence. This defect gravely undermined the objective of British tutelage throughout the Mandate and Trusteeship periods in the Territory from 1922-1961.

Critical in any balanced account of the History of Cameroon since Reunification is the primeval role played by "Southern Cameroons," which alone underwent the birth pangs that begot the 'Federal Republic of Cameroon': the reunion with "equal status" of the former

United Nations Trust Territories of "French Cameroun" and 'British Southern Cameroons.' It took the two to unite but the rigours undertaken towards the plebiscite applied only to the latter. Much earlier, Britain had arbitrarily by an Order in Council carved out "British Northern Cameroons" on 26 June1923, when it was still a Mandated Territory of the League of Nations. This created as a matter of administrative convenience for theme eventually resulted in the reality of two separate entities: British Southern Cameroons and British Northern Cameroons not originally previewed in the League of Nations Mandate which formally divided the former German Kamerun colony between Britain and France on 20 July 1919. Originating provisionally as "Provinces" within their Nigerian colony for easy administration, they calcified and became de facto distinctive political entities as carefully designed by Great Britain. With intensified British machinations the gulf between them so greatly widened that as independence approached in 1961, one section voted for integration with Nigeria, while the other which resisted British pressure chose reunification with the Republic of Cameroon. For this recalcitrance the British sought unmitigated vengeance through setting up inescapable traps for them.

Double British Standards

These clandestine manoeuvres were brought out to the surface with the publication of the declassified British secret papers in which it was openly stated that as far as British interests were concerned, compared with Northern Cameroons, "Southern Cameroons was expendable." Throughout the Trusteeship period, everything was done to ensure that the "radicalism" inherent in the latter did not infect the former. Consequently, when it came to the plebiscites, which were largely concocted through British intrigues, the split of British Cameroons in 1923 was concretized and they were henceforth recognized and treated as two separate political entities. In fact, as a result of this ploy over time, they became widely different in several ways; such that, describing Southern Cameroons as suffering from "benign neglect" under British rule the situation of Northern Cameroons was dismal.

It was so socio-politically and economically stagnated that the first indigenous political party, the "Northern Cameroons Democratic Party" (NKDP), literally an extension of the KNDP in Southern Cameroons was only created in 1959. Understandably, it was highly critical of the British Colonial Administration and campaigned either for an independent sovereign status or a reunified state with Southern Cameroons and eventual unification with Republic of Cameroon. Obviously just like with the KNDP, these options were anathema to British policy. The other political parties there such as: the Fulani dominated Northern People's Congress (NPC) and the Northern Elements Progressive Union (NEPU) were entirely Nigerian based. These were all disagreed on the way forward.

To ensure that the results of the impending plebiscites reflected the British aspirations of integration with Nigeria, they proposed to the United Nations Trusteeship Council that: the Northern Cameroons plebiscite should take place simultaneously with that in Southern Cameroons; the electors asked the same questions, but that the votes should be counted separately as well as the declaration of results. To further confound issues for an already confused electorate, the Northern Cameroons was made to participate in the Nigerian Federal Elections. In fact, two plebiscites were conducted there; the first in November 1959 in which the people advocated for continued Trusteeship under Britain, which was easily interpreted as a vote against integration with Nigeria.

However, since the direction of the wind had been made clear after that first plebiscite, Britain working with the Nigerian based political parties did everything to turn the tables before11 February 1961. As expected, integration with Nigeria in the second plebiscite won by a wide margin of 146.296 to 97.659 votes. However, had provision been allowed for tallying the votes of both British Northern and Southern Cameroons, reunification would have won handsomely since combining the votes would have amounted to Southern Cameroons' 233.571 votes being added to those of Northern Cameroons: 97.659 making a total of 332.230 votes; while integration with Nigeria for Southern Cameroons with:97.659 votes added to those of Northern Cameroons: 146.296 would have totalled 244.037 votes leaving reunification (331.230 – 244.037 votes)with a distinct victory margin of87.193 votes.²

The entire history of 'British' Southern Cameroons is exceptionally, the unfolding of the process that ended up in its reunification with the Republic of Cameroun on 1 October 1961. In French Cameroun, the "Kamerun Idea" fossilized in the hands of the Unions des Populations du Cameroun (UPC) in 1948.³ It was so glaring that during the presentations before the United Nations Visiting Mission (UNVM) of 1958, they ruled out the need for any referendum in the case of French Cameroon as was the situation in British Southern Cameroons. The form of that union might have been different but the ultimate objective of reunification never really wavered on either side. While the antecedents of that event for British Southern Cameroons stretched as far back as to the 1940s, when the idea was first mooted, the process acquired an unprecedented momentum and dimension of its own during the decisive years running from 1958 - 1961.

This is largely the period dealt with in the interview as well as the substance of this exposition.⁴After achieving independence on 1 October 1961, Southern Cameroons metamorphosed into 'West Cameroon', an appellation by which it was known until 24July 1972; when a Presidential Decree set up seven Provinces to replace West and East Cameroon.⁵ This was a transient existence of barely a decade, and a period⁶ far too short for it to have proven itself either as a success or a failure, when juxtaposed with nations that have survived for centuries

---

²*Cameroon Tribune, Hors Serie Octobre* 2011. pp. 74-76., Kimeng Hilton, "Unease with Northern Cameroons Results."

³ Their own demand like that of the One Kamerun party (OK) party which replaced them after they were banned by the Endeley Government for their radical communist sympathies and a predilection for violence in 1957 was for immediate "independence and reunification". It is also insinuated that their inclination towards an alliance with the KNDP posed a threat to Endeley's KNC.

⁴ Ngoh's, the *Untold History of Cameroon* Reunification published after the Summit Magazine interview equally covers this period.

⁵ Read Victor LeVine, "Political Integration and the United Republic of Cameroon", p. 279, in David Smock and Kwamena Bentsi-Enchill, eds., *The Search for National Integration in Africa*, (New York, The Free Press), 1972.

⁶ There are current debates as to whether what took place as the "Peaceful Revolution" of 1972 could qualify for a valid referendum comparable to the 1961 plebiscite in Southern Cameroons; more especially as it violated Article 47(1) of the constitution of the Federal Republic of Cameroon.

and even millennia and are still evolving[7]. This was essentially the scheming of President Ahmadou Ahidjo ironically the one individual whose responsibility it was to secure its invincibility.

A Broad Analysis of the Issues

However, broadly talking about "Southern Cameroons Fifty Years After Reunification," could take more than one perception; as, it could arguably mean the entire period covering 1961-2011, when it was politically and "geographically" transformed[8] through the stages of the Federal Republic, 1961-72; the Unitary State,1972-84 and, finally, simply subsumed into the "Republic of Cameroon," 4 February 1984 – date.[9] Throughout this period the erstwhile Southern Cameroons however, has maintained its basic essence and therefore within the context implied in this book; revisiting "Southern Cameroons 50 Years after Reunification" implies more or less, a re-visitation of the events affecting the inhabitants encapsulated in this geographical circumscription.

As a matter of course, the persistent arguments and complaints by North and South-Westerners as exemplified in the interview over issues such as: "bad faith," "marginalization," "assimilation," "annexation," "absorption", second class citizenship and the like are symptoms that unlike "independence," which was a single, finite "act" - an event that took place at midnight on 1st October 1961, "reunification" on the other hand is an ongoing, multi-dimensional and emotionally charged process. This is best expressed by the Cameroon Anglophone Movement (CAM) in their memorandum to the Head of State on constitutional reform with reference to the political unrest

---

[7] Britain is presently undergoing throes of devolution with Ireland, Scotland and Wales seeking autonomy after centuries of centralized administration from London.

[8] Examples abound, Britain alone has had to review the Acts of Union with Ireland, Scotland and Wales dating back to the 18thCentury in favour of dialogue, peaceful coexistence, devolution and even independence.

[9] Law No 80.001, abolishing the United Republic of Cameroon and resuscitating in its place the Republic of Cameroon which at independence on 1 January 1960 became a member of the United Nations with defined internationally recognized boundaries. See, Albert W Mukong ed., USA, The Case For Southern Cameroons, 1990, p.21.

that gripped the nation in the early 1990s. In it, referring to the plight of Anglophones, they reiterated:

> The frustration born of oppression, subjugation, marginalization and neglect finally led some Anglophones in desperation to organize political dissent in May 1990, to which the Cameroon Government responded by shooting dead six persons in Bamenda and telling Anglophones to go elsewhere. But Anglophones do not want to go anywhere else; their demand is for a return to the legality of the 1961constitution of the Federal Republic of Cameroon.[10]

The coming together of the two former UN Trust Territories torn apart by the vagaries of colonial intrigues for forty years was much like a marital union calling for a genuine conversion and bonding of hearts, minds, wills, thoughts and actions of the parties and not merely a matter of legality, lip service and form.

In fact, this dismal situation is more pungently expressed in Foncha's words in his Letter of Resignation from the CPDM in1990; as the one man who had fought for reunification and won by a landslide majority of 233. 971 votes (70.49%) to 97.471 (29.51%) votes for integration. After enumerating the ravages that Southern Cameroons had gone through economically, socially and politically since reunification, he wept over the plight of his people reiterating:

> The Anglophone Cameroonians whom 1 brought into the union have been ridiculed and referred to as "Les Biafrais", "Les Enemies Dans La Maison", "les traitres" etc. and the constitutional provisions which protected this Anglophone minority have been suppressed , their voices drowned, while the rule of the gun has replaced the dialogue which the Anglophones cherish very much.... The national media has been used by the government

---

[10] See, "Cameroon Anglophone Movement: a socio-cultural association", Douala 5 December 1991. Chief Dr. HNA Enonchong was chairman; see also, the Epilogue in Ndi, Mill Hill Missionaries in South-West Cameroon, (Pauline's Press Nairobi, 2006).

through people who never voted for unification to misinform the citizens about Bamenda.[11]

Of course, this is the machinery that has deliberately but subtly been put in place to drive wedges between peoples of the two Regions for easy manipulation.

The Paradox

When historically contextualized today with the North and South West Regions simply reduced to two of the ten Regions (former Provinces) that constitute the Republic of Cameroon, the product is something of a freak, a contradiction in terms. This, essentially, because prior to reunification in 1961, Southern Cameroons had already attained and enjoyed all the attributes and privileges of statehood stretching to as far back as 26 October1954, when as a State with a Quasi Federal status within Nigeria, it had an Executive Council led by Dr. EM L Endeley as Leader of Government Business. The state was adequately defined with a specific geographical circumscription, a permanent demographic population with its own Legislative Assembly, independent judiciary and executive paraphernalia which qualified it for internal self-government. However, in matters of defence and international relations it depended on Great Britain, the administering authority. In essence, it had all that it took to be identified on the basis of possessing: executive, legislative and judicial arms of government with its own territory and nationality laws.

Southern Cameroons Refused Independence

This status was vastly extended in the Southern Cameroons Order-in-Council or indeed, the Constitution, which went operational on 1 October 1960, before the plebiscite and one whole year before independence. By it, the House of Assembly was significantly enlarged and comprised three ex-officio members, 26 elected Members of Parliament, an Executive Council headed by a Premier, who could

---

[11] Foncha's Letter of Resignation from the CPDM, 9 June 1990.

appoint up to seven ministers and three Parliamentary Secretaries with the Commissioner of Southern Cameroons playing the role of Her Majesty the Queen's Governor.[12] There was a High Court with a Judge, financial autonomy and a Public Service Commission with a Chairman. Finally, a House of Chiefs, a sort of Upper House (House of Lords) was granted.

So far advanced, the Trust Territory was just one short step away from the final goal of total sovereignty or independence, the obstacles to which as will abundantly be demonstrated in this thesis, inexplicably were mounted and masterminded by Great Britain to which it was trustee. Great Britain had solemnly, conventionally and legally by Article 76(b) of the Charter of the United Nations undertaken to guide Southern Cameroons towards that grand objective. In fact, the atrocious manner in which Britain did this constitutes the most important missing component in the Summit Magazine interview which consequently, an extensive portion of this treatise sets out to redress.

This attitude by Britain clearly amounted to an act of a grave betrayal of trust. Above all, it largely continues to account for the bulk of the woes that "Southern Cameroonians" face and complain about till today.[13] The other paradox is that having evolved so far and finally become an ideal 'state' savouring the flavours of internal autonomy for close to twenty years: 1954-1972, it was systematically demoted first, to the status of simply being regarded as one of the seven Provinces of the United Republic of Cameroon: 1972-1984 and, finally, inexplicably split into two, namely, the North and South West Provinces, 1984 - date of the Republic of Cameroon. Put in proper perspective this has been a traumatizing experience, tantamount to the loss of self-identity; in short, to anonymity and obscurity having first acquired formal statehood within the Federal Republic of Nigeria and then within the Federal Republic of Cameroon (FRC).

---

[12] The 1961 elections to the enlarged parliament were massively won by the KNDP, which swept 29 of the 34 seats leav2in1g the CPNC with barely five seats thus confirming the political landscape earlier shaped by the hotly contested plebiscite. Later, these were reduced to a rump of two; Endeley and Mbile.

[13] See the Legal Criteria for Statehood as defined by the 1932 Montevideo "Convention on Rights and Duties of States"; Article 1(a, b, c & d).

This, for a people who since the 1940s had been searching for a corporate individuality and identity becomes paradoxical. It should equally be recalled that had Southern Cameroons opted by the Plebiscite in 1961 for integration with Nigeria, it would have been granted the status of a full autonomous region equal in every way to that enjoyed by the other regions (states) in the Federation of Nigeria. This conundrum is examined in all its ramifications within the context of the "Ahidjo Factor" as well as under the compatibility of the North and South West Regions[14].

Taking a more detached and mature penetrating observation of the situation, Christian Cardinal Tumi observes that, "The Anglo-Saxon Minority Needs Protection". Going further he points out that:

> The formal agreement of 1961 in Foumban foresaw neither the assimilation, nor the dilution, nor the complete disappearance of the personality of the English-speaking part of the country. It is obvious that Ahmadou Ahidjo, making absolute use of the absolute and exceptional powers the president had, did away with his Anglophone partners in Foumban by imposing on them a gradual and political change and development which was completely different and opposed to their own political ambitions.[15]

---

[14] For details see Chapter 3.

[15] Christian Cardinal Tumi, *My Faith: a Cameroon to Be Renewed*, (Les Editions Veritas, Douala, 2011), p. 38.

Christian Cardinal Tumi

A Popular, Outspoken and Fearless Prelate

The popular, outspoken, erudite and fearless, prelate identifies fully with the political analyst, Shanda Touré, who argues that the so– called Peaceful Revolution of 1972 organized at a time, when the country was ruled with a rod of iron; citizens had no freedom of speech; they had no right to vote nor the right to be citizens in the real sense of the term; the 20thMay can only have an unhappy significance. Tumi concludes with Shanda: "We have no right whatsoever to attribute to a people the results of a Referendum that was organized by a bloody dictator".[16] Referring to the English - speaking Cameroonians, Cardinal Tumi, who is best placed and knows intimately about his people, minces no words when he literally propounds:

> These fellow countrymen and women, whether they occupy important or unimportant places in the social and political hierarchy, make known in private, their deep sentiments of disgust, of deception and of repulsion. All of them are convinced that they are oppressed marginalized and deceived in many ways.[17]

---

[16]Shanda Touré, article *in* Le Messager No. 2133 of 24/05/06 quoted in Tumi; My Faith: A Cameroon to Be Renewed, pp. 38-9.
[17] Ibid.

For the solution, quoting Professor Bernard Fonlon, he proposes three things; including, the basic principles of the culture, which should undergo a thorough objective and scientific examination, followed by a logical and decisive choice that is not passionate and finally, the modalities of choice that should be judiciously and energetically put into practice.[18]

Nature, Reason and shape of Reaction

Initially, after reading the interview on this sensitive, emotive and rather thorny topic, I was minded to react in much the same way as those who did so spontaneously over the airwaves and in the press.[19] However, on further reflection of the fact that Professor Ngoh was selected by virtue of the fact that he is a seasoned historian, writer and university professor, I decided to tackle the response from a purely historical perspective, the proper medium for intellectual discourse. This way, the points made could be seen holistically in their broader, less distorted historical context instead of selectively picking up each of the myriad of indictments pitched in the interview against John Ngu Foncha as lowest points in British colonial history. Malcolm Milne attempts to throw further light on why he had been so grossly misled.an individual, the Kamerun National Democratic Party (KNDP), its leadership, the Southern Cameroons political elite and people as a whole.

For yet another reason, this response could come in handy for those who might not have read the particular issue of the Summit Magazine that carried the classic interview[20] and could therefore serve as a historical document for further debate and future reference. The most important reason however is that Dr. John Ngu Foncha, specifically targeted in the interview bears little resemblance to the man I knew personally in practical life or from literature and ubiquitous public opinion about him having already undertaken substantial

---

[18] Ibid., p.40.
[19] There were hot exchanges between Profs. Victor Julius Ngoh vs. Verkijika Fanso and Jonny Nfonyam, which were carried in e.g., *The Post Newspaper* and other publications.
[20] For the sake of clarity and easy cross-referencing the interview is reproduced in its entirety as the "Epilogue".

research towards writing his biography. Much of what resonates in the interview is a nauseating repetition of the conspiracy theories that for years have been peddled about the man. It is time long enough for the records to be straightened on this, as on similar issues.

Having said that, it should quickly be added that putting together this account has been a traumatizing experience; given that it did not evolve as an original, spontaneous option, but sprouted in reaction to an external agenda consisting of the litany of indictments mounted in the interview on widely disparate subjects. An attempt has been made to reclassify these into themes or chapters that carry a sense of cohesion. Consequently; the approach unavoidably leans heavily towards rectification of the mostly skewed information that abounds in the journal and other literature on this topic. Therefore, it is advisable to browse through the Summit Magazine interview which is reproduced in its entirety in the epilogue, where necessary to stay focused.

The presentation was flawed in several ways and historically by the sketchy or near total absence of reference to the "declassified British secret papers" made public as far back as 1998. These were further confirmed and consolidated by Malcolm Milne's denunciation of the entire British Colonial Policy in the Trust Territory. Taken together; the disclosures emanating from these sources have literally revolutionized thoughts and trends in Southern Cameroons history in particular and Cameroon history as a whole. In these, the intrigues organized by the Colonial Office and faithfully executed by Messrs Johnson O Field and Malcolm Milne, the Commissioner and Deputy Commissioner of Southern Cameroons together with CE King the British Ambassador to Yaoundé[21], Cameroon are laid bare. Their total omission on a topic in which they were the fundamental executors can hardly be justified.

The other yawning chasm is the near absence or sparse reference to the odious role played by President Ahmadou Ahidjo, whose brazen and insatiable craving for power was matched as much by his "absolute" cynicism with reference to federalism and democracy. Unfortunately, this was not as obvious to his contemporaries as it has become presently with hindsight. Coincidentally, like what the

---

[21] Ibid., PRO Co 554/2254 XC 4478.

declassified British secret papers and Malcolm Milne ended up doing in recanting British colonial policy in Southern Cameroons, so also are the disclosures of how Ahidjo was contemptuous and sceptical over the idea of reunification and federalism. Consequently, re-examining the facts available, "Fifty years after Southern Cameroons Independence," it is obvious that nobody and nothing could have stopped his determination to dismantle the Federal Republic of Cameroon for which he had no regard and in which he had no faith *ab initio.*

Intellectually, we cannot disclaim or ignore what is now so widely available; information emanating from the declassified British secret papers as well as that on President Ahmadou Ahidjo; reasons that have occasioned my response through this exposition. Historians owe it as a duty to posterity just like the medical corps do in the "Hippocratic Oath," to reconstruct the past authentically and to render the truth and nothing but the truth within their competence to the public.[22] Absolute truth as such may not be possible; since the humanities and the social sciences to which history belongs are approximate sciences. Nevertheless, the public should be afforded what it takes to make informed opinion, distinguishing between an author's views and facts on any given issue, aware that in matters of history as in all academic pursuits subject to continuing research, no one has ever put a finite conclusion on any topic. This is most applicable to History, which by its very definition refers to: "enquiry" and first hand, uncorrupted report; all of which points at continuous, relentless research and investigation. History above all else, is dynamic as each generation is challenged to rewrite the history of its past in the light of unfolding information and techniques of research, reconstructing the past in the perpetual search for authentic truth or, as EH Carr better puts it: "History is the continuous process of interaction between the historian and his facts, an unending dialogue between the present and the past."[23]

---

[22] See Chapter 10 Section on Methodology in this volume.
[23] EH Carr, *What Is History?,* (London; Palgrave , 2001).

Milne's Revelations Revolutionize Cameroon History

A personage whose conversion and revelations have done much to uncover and radicalize the history of Southern Cameroons is Malcolm Milne, the Deputy Commissioner for Southern Cameroons, who amazingly featured prominently in many accounts as the administrator par excellence. But, for yet another reason not so obvious in the interview is the fact that he and his boss, Johnson Field, the Commissioner of Southern Cameroons were the central actors, in effect architects and executors of British colonial policy in the Trust Territory of British Southern Cameroons especially during the critical period of 1958-1961. However, Malcolm Milne further distinguished himself as one person, who has elaborately documented most of what transpired during this period in his autobiography.[24] In this respect, he profusely regrets:

Johnson O Field

Commissioner of Southern Cameroons and Malcolm Milne's Boss

---

[24] Ibid., Milne, *No Telephone to Heaven*: This, to say the least marks one of the lowest points in british colonial history. Malcom Milne attempts to throw further light on why he had been so grossly misled.

[What] I had not come to terms with the conviction myself – was that we were doing the Cameroons a wrong. We should have struggled harder to continue our trusteeship for several years longer. But the forces against us were too strong and l judge now that had l, as Commissioner of the Cameroons taken this line in 1959 – 61, l should merely have made a great nuisance of myself and achieved nothing.[25]

Consequently, he is attributed a substantial section in this work and so are: the plebiscite, President Ahmadou Ahidjo, John Ngu Foncha, the Foumban Constitutional Conference and the supposed North /Southwest divide of the so-called: "Cameroon West of the Mungo" or "Anglophone Cameroon". The sections on Ahidjo and the Foumban Constitutional Conference are further enriched with recent accounts by first hand reporters revealing inconceivable snares that were carefully hatched to lure the Anglophone delegates at the Foumban Constitutional Conference into complacency and impotency.

Malcolm Milne's views after his rather theatrical and mysterious conversion are powerfully corroborated by those of his compatriot, John Percival, who came out to Southern Cameroons on a United Nations ticket as one of the twenty-five Plebiscite Officers, recruited by the British Government and seconded to the UN. Thus his background and even temperament were totally different from those of his countryman. It is amazing that these two gentlemen approached the question of British colonial administration in Southern Cameroons from two vastly dissimilar, literally opposite experiences but arrived with mathematical precision at the conclusion that the British had made an awful mess of their mandate in the Trust Territory. Equally, they concluded that they (the British) ought to right the wrongs done to these nice trusting, loyal people. Actually, Percival, a liberal and critic, after a careful study of the situation was totally disenchanted and took the view that the British Government had neglected its responsibilities forcing the people to make a difficult decision with far reaching consequences having failed in the first place to adequately

---

[25] Ibid., p. 395; see also NAB, Vb /b/ 1962)2 *Press Release* No.1498"Southern Cameroons discussed in British Parliament"

prepare them economically and politically for selfhood. He categorically took note that:

> Many Southern Cameroonians continued to plead for the colonial administration to be prolonged for a little longer, to give them a chance to make informed decision about the future, but both the UN and the colonial authorities had refused to countenance this option. ... with Ian Macleod as colonial secretary, the British Government of the day was only too eager to wash its hands off the Cameroons... as quickly and painlessly as possible.[26]

Consequently, Percival rejected the tinted view of the deplorable British Administration in Southern Cameroons and argued fervently in favour of independence. In fact, in many ways, though an Englishman engaged in the service of the United Nations, he was more radical in his castigation of both establishments, Britain and the UN, than Malcolm Milne. After six months in the country, he declared: "The experience awoke me to the consequences of colonial rule. I still believe that Britain should do its best to ensure the lasting welfare of territories it once ruled." Far away in Wum, he was shocked to discover that:

> People who lived only a morning's walk from the DO ... had spent the best part of a life time under British rule without setting eyes on a white man. And now that they were setting eyes on one it was the closing days before independence.[27]

This is a brutal indictment and speaks volumes on British neglect of Southern Cameroons and further elaborates their attitude to the people and their leadership as independence approached. To Percival, even then, the people were well informed and knew exactly what they wanted. And, of the plebiscite, he made the cryptic observation:

---

[26] John Percival, *The Southern Cameroons Plebiscite, Choice or Betrayal* (Langaa Research & Publishing CIG, Mankon, Bamenda), Pp.77-78. In other words, the KNDP stand for extended trusteeship fairly represented the wishes of the people.

[27] Ibid., p. 33ff.

It was quickly made clear to me that they wanted no part of it and that they saw the whole thing as a sham, a cosmetic exercise in democracy. The only decision they were allowed to make was to choose whether to throw in their lot with Nigeria or French Cameroon, and they wanted neither of them. All the other decisions had been taken thousands of miles away by officials who thought they knew what they needed better than the people themselves.[28]

Many of the people wanted the white man to stay at least for the time being, and were hurt and angry to think that the British were going to abandon them forcing them to choose between the Nigerians whom they considered "cannibals" and "Frenchy people" whom they saw as robbers. The real choice of "independence" was denied them.[29] It is also amazing and a lot more than a mere coincidence that these two men; Malcolm Milne and John Percival, like numerous other administrators, missionaries, casual visitors and tourists commonly arrived at the conclusion that Southern Cameroonians were exceptionally hospitable, kind and trustworthy. Consequently, of these "wonderful people," Percival like Malcolm Milne concluded as recently as 2008, when he passed away: "I still retain to this day, a powerful affection and respect of the Bamenda Grasslands and the beautiful country where they live".[30]

It is in this connection and, with this knowledge that one can hardly resist the endorsement of the compelling penultimate concluding statement in the editorial of the Eden Xtra Magazine No. 001 of October 2011, in which the editor in his wisdom predicts: "We may yet fall back on the relevance of history to correct today's wrongs and fashion the tomorrow that we desperately hope to attain."[31] This statement encapsulates the expositions in that timeless version of the paper especially, when juxtaposed with the prediction by Malcolm Milne that the British would not only regret for their misdeeds but would be held accountable for them some day. Possibly, this is where

---

[28] Ibid., p. xiii.
[29] Ibid., p.32.
[30] Ibid., p. 103.
[31] *Eden Xtra Magazine* No. 001 October 2011, p. 5.

law would capitalize on the excavations of history to redress and rekindle the blighted aspirations of a suppressed promising nation that once was. This after all may not be too farfetched taking the cue from the redress presently being awarded by the British Government to the victims of the Mau Mau independence movement in Kenya in the 1950s.[32] In a nutshell, challenged by the plethora of issues and questions raised in the Summit Magazine interview, an endeavour has been made in this work to identify the sources, context and nature of the woes that have bedevilled Southern Cameroonians since "Reunification and Independence", fifty years ago. These can roughly be placed in the hands of an odd triad comprising: in the first instance, Britain, the administering power of the Southern Cameroons Trusteeship;[33] secondly, the Southern Cameroons political leadership and thirdly, the regime of President Ahmadou Ahidjo.

Of these three, the Summit Magazine interview focused exclusively on the Southern Cameroonian political leadership literally to the exclusion of the British Colonial Administration, one of the powerful props of the tripod and President Ahidjo.[34] Massive evidence that the British covertly and overtly obstructed all attempts at secession from Nigeria, extended Trusteeship or much worse, "independence for Southern Cameroons" led by the Foncha Administration, lay hidden in the archives until this masquerade was unmasked with the publication of the declassified British secret papers in the late 1990s. Further missing links and lingering doubts were amply divulged in the unnerving confessions paradoxically by Malcolm Milne himself, the erstwhile Deputy Commissioner of Southern Cameroons, and practically one of the hatchet men who executed the colonial atrocious plots against that Trust Territory.

Ultimately, he came clean and took revenge against a system that had used him as tissue paper, against the people of Southern

---

[32] In the 1950s, towards Kenyan independence: a secret nationalist Kenyan organization set up in 1952 with the objective of forcing European settlers from the land and ending British rule in Kenya. Microsoft® Encarta® 2009. © 1993-2008 Microsoft Corporation. All rights reserved.

[33] Secondly, the Southern Cameroons political leadership itself.

[34] Even when referring to President Ahidjo, this is done with a slanting rather reverential, benign approach. Interestingly, existing historical evidence and simple logic bear heavily on them.

Cameroons and their political leadership. Most interestingly, at the end of the day, though reluctantly, he graciously conceded that these political leaders were the best breed of people he had had the occasion to work with throughout his long career in the colonial service spanning from Eden and Gold Coast to Nigeria. In the ultimate analysis as atonement he played the role of advocate for the people of Southern Cameroons whom he thought had been gravely wronged by the heartless British Administration operating from Whitehall.

The Foumban Constitutional Conference and the Federal Constitution resulting from it with all possible shortcomings was never the less the best thing that could have happened to Southern Cameroons in the prevailing circumstances. This is precisely what it failed to become in the hands of President Ahidjo, who as pointed out was innately antidemocratic and could not contemplate sharing power with anybody. The eventual result was the decimation of the ten year old budding democratic State of Southern-West Cameroon, which had enjoyed Self-Government since 1954 with its own legislature; House of Assembly and House of Chiefs, Executive and Judiciary, each of which by the Westminster parliamentary democratic principles and procedures was thoroughly conscious and jealous of its rights and prerogatives. There was a distinct separation of powers and the exercise of checks and balances among them. It could be said that the blossoming Federal Republic of Cameroon within which it existed was blighted at birth and, with it, their dreams, aspirations, visions and expectations; leaving behind a dazed community in total disbelief. Herein lay the source of most of the woes; problems that have erupted and continue to fester in a fluid state of affairs without a clear vision of the way forward or an appropriate means of expression and dialogue by the aggrieved party.

In a sort of conspiracy of circumstances arising from the lack of understanding of the historical background of these issues; prejudice or ignorance, Foncha and his administration who, in a proper analysis of the manifest historical data available should rightly be regarded as "victims" crushed in between these imponderable forces, have instead been made to appear as culprits placed in the dock at whom accusing fingers are continuously directed. This is the paradox of Southern Cameroons history but as Malcolm Milne concludes, the British would rue it one day. Within this logic, it is just possible that law and equity could tango with history to right the wrongs done to the "nice trusting little people of Southern Cameroons" manhandled in the first place by a mindless colonial machine remote controlled from Whitehall in London, on the one hand, and then thrust into the claws of an insatiable, supposedly "fraternal" and benign regime on the other. That precisely is what this treatise attempts to lay bare.

Chapter 2

Reunification Account: Setting Basic Records Straight

So far it is obvious that there was indeed not only a plethora of indictments but as well, several controversial topics which sprang out from the epic Summit Magazine interview. The bulk of these will be dealt with later in the course of this exposition. Nevertheless, there are a few pungent ones which call for urgent preliminary examination to clarify issues fundamental to the themes that resonate throughout the discussion. Together with these, are generic expressions which need to be harnessed for common understanding. The idea therefore is to simplify these disparate topics so that everyone is taken on board.

The preliminary challenges raised touch on: the intrinsic historic notion of "reunification" seeded in the "Kamerun idea"; the indisputable political maturity of Southern Cameroonians; the identification of victims from predators and oppressors in Southern Cameroons history; the place of bad faith and lack of political will in the Ahidjo Regime; the uniqueness of the Summit Magazine as a journal and a brief check out on who John Ngu Foncha was in the context of this essay, since he is at the heart of the indictments in the discussion. An early X-ray and proper situation of these lurking hurdles in their proper Cameroon historical context would facilitate the sense in which they are used in this work. This ensures that controversial interpretations are reduced to the barest minimum.

Golden Jubilee Celebrations Whet Appetites

Beyond the glitter, glamour, nature and expectations of the political setting of the public festivities marking the Golden Jubilee celebrations, there has been a heightened awareness coupled with anxiety, curiosity and great expectations, especially among Cameroonians of the North and South West Regions about the circumstances surrounding their rather misty common past. Many of the educated and enlightened elements think that it is also an opportune moment to stop and deeply reflect on: how and why we got here and who really is responsible for all that happened at reunification and has continued to be experienced since then. These are legitimate concerns which constitute the recurrent substance of discussions, gossips, questions and worries raised by inquisitive individuals, students, civil society organs and more vehemently by radical political movements at home and abroad. These vocalized anxieties and complaints range from feelings of: discrimination, marginalization, assimilation and perceived annexationist tendencies, as well as questions of the citizenship status of former Southern Cameroonians within the State of the Republic of Cameroon. Put together, they constitute the so called "Anglophone problem", their woes so to speak.[35]

In all of this, fingers are continually pointed at the majority French Cameroonian political elite but even more significantly, inwardly, the extent to which the Southern Cameroonian political leaders themselves were answerable for their own predicaments. The magazine interview liberally wrapped up numerous controversial issues thus laying bare, grey historical areas that necessitate attention and clarification. Open reactions to it so far, have been made by eminent scholars, historians, jurists and the public at large in diverse ways and at different levels, which academically, should be stimulating, enlightening and welcome.[36]

Having said that, in anticipation of the mega celebrations marking the event much ink continues to flow but nothing as rocking as the Summit Magazine interview, also, perhaps because it fired the first salvo that has initiated the discussions.

---

[35] This essay is not about the socio-political and economic achievements made or not made by Southern Cameroons over the past fifty years but focuses on the leadership and institutions as portrayed in the interview that were responsible for determining their woes. This clearly defines the boundaries of the discussion. The emphasis on woes is indicative of the looming lapses largely in the sphere of autonomy, governance and equitable distribution of national resources.

[36] Prominent among them are Prof. Fanso, Prof. Jonny Nfonyam. The latter gives a critical legal touch to the criticism in *The Post Newspaper No,* 01266 ofFriday , 22 July 2011.

Distinction of the *Summit Magazine* interview

By and large, three qualities mark out that interview as being unique: firstly, that it was granted by the Summit Magazine, a journal of choice for many, highly rated, exalted and acclaimed nationally and internationally. On initial encounter, it strikes one as an attractive, glamorous and an accomplished journal, which in essence produces articles of class. It further distinguishes itself in bringing out to the public arena the biographies and life styles of celebrities, role models, heroes and heroines. In a country like Cameroon dearth of exemplary leadership, who can be showcased for emulation by the youth, this indeed is a noble mission the editorial board of the paper has assumed and is of inestimable value for nation-building. Without bothering to cite any specific examples, all, indeed "all" the journals are awash with news of startling scandals dealing with the embezzlement of state funds and corruption naming and shaming high government officials from the Prime Minister through Ministers of State to top ranking directors of state corporations who are behind bars in the maximum prisons in Yaoundé and Douala, besides ongoing investigations and persecutions.[37] Secondly, the editorial team most aptly captured the mood of the moment during this year of celebrating the Golden Jubilee of Southern Cameroons Independence and "Reunification, Fifty years After" as an apt caption for deep reflection, stock taking and charting the way forward into the future, mindful of the stumbling blocks of the past and experiences of the present.

Thirdly, of everything, the greatest good effusing from the iconic interview coupled with the immediate robust reactions to it, is that the various grey areas and aspects of Southern Cameroons history were thrown wide open to academic debate. Beyond the press, this challenge taken up by professional and budding researchers would definitely revolutionize the approach, content and the entire Cameroon historical thought.

---

[37] Cameroon journals, especially the dailies and biweeklies, literally without exception presently compete in carrying mindboggling in-depth disclosures on these issues especially those affecting the top ranking officials – court trials and sentences meted out to the former: PM, Ephrain Inoni, Secretary General at the Presidency, Marafa Hamidu Yaya, Jean Marie Mebara, director general of the Cameroon shipyard, Zac Fornjindam among others feature in these papers.

Finally, and of equal importance was the choice of Professor Victor Julius Ngoh, a renowned, prolific author and teacher, who has written widely on Cameroon, African and World History, as their guest. He is also appropriately described as: "one of the few authoritative researchers in Cameroon History," who "has always stood firm on the truth about the process towards reunification".[38]

His other attributes as (former Head of the Department of History and Acting Dean of the Faculty of Arts, University of Buea) immediately attract more than just the ordinary reading public. By the same token and above all, it invoked the rapt attention of his former students, scholars, politicians and watchers of the Cameroon socio-political scene. It is little wonder therefore, that the interview received varying commentaries from some university dons, jurists, scholars and journalists in the press and over the radio; largely also because of the wide range and controversial nature of the issues it raised. Consequently, the interview positively served as a launching pad for highlighting the grey areas of Cameroon history that need collective illumination and invigoration.

On the other hand, the mainstream of those who read the Summit Magazine article on this topic would be those who were too young or who were not even born by 1961, when the plebiscite was organized and consequently will not have any personal knowledge to rely on. Furthermore, besides reading the papers, few are those who would have studied or will venture to study Cameroon History to any appreciable depth and so the tendency would be to take all that has been published in the Summit Magazine and elsewhere as the gospel truth. There is therefore a grave need to set the record straight.

One positive outcome of the interview as indicated is that it has highlighted some of those areas of Cameroon History generally taken for granted as "common knowledge" for the average educated person in this country. However, after browsing through the interview a second time, and reflecting on statements commonly made by apparently well-informed compatriots, whom one would normally

---

[38] See Epilogue for the rendition of the entire interview. Professor Ngoh's publications, especially his Constitutional Developments in Southern Cameroons 1946 -1961, From Trusteeship to Independence, has held unrivalled cen- tral ground in the history of that period in Southern Cameroons historiography.

assume should know basic Cameroon History, it is baffling to discover the prevailing degree of gullibility, superficiality and outright ignorance displayed on the knowledge of our common past. This is the invaluable enlightening service which journals like the Summit Magazine and others render to the nation, when they pick on specific topics of public interest for in-depth examination and education.

The Response: Inherent Limitations

However, any honest attempt at a befitting "critique" on the issues raised in the epic interview would at first sight in these circumstances, give the impression of a rebuttal or even of taking sides in the debate to debunk the interminable charges levelled against specified individuals, structures and processes. Yet, this would only be apparent. The approach adopted in this exposition is deliberately and basically intended to highlight points of fact, logic and history that have seemingly or deliberately been glossed over, ignored or distorted. As a result, what follows is a straight forward presentation of open facts backed by historical data available to all who can find the time and means to investigate. Of course, this has entailed double bending backwards to garner appropriate information to meet basic standards of authenticity, conscious that credible history does not merely consist in citing such facts, but in ensuring that the facts arise from critical analyses and that the root sources from which they are extracted stand the test of stringent credibility as well.

The other limitation with this exposition is its brevity given that the range of issues addressed is enormous. Basically, therefore, the presentation largely though not completely targets the indictments propounded in the interview, and, for that reason cannot exactly be as seamless, chronological and all-encompassing as with a spontaneously conceived piece of work. However, this is balanced by the fact that since for the most part the treatise seeks to respond to indictments made in the discussion; an added effort is made throughout the account to let the political actors and actions speak for themselves as in a sort of stage show. In other words, most of the quotations in this work are elaborate and made in extensor with paraphrasing and explanations reduced to the minimum. This is intended to leave the individual readers, the liberty as far as possible to arrive at independent, informed and empirical conclusions. This basically is the role historians should play, to stay above board. Arthur Marwick, an authority in historiography aptly warns that: "It is history and not the historian that society requires".

The approach pursues the adage that historically, "We think globally and act locally". Hardly are issues, events and personages such as: John Ngu Foncha, EML Endeley, PM Kale, AN Jua, ST Muna and their colleagues examined in isolation. They are always seen in the particular context, circumstance and time. Taking Foncha the most targeted, for example; as a historical figure, there were certainly those who went before him, those who succeeded him and especially those contemporaries with whom he interrelated either as colleagues, opponents or detractors. Of equal importance is the epoch within which the characters examined lived and functioned; this is crucial because all individuals are products of their time and circumstances. Events should therefore be examined with all their ramifications. Historical figures should generally be seen within context, and in comparative terms since no person is an island. This is dealt with more profoundly in the subdivision on methodology in History.[39]

It is in the realization of such commissions, omissions and the fact that these systematic attacks have not been given a proper historical response that I have decided to throw in some light even before I complete my major preoccupation on John Ngu Foncha's biography. At a personal level, I take it as the fulfilment of an obligation and commitment not only to the man and to posterity but to history itself, which more and more is being distorted. Practically, therefore, this exposition is an intermediate measure of "damage control" in the circumstance.[40] It indicates sign posts for constructive research in national integration and nation building.

---

[39] This is lightly handled as a section of Chapter Three in this book.

[40] Nonetheless, a major positive challenge ensuing from the Summit Magazine discussion is the urgency for me to complete that major project on Dr. John Ngu Foncha's biography. Apparently much of the interview was targeted at his person. The *Summit Magazine* aspointed out is a journal of repute and held in high esteem but strangely, in the interview both the interviewer and the interviewee were openly partisan. There was open bias and hostility not only against Foncha, his cabinet, the KNDP leadership and the North-West Region but open defence or extolling of Dr.

Reunification: Certainly, Not a "Gamble"!

Even before the issues raised in the Summit Magazine interview are appropriately tackled, the sub-title used in the interview referring to: "The Reunification Gamble: Setting the Records Straight" requires urgent attention to really set the records right. Reunification with Republic of Cameroon is easily the greatest thing that has happened in the history of Southern Cameroons and therefore deserves a critical clarification. Judged by the circumstances and statistics available, and in the context of the epoch, it would be most inappropriate to describe the momentous event that originated with the Plebiscite of 11 February 1961 throughout Southern Cameroons resulting in the landslide victory for Reunification followed by the famous Foumban Constitutional Conference of July 17-21, 1961 and finally, consummated on 1st October 1961 by Independence and Reunification cannot simply be dismissed as a "gamble".[41] This would be a total misjudgement of the facts.

Of all the defects and adverse comments that can be made, the events building up to the Plebiscite, the Buea Tripartite Conference, the Bamenda All Party Conference, the Foumban Constitutional Conference and leading from there to independence and reunification remain incontestably the most significant in the history of Cameroon as a whole and not just Southern/West Cameroon. Actually, it can be argued forcefully that reunification combined and transcended a concept higher than the "political will" of Cameroonians on both sides of the divide. Its umbilical cord is found in the treaty of annexation signed by Dr. Gustav Nachtigal the explorer with Douala Chiefs for the German Empire on 12 July 1884. It inaugurated the thirty year period of German Colonial rule: hence "the German idea" imbedded in all Cameroonians, to whom this territory is "Motherland" and who *ipso facto* have equal right to its patrimony. The UPC ideology, which

---

Endeley, the CPNC leadership and the SW Region. Wherever mention is made of Foncha and his collaborators and the KNDP it is entirely negative: to blame, accuse or denigrate almost without exception. This can quickly be crosschecked in the epilogue.

[41] The caption of the magazine, see Epilogue; "Foreword" (sic) 'Setting the Record Straight,' *Eden Xtra*, No. *001*, October 2011, p.5. It carries a terse description of the processes enclosing the event.

vocalized this view in its ideology of immediate independence and reunification came to be adopted or more appropriately pirated by Ahidjo's UC as amply demonstrating the will of French Cameroonians. this explains why there was no demand for a plebiscite to ascertain what was already so obvious before the United Nations Visiting Mission in 1958.[42] On the balance, in Southern Cameroons reunification was the espoused battle cry of the FCWU, KUNC, half-heartedly taken up by the KNC and finally realized by the KNDP.

Granting "Reunification" the primordial importance it deserves in the national integration of Cameroon, Professor Martin Njeuma squares it in its proper historical perspective contending that:

> Since 1916 when the British and French partitioned German Kamerun, the reunification of Cameroon has been an important political issue. In modern times many politicians have risen and fallen depending on their skill in handling the implications of reunification. The point is that the very survival of Cameroon, in terms of national integration and harmonious development, depends largely on a profound understanding of the role that the quest for reunification has played in Cameroon's political history.[43]

In other words, the Plebiscite of 11 February 1961 broadly manifested the popular yearning within the Southern Cameroons to reunite with la République du Cameroun. As solidly demonstrated in the editorial of the Eden Xtra of October 2011, it must be emphatically stated that: "Reunification was not based on any real or imagined weakness on the part of the former or on the alleged and often bloated magnanimity of the latter".[44]

---

[42] The UPC from 1948 espoused the radical ideology of immediate independence andreunification.

[43] Reunification and Political Opportunism in the Making of Cameroon's Independence by Martin z. Njeuma, http://lucy.ukc.ac.uk/Chilver/Paideuma/paideuma-REUNIFI.html.(07/07/13) .

[44]*Eden Xtra,* October 2011 p.7.

Best Decision Everything Being Equal

The paper further captures the essence of the entire process that took place in Southern Cameroons during the critical period from 1958-1961 and concludes:

> On the contrary, it was a heroic and historic act consummated from the heart, with the best of intentions and with the ultimate hope that each sector will be its brother's keeper. In harbouring this dream, Southern Cameroonians hoped that their compatriots on the other side of the aisle would grasp the substance and significance of this dream and make Cameroon stand tall if not tallest among Africa's emerging nations.[45]

This was equally the spirit of Foncha's vision expressed in discussions with Ahidjo in July 1960 after "independence and reunification" had been imposed on him at the UN, he declared: "Cameroon can be transformed into a paradise in Africa". This was, everything being equal, with good will, transparency, honesty, the political will and determination to make it succeed by those who held the reins of authority provided they had the intrinsic interest of the Cameroon nation truly at heart.[46]

Indeed, critically examined it was Southern Cameroons which alone took the critical steps that brought the new Federal State into being. Furthermore, the point should be made that this historic event initially took place at Tiko International Air Port (and later at Buea Mountain Hotel) on the eve of 1 October 1961, on this side of the Mungo with President Ahidjo presiding and PM Foncha, Endeley and others in attendance watching as the bright green, red and yellow striped flag with two golden stars was hoisted for the first time, while the Union Jack of Great Britain was lowered and "God Save Our Gracious Queen" sung for the last time.[47] That is how the brand new

---

[45] Editorial by Chief Zachee Nzohngandembou, "Reunification: Paradise Not Yet Lost" in, *Eden Xtra*, October 2011, p.7.
[46] *Cameroon Life*, March 1991, p.9., "The Plebiscite: Thirty Years After, The Choice between Fire and Deep Water", by Francis K Wache.
[47] As it wasthe first.

nation, the "Federal Republic of Cameroon" (FRC) comprising two states: East and West Cameroon of equal status was ushered into the comity of nations.

Dr. EML Endeley easily is the one person, who should have contested this event as the leader who fought the most steadfast and relentless battle against reunification. Consequently, there can be no gainsaying the significance of the declaration he made at the CPNC Congress holding at Tabenken in Nkambe in 1965. He maintained that he as an individual, not only as party leader, had sacrificed more than anybody in the struggle for integration with Nigeria but that after the defeat at the polls, he had reflected and fully embraced the fact of reunification. Earlier, right on the conference floor at the Foumban Constitutional Conference this great patriot, who above all fought for the realization of the coming into being of the "Cameroon Nation", finally, wholeheartedly, embraced reunification and invited the "maqizzards" to abandon the jungle and join in the process of nation building as he and Foncha had demonstrated. Endeley declared:

> Many thought that this conference would be a failure and that it would not work;[48] succeed. And, therefore, Mr. President, 1 am appealing to those brothers who have gone wild to cease fire and cooperate with us and come back to help make Cameroon a peaceful country. We should not use our arms against our brothers; we should use them against our enemies.[49]

If in time this great achievement has been messed up with, then that is another story altogether. The brave political "nationalist" hunters courageously fought and safely brought home the game, the problem therefore, has been the manner in which it (the cake) has been distributed. This does not in the least dent the collective accomplishment of these courageous patriots. By the same token, Dr. EML Endeley, after all is said and done, remains the statesman, man of vision and conviction, qualities he shared with his valiant colleagues in

---

[48] PRO CO 553/2265 XC C3406 of 21 July 1961, also, the Foumban Constitutional Conference

[49] More of this is discussed under the Chapters on the plebiscite and the political culture in Southern Cameroons.

the reunification struggle. The qualities cherished here are those centred around the political will to build a nation on reconciliation and shared values. To different degrees this whole thesis sets out to espouse without any attempt at triumphalism the virtues in these dedicated leaders who worked with very limited means to lay a solid foundation for this nation.[50]

Forging a Unique Identity

Consequently, the facts largely belie the assertion that "reunification was a gamble." Rather, on closer examination, a great deal could be made of the massive impact of the political sensitization that engulfed not only the politicians but the entire Southern Cameroons public especially the electorate beginning from the elections into the Eastern Nigeria House of Assembly in 1951, through the Eastern Region Crisis; the evolution of the "Benevolent Neutrality Bloc" in Nigerian politics by Cameroonian Members of Parliament, followed by the; 'All Party Conference at Mamfe' in 1953. These political landmarks could hardly have left anybody indifferent. The ultimate impact was that the struggle yielded the first truly 'national' (nation-wide) political parties in the "United Nations Trust Territory of Southern Cameroons": viz, the Kamerun National Congress (KNC) and the Kamerun People's Party (KPP). These developments including the constitutional conferences held in Nigeria and London earned the "Quasi Federal" status for Southern Cameroons within Nigeria. Here the emphasis all along had been that of the "identity" of Southern Cameroonians as a unique people, with a common political past, culture and vision.

The sum total of these experiences was that the people increasingly saw themselves as "belonging together" to a homeland, a motherland, with a common history, geographical circumscription, ambitions, fears, challenges, disappointments, achievements and above all a common vision as Southern Cameroonians. Reminiscences of Dr. Endeley and his colleagues exhibiting stones throughout as they toured the length and breadth of the territory purported to have been shot at them in

---

[50] NN Mbile, *Cameroon Political Story; Memories of an Eye- Witness* (Presbyterian Printing Press, Limbe), p.174.

Nigeria could hardly be expunged from the memories of those who lived that dramatic experience; hence the undivided loyalty the entire nation gave him. Put together this is what bore dividends in 1961 even, if in the course of time some of the leaders including Endeley himself had wavered.

With this strategic political evolution Southern Cameroons was accorded its own House of Assembly, which met for the first time on 26 October 1954. From then, it began enjoying an appreciable measure of "internal Self-Government" with Dr. Endeley; first, as Leader of Government Business (LGB) from 1954-1958, and then as first Premier of the Trust Territory. So, constitutionally, Southern Cameroons was way ahead of French Cameroon which was still dabbling under the status of a French Overseas Territory only attaining internal autonomy or self-government with the appointment of Mr. Andre Marie Mbida as Premier in 1957 after the "Loi Cadre" or the Enabling Act, but it was not until 1959, the year before full independen5c0e that it was granted internal autonomy. That is to say, long before reunification, Southern Cameroonians had been self-governing for seven years and definitely the people knew what they were doing. Proof of this political maturity until 1972 largely comprises the essence of this book.

Southern Cameroons: Political Maturity

Subsequent to these developments, there were hotly contested legislative elections in the territory in: 1951, 1953, 1957,1959 and 1961 excluding the plebiscite which stood a class of its own. Thus, within ten years, these Southern Cameroonians went to the polls five times or an average of one election every 1.7 years! Taking into consideration the political sensitization that preceded each election, this was a unique experience. These were usually accompanied by mutations, leading to the formation of rival political parties, coalitions and carpet crossings. For the plebiscite in particular, note must be taken of the rigorous politicization and conferences: at the UN, Mamfe, in the West Cameroon House of Assembly, then back to the UN and London before proceeding to the polls on 11 February1961. This was followed by the Buea Tripartite Conference, the "Bamenda All Party

Conference", prelude to the Foumban Constitutional Conference and finally the Yaoundé Tripartite Conference. Mbile, who initially had complained about having not been given a copy of the draft constitution from Ahidjo earlier; captured this special experience when he logically boasted; "We may not have done more if we had spent five months instead of five days in writing our constitution at Foumban."[51] This was on the strength of the argument that the Southern Cameroonian delegates to the Conference did so as mature politicians. In his words:

> Indeed, against the background of having attended four conferences, three in London, and one in Nigeria, several of us in the West Cameroon contingent felt confident to be more than a match for our Francophone counterparts for none of them could claim the experience of more than four months…and lobbying in the corridors and committee rooms of Lancaster House, London and Lagos. In men like Endeley, Foncha, Muna, Jua and my humble self, to name only these the feeling was that in wrestlers on hearing the drums and music of their popular sport….[52]

This is ample proof of the political maturity of Southern Cameroons as finally confirmed by the result of the Plebiscite. Thus to find fault with Foumban is sheer rabble rousing. In fact, he turned up with half the number of Anglophone delegates at Foumban and even if he had special French advisers as alleged there was no provision for such inputs on the conference agenda.

Special UNTC Status and Privileges

In making any such evaluation note should be taken of the privileged position accorded Southern Cameroons as a UN Trust Territory. Southern Cameroons like British Northern Cameroons and French Cameroon, extracted from German Kamerun, by Article 76(b)

---

[51] Ibid., p.165.
[52] *Cameroon Tribune Hors Serie* Octobre 2011. Reunification One Cameroon, A Dynamic Story, pp. 126-7. See, striking article on Northern Cameroons by Kimeng Hilton Ndukong4.7CNH and KUNC produced the KNC

enjoyed a special status, distinct from other colonies at the UN. Southern Cameroons was a Trust Territory under the tutelage of Great Britain, which they administered as an integral part of their Nigerian colony until First October 1961. In fact, it could be said that most of the difficulties faced by the former Southern Cameroons today, fifty years after reunification and independence result from that original error; because, when the time came for secession and, "independence for Southern Cameroons", the British Colonial Administration placed treacherous hurdles on that path. In the case of British Northern Cameroons, they succeeded in manipulating for its integration with Northern Nigeria.[53]

By this UN statute, Britain was obliged to report periodically, responding to a barrage of penetrating questions, explaining what exactly it was doing to ensure that the territory was being adequately prepared: economically, socially and politically towards self-government and ultimate independence. As a further control measure, the United Nations Trusteeship Council (UNTC) was set up and from 1949, routinely dispatched United Nations Visiting Missions (UNVM) to the Southern Cameroons to ascertain the situation on the ground for themselves. During such visits, apart from spot checks and field trips, they received: petitions, complaints, requests, memoranda, letters of all sorts from socio-cultural, economic, development and political groups and associations. These were transmitted to the UN, where they were critically examined at various levels of the UNTC and UN General Assembly. The extent to which this process alone contributed to the socio-political and economic sensitizing exercise is amply demonstrated by the volumes of reports available in the National Archives at Buea and Yaoundé besides those that could be found in other archives in Nigeria and Britain.

As a consequence of this special status, the Territory was visited triennially by the United Nations Visiting Missionsin:1949, 1952, 1955 and 1958. These were privileges unknown to the rest of the colonial territories not only in Africa but everywhere else in the post-World War II colonized world. During each of these visits, Southern Cameroonians as indicated through organized socio-economic, cultural; development and political groups and associations had the

---

[53] CNH and KUNC produced the KNC.

opportunity to report directly and comment on the way and manner they were being governed by Great Britain, the administering power. The political impact of these visits cannot be minimized as some of these groups subsequently evolved from proto-nationalist organs to fully fledged political parties that ushered in independence.[54]

This lengthy and intensive process of political tutelage not available to all colonies cannot by any stretch of the imagination simply be dismissed by a wave of the hand as of no consequence or as having no significant impact on the political consciousness of the populace such that they could be said to have taken "a leap into the dark" during the plebiscite of 11 February 1961. The fact that 95% of the registered electorate throughout the territory finally, consciously went to the polls under sun and rain and decisively exercised their franchise, did so, as mature, intelligent people. And, for that matter, that they made some truly difficult choices says it all.[55] Nor is there proof anywhere that there was cajoling from any quarter. Without a doubt therefore, reunification in the circumstances could not be described as a mere "gamble."[56]

A Case of Sheer 'Bad Faith'

What is not so obvious at first sight is that there was certainly a huge problem; which incidentally had little to do with the nature, shape or form of the Foumban Constitutional Conference or the tortuous path undertaken by Southern Cameroons leading up to that event.

---

[54] PRO COS54/2412 XC 3343: John Martin of 7 October 1960, notes "clear majority for independence;. Deadlock faces summit: 3 ideological blocs emerge; Foncha for secession, continued trusteeship pending union with French Cameroon at a later date4, 8Ntumazah, immediate unification and independence". Daily Times, Thursday 13/08/59.

[55] Since this point cuts right through the heart of the interview it is pursued in depth further on in this work. Alone, they constitute a huge chapter in the political evolution of Southern Cameroons.

[56] See "Foreword" (sic) 'Setting the Record Straight' *Eden Xtra*, no.001, October 2011, p.5. It carries a terse description of the processes enclosingthe event, also LeVine's "Political Integration and the United Republic of Cameroon", in David Smock and Kwamena Bentsi-Enchill, eds., *The Search for National Integration in Africa*, (New York, The Free Press, 1972.) He unveils how Ahidjo unconstitutionally dismantled the Federal System.

Rather, this resulted from the lack of political will and trust or in short, sheer "bad faith" by the 'highly rated 'Francophone brothers, and protagonists in the union, who even that early, engaged treachery against their unsuspecting guests. Specifically, the dismantling of the Federal Republic of Cameroon had to do with the character, intent and determination of the individuality of "President' Alhajj Ahmadou Ahidjo, the accredited creator and custodian of the constitution of the new Federal Republic of Cameroon".[57] Within the context of the termination of the Federal Republic of Cameroon, indeed, of the history of Cameroon until his own enigmatic exit in 1982, an excellent case study could be made of "President Ahmadou Ahidjo" as a "Factor" in the destruction of both the Federal and Unitary constitutions, the very foundations on which the state of Cameroon was constructed.[58]

For Southern Cameroonians, the "ultimate" was the letter of commendation for their maturity in the process leading up to and during the plebiscite from the hands of Dr. Djalal Abdoh, the Iranian UN Plebiscite Commissioner. As soon as the plebiscite results were declared, he was much relieved. He noted with an air of satisfaction and in his report to the UN General Assembly was full of appreciation for the maturity of the people of Southern Cameroons: to this effect as reported in *Cameroon Life* "The people of Southern Cameroons had the opportunity to express their wishes freely and secretly at the polls concerning the alternatives offered in the plebiscite."[59] On the other hand, in his report, Dr. Abdoh noted:

> One of the outstanding aspects of the plebiscite in Southern Cameroons was the remarkable calm, which prevailed during all its phases, despite the density of the political campaign during the last weeks preceding the polling. It is with great satisfaction that I pay

---

[57] Richard Joseph, *Radical Nationalism* and *Gaullist Africa*, for graphic details of the brutality of the Ahidjo regime.

[58] "The Plebiscite: Thirty Years After, The Choice between Fire and Deep Water", by Francis K Wache, in *Cameroon Life*, March `1991, p.10.

[59] The UN Plebiscite Officer's Report to the General Assembly 1961, Addendum to the agenda, item 13 para.112.

tribute to the people of Southern Cameroons for the respect they showed for law and order.⁶⁰

He is the single most competent person who could have made such an assessment of all that transpired during that highly profiled political event in the history of this country. For the same people to be regarded as illiterate, misguided and misled, sounds much like insolence. This becomes all the more inadmissible when the numbers and circumstances involved in the plebiscite phenomenon are taken into consideration.

In fact, what further engraves this conclusion in gold are the expressions of Dr. EML Endeley and NN Mbile, leaders of the opposition CPNC on the solidity of the plebiscite, after sober reflection. Taken together, these make criticisms of the plebiscite so much idle talk.⁶¹In comparative terms, whether with Nigeria with which Southern Cameroons was administered for forty-one years or Republic of Cameroon, with which they have been cohabiting for the past fifty years, the former "Southern Cameroonians" had achieved by far amore highly evolved political culture than the Summit Magazine caption suggests.

The comment in the Cameroon Times, a leading newspaper at the time of reunification bears ample testimony to this assessment. In an editorial in 1961, the paper critically but appropriately asserted:

> We are bringing into this union a great inheritance viz: democracy, the English have not given us fine roads and fine buildings but they have given us something far more valuable: "a democratic way of thinking and a fine educational system. With these we need not be afraid to meet our brethren across the border for we are not coming empty handed."⁶²

---

⁶⁰ These are better examined under the Chapter Three on the Plebiscite.

⁶¹*The Cameroon Times*, n.d 1961, the leading newspaper at the time; quoted in The Golden Age of Southern West Cameroon 2005. p.41.

⁶² Daniel N Lantum (ed). *Tribute to Dr. John Ngu Foncha,* by Southwest and Northwest Elite , Eulogy by ET Egbe p.10.

Given a level playing field, the size and power of the Cameroon Republic "elephant" would adequately have been matched by the agility and prowess of the West Cameroon "tiger". What was and has been absent all along since Foumban is the level playing field resulting from a solid political will by the political leadership. The Federal Constitution that resulted from the famous "Foumban Constitutional Conference" as will be seen shortly certainly remains the best thing that could have happened to Cameroon at the time, noting that there is nothing like a "perfect constitution". What generally counts as they say, is not the "letter but the spirit of the constitution".[63] Those who crafted that document certified it as "excellent", ready for operation, and gave it a clean bill of health.

Two Critical Omissions and a Flawed Target

Central in any serious discussion on the topical issue of "Fifty Years after the independence of Southern Cameroons", is the process that led up to the 'reunification' of Southern Cameroons with Republic of Cameroon. This was the period spanning from 1951 to 1961, and possibly up to 1972. This immediately conjures two overriding factors; first, the British colonial policy in Southern Cameroons, which dominated political life in the period leading up to: the plebiscite, the Buea Tripartite conference, the Bamenda All Party Conference, the Foumban Constitutional Conference and the Yaounde Tripartite Conference during the phase, 1959-1961. This constituted one huge hoax, whilst that from 1961-1972 and, beyond was dominated by the enigmatic figure of President Ahmadou Ahidjo. At the heart of the first, are the declassified British secret papers which have disclosed the ugly undercurrents that characterised British colonial policy, while on the other hand is President Alhaji Ahmadou Ahidjo, who practically personalized the administration of the Federal Republic of Cameroon. His domination of the entire existence of the Federal Republic of Cameroon, (1961-1972) was overshadowed by the fact that he could not brood sharing power with any individual or institution and was allergic to any form of opposition to his authority. As will be

---

[63] Nicodemus Fru, in Africa Today Vol. 47, No. 2 "The Reunification Question in Cameroon History: Was the Bride an Enthusiastic or a Reluctant One?"

demonstrated, he was a matchless dictator especially in his ambivalent dealings with Southern/West Cameroon.

Victims, Predators and Oppressors

Consequently, if "Fate" could be accepted as part of a people's history, then the factors identified above were the catalysts that got factored into the developments that have shaped the destiny: woes of Southern - West Cameroonians so far. Southern Cameroons as a State together with its political leadership was simply squeezed and crushed in between them. Critically examined, the whole political line-up (both government and opposition – KNDP/CPNC), in Southern-West Cameroon were unmitigated victims of intractable "external" forces towards which they were simply prostrate; in short, helpless. The point is that the Summit Magazine interview clearly botched in its analysis to identify the victims from the predators and oppressors. Consequently, it was the victims who instead were targeted as culprits.

The extent to which the Southern/West Cameroonian political leadership and people could have wangled themselves out of the web of "traps" that were wrought against them by the British colonial administration as clearly demonstrated by Malcolm Milne and thereafter under the hidden claws of President Ahidjo as revealed by his Prime Minister, Charles Assale were extremely limited. Assale maintains that Southern Cameroonians imposed themselves on Ahidjo and as a result, he was not committed to their welfare.[64] Actually, Assale was basically stating the partial truth excluding the disclosure that he and his boss were brazen opportunists, predators and double dealers. Ahidjo's lukewarm attitude towards reunification partly evolved from his cultural background. Here Njeuma who has researched on the area points out that:

> In the predominantly Moslem north ... There was little interest in reunification because religious and linguistic solidarity over a wide area bred permissive habits towards frontier regulations. Ahidjo was never excited about reunification, and so played down

---

[64] Ibid., MartinNjeuma.http://lucy.ukc.ac.uk/Chilver/Paideuma/ paideuma-REUNIFI.html.(07/07/13)

its structural implications. His political programme dealt exclusively with East Cameroonian politics... In fact, Ahidjo and the East Cameroon population were largely indifferent to it because the ultimate form of independence of his part of Cameroon had already been decided by the end of 1958.[65]

The demonstration of the odious roles played by these forces in laying mine fields, which have become the sources of the woes that present day North/South West Anglophone Cameroonians have been encountering largely constitute the essence of this work. It is regrettable, that in the interview these predators were so easily led off the hook. This in no way insinuates that the domestic politicians could be described simply as helpless victims. There is not much they could have done to resist the onslaughts which at best could only have delayed but not prevented the final outcome. This may be open to debate, but clearly the general trend and flow of events was not within their competence; situation pessimists would term "fate". The elucidation of this dilemma constitutes the essence of this exposition especially as between these two missing factors are to be found the vectors responsible for Southern Cameroons' woes.

A Common Patrimony

However, referring to "fate"; placed in the historical context, the Humanist Philosophy of the Renaissance provides the clue. This emphasizes the dignity, self-worth of the individual and community, maintaining that human beings are rational beings who possess within themselves the capacity for truth and goodness. Furthermore; while "man" cannot alter his past, he is responsible for shaping his future, and no dynamic situation can be taken as finite.[66] The challenge is for Cameroonians to analyse and re-examine their past taking keen note of the pitfalls in order to shape a better future for every single citizen. The Cameroon motherland belongs in equal measure to its entire citizenry and no one has greater right to the patrimony than the others. From lessons of history, we know that this is best achieved through

---

[65] Danto, Arthur C Humanism, Microsoft @ student 2009, (DVD), WA: Microsoft Cooperation 2008.
[66] *Eden Xtra*, p.22.

democratic principles and the equitable distribution of the national cake. Born and bred in this land, we all are shareholders and owe a debt of gratitude to our common ancestry to improve on it for posterity. Every generation should leave its patrimony better than they merit. This is the essence of authentic nation building, with which patriotic citizens proudly identify themselves and are ready to lay down their lives in its defence. It is a birth right.

As for the continuous evolution of Cameroon as a state like other nations of the world past and present, Professor Daniel Abwa emphasizes the holistic notion that all Cameroonians contributed to reunification and adds the critical observation that Cameroon is a country on the move propelled by the unstoppable winds of history. As a result, he maintains that:

> Nobody from wherever should question this part of our history. We take collective responsibility for it. Perhaps, it must be said that reunification is not the end of the history of Cameroon, since Cameroon is a country on the move, a nation undergoing permanent construction. Without renouncing our history, we have no right to stop the movement of the history of our country much as we celebrate and assume the United Republic of Cameroon as well as its République du Cameroun. All of this contributes to the evolution of our history and all Cameroonians have to play their role to bring about the harmony, much needed for every positive evolution.[67]

For one thing, it should be borne in mind that the "Cameroon State" is still in its embryonic early days, in the course of evolution

---

[67] Victor T Le Vine makes the distinction between constitution octroyee, handed down from on high and constitution evoluee, the product of political development, which embodies the values, goals, and aspirations of those who write them. The Cameroon constitutions of 1961 and 1972 were options selected by the leaders of the people. See Victor T. Le Vine, , "Political Integration and The United Republic of Cameroon" in, *The Search For National Integration In Africa*, David R. Smock and Kwamena Bentsi – Enchill, (the *Free Press*, Collier Macmillan Publishers, London). 274

towards becoming a viable "nation".⁶⁸ No good student of history will jump to any peremptory conclusion since what we are experiencing yet is a process, obviously transitional as demonstrated in the rise and decline of great and powerful nations in history such as Greece, Rome, the Holy Roman Empire and recently the shattering of colonial empires and even of Cameroon's own recent past. In the course of time, nations like the living human beings whom they represent, or better still who constitute them: grow, age, mutate and either balkanize or coalesce. They do not remain static and Cameroon is no exception. The simple principle is that any consensual course the nation undertakes with the interests of the masses at heart hardly ever falters. This is another definition of democracy, which is universally applicable.

The "Royal Presidency of Alhadji Ahmadou Ahidjo"

It is easy for one reading about President Ahidjo to conclude that descriptions of him are exaggerated. This is until such a reader is fully introduced to whom actually he was - and it is clear that no better descriptions can be found to qualify his hegemony. In the specific instance of the dismantling of the carefully crafted constitution of the Federal Republic of Cameroon, President Ahidjo's egomania, megalomania and manifest bad faith came powerfully to the surface. A flash back to his "Royal Presidency"⁶⁹ would abundantly reveal that nothing and nobody could have stood on his path to shake him out of power or in his quest to create the highly centralized state system of his design. Regarded by *griots* as: "Father of the Nation", "Pioneer of Negritude," "Prophet of Pan- Africanism", "Defender of African Dignity" and other sycophantic praise names, Bayart however adds that:

> Any and everything was done to preserve power in the hands of Ahidjo, his confederates, clients and constituents, that is, the regime's nascent ruling class. This meant not only

---

⁶⁸ PRO, Ref.CO554/XC 3406 Yaoundé, July 19 1960; Patrick Johnston, Report on Tripartite Conference in Buea.

⁶⁹ Bayart, *L'etat au Cameroun,* (Paris, P*resse de la Fondation Nationale desSciences Politiques,* 1979). Quoted in Cameroon, Politics and Society p.46.

> avoiding the uncertainties of electoral competition, but arranging periodic staged symbolic demonstrations of popular support (elections) referenda, party holidays, public manifestations of thanks) ... an elaborate system of patronage that rewarded loyalty to the regime and maintaining the political supremacy of Ahidjo's so-called 'Northern barons', while balancing the competing demands of various competing regional interests.[70]

His, was far higher than any mere elective office, he "reigned" rather than just "ruled" as nothing really limited his authority. With hindsight, this became apparent soon after he put his seal on the Foumban accord. From the perspective of his political philosophy it is probable that Ahidjo read Machiavelli's "The Prince"[71] because his administration abundantly epitomized most of the features espoused in that treatise. In fact, Ahidjo spent his time in office from 1962-1982 as the "President", protector and guarantor of the constitutions of the Federal Republic of Cameroon, which he approved, and that of the United Republic of Cameroon, which he "singlehandedly" designed, manipulating these "sacred" documents to centralise power on himself. Specifically, this was against the stipulation in Article 8.1 of the Federal Constitution in which it was inscribed:

> The President of the Federal Republic, as the head of the federal government, shall ensure respect for the federal constitution and the integrity of the federation and shall be responsible for the conduct of affairs of the Federal Republic.[72]

---

[70] See well researched article on: "The influence of Machiavelli on contemporary African politics" by Kevin Sakwe and Frankline Javlon in *Searchlight Magazine*, published by the St. Thomas Aquinas Major Seminary, Bambui, No, 101, June 2011 pp.6-11.Also, "Proposals for The Federal Constitution", in Report by Patrick Johnston PRO No. CO554/2249 XC 3406 of July 19 1960.

[71] Epilogue; the Federal constitution and also: the editorial, *The Post Newsmagazine*, October, 2007, pp. 8-10.

[72] Joseph, *Radical Nationalism in Cameroun*, pp. 349-50.

Rather, President Ahidjo shrewd and astute as he was, gradually but deliberately, surreptitiously and systematically tore, literally to shreds, the very constitution of which he was the ultimate custodian and guarantor. Well after the 1972 debacle, he continued relentlessly to mutilate, "doctor" and "panel beat" not only the Federal Constitution but even the unitary one, which he had literally, single-handedly designed to substitute it; tailored to suit his moods, whims and caprices. Each time this took place Ahidjo's objective was to garner more and ever more power into his hands. He ruled by decree, without parliament in 1961 for six months and then again for an extended period of twelve months in 1972.[73] In actual fact, after the creation of the one party system in 1966, whatever the president wished, was sure to materialize and be implemented without any felt opposition. He had become almighty wielding power and authority in the triple capacity of Head of state and head of government and the head of the political party controlling the government and therefore, enjoyed the powers of hydra-headed dictators known in history. The parliament was reduced to a rubber stamp; the judiciary was also under his control; he could appoint, promote and dismiss its personnel. In effect, the constitution had no provision for the division or separation of powers.[74]

To fully illustrate this point could constitute a whole challenging topic for research as the entire history of Cameroon whether as the federal or unitary state is littered with fragments of this manipulation process. Mbile who belonged close to the centre of political power and authority equally maintains that Ahidjo instituted a culture of fear and repression in the country to instil his authoritarian rule.[75] Actually, more like a Monarch, President Ahidjo considered it below his status to sit in cabinet with his ministers and only accepted to do so in 1965. His role was to define policy and make high appointment and not to be involved in discussions and debates.[76] Richard Joseph,[77] an erudite

---

[73] Emmanuel A Aka , *The British Southern Cameroons, 1922-61: A Study in Colonialism and Under Development*, (Madison, Nkemnji Global Tech, Platteville, 2002), p. 91.

[74] Ibid., Mbile, *Cameroon Political Story.*

[75] See Jacques Benjamin Tr. Jatyem Jotanga, *West Cameroonians: the Minority in a Bi-Cultural State (Les Presses de l'Université de Montreal, Canadea* n.d) p.60.

[76] Rechard Joseph, *Radical Nationalism in Cameroon*, (Oxford, Clarendon Press 1977), pp. 349-50.

political scientist and historian referring to the views of certain political analysts on the question of the most successful political systems in Africa was led to comment in comparative terms as follows:

> In the opinion of others, however, the political order which exists [in Cameroon] is maintained by a powerful military presence, a ubiquitous secret service, the ruthless repression of any form of political opposition, the use of torture in concentration camps and a rigid censorship of all forms of expression.[78]

Nor was this all, to the point that critical analysts came to refer to him as being a megalomaniac and egomaniac, some sinister anecdotes are repeatedly quoted. Of the audacity of the Southern Cameroons press: During the oppressive years of the much dreaded censorship, if a journalist dared to criticize the administration, he would be made to disappear from his home during the wee hours of the morning to an unknown destination. His papers would be seized and those who dared procure early copies would burn them for fear of their homes being searched.[79]

Reference is made to the legendary Tataw Obenson who still found ways of satirically criticising the system and paid dearly for it. Thus:

> All through his almost 20 years tumultuous publishing career, the daring Late Tataw Obenson was a constant visitor to the underground cells in Buea and Yaoundé, for his effrontery to print some flaws in the Ahidjo Administration...even right up to the nineties, some print media journalists were incarcerated for having the audacity to suggest that the one party state had become an anachronism... the case in the sixties, Paddy Mbawa, was forced thereafter to become a tenant in one of the underground cells.[80]

---

[77] Ibid.

[78] Ibid., *Eden Xtra*, p. 50 Paul Kode, "The Cameroon Press in Retrospect".

[79] He was easily one of the most audacious Southern Cameroonian journalists, who used satire to criticise the system and was indifferent to torture and stints in jail.

[80] Ibid., This continued to be the case until after the 1996 Law on Liberty of the Press.

This topic in the meantime is given a little more attention further on in this book (but especially in Chapter Five Volume Two devoted to him). It should however be stressed that the essence of this essay is not so much about the merits and demerits of the epic *Summit Magazine* interview as it is of the historical virtues and challenges of Southern Cameroons history, which it triggered. In this light, though largely limited to the questions issuing from the interview, such topics are examined in their widest historical ramifications possible following the adage that in history we think globally and act locally so as to see things in their proper comparative and holistic perspective. The other notion being emphasized is that "democracy" is not merely a game of numbers; it has cardinal principles, values and ideals among which is the respect for the views of significant minority groups. In the case of Southern Cameroons it was not a minority as such but a viable political entity, and possibly a threat to Ahidjo's hegemony which he could not tolerate.

Members of the newly formed Northern Cameroons People's Democratic Party, 1959 With the Southern Cameroons KNDP Leadership

Chapter 3

Southern Cameroons: Political Maturity

An Evolved Political Culture

This chapter, elaborately, and in comparative terms demonstrates using various parameters, the extent to which Southern Cameroons up to the mid-1960s, had extensively developed an evolved, mature, political culture. It was amazingly led by a range of: simple, visionary, austere, honest, peace-loving and realistic leaders, almost without exception – vintage products of their epoch. Distinguished by good governance; throughout it organized frequent free, fair and transparent elections, peaceful handover of power and enjoyed free primary adult education. It was further crowned with an ideal, efficient civil service, literally, corruption free.

In fact, the period, 1955-1965 in the history of Southern Cameroons qualifies as a "Golden Age"[81] for that nostalgic state, whose citizens were repeatedly referred to as "nice, peace loving, good and hospitable people" by administrators, missionaries, visitors and those who got to know them closely. The most remarkable observation was that finally made by Malcolm Milne himself who noted that during his last couple of years in the Southern Cameroons administration, he dealt with: "People of high intelligence who knew exactly what they wanted."[82] However, in the interview repeated and derogatory references are made of the people in general and to the fact that: "Foncha and Muna were not well educated;" the 'KNDP lacked sufficient qualified personnel, therefore their negotiations were weak. In yet another interview granted to; Time Scape Magazine, Ngoh is blunt and categorical maintaining that:

---

[81] Ibid., Ndi, *Golden Age of Southern (West) Cameroon – Impact of Christianity,* (Full Gospel Press, Bamenda, Cameroon), 2005.

[82] Ibid., *No Telephone,* p.254.

British Southern Cameroons came out with a very poor deal because the KNDP politicians were ignorant and self-centred. For example on the 20thof June1961, Ahidjo and Foncha had a secret agreement that the latter would be made Vice President in the draft constitution of the Federal Republic of Cameroon, this secret arrangement was leaked and it scared Southern Cameroon politicians who quickly fought for their own interests.[83]

All of this squares up with the Colonial Office correspondence by Malcolm Milne in which he quotes his colleague Foley Newn, who says:

> The present government in Southern Cameroons made up almost totally of inexperienced and naïve ex-primary school teachers with good intentions is incapable of grappling with the tremendous problems which face it, leadership in Southern Cameroons is inexperienced, untrained and naïve"(sic).[84]

This is despite the fact that other than Endeley as an individual; on a one on one basis as will be seen shortly, the KNDP leadership was of the same calibre as their CPNC colleagues if not better.

In fact, described as "ex-primary school teachers", practically all of whom had served as "headmasters", they were the best any locality could boast of across Nigeria and Southern Cameroons at the time. On the other hand, none of the CPNC leadership but for Dr. EML Endeley, held qualifications higher than the West African School Certificate, while others were Pastors and holders of the Standard Six certificate. Some of these were amateur journalists and newspaper vendors, who had access to, and maximally used the local press to lambast, criticize and ridicule their KNDP opponents as testified by the terse provocative newspaper captions crafted by Motomby Woleta and Nerius Mbile.[85] This is abundantly demonstrated in the Endeley

---

[83] Ibid., *Time Scape Magazine* Vol: 02 no. 006, March-April 2011, p.18. For more on the so-called Secret Deals, see Chapters Four and Five.

[84] Ibid., Epilogue, Summit Magazine.

[85] Ibid., *Sunday Times* 21 June 1959, Foncha is referred to as: "Mr. 14:12- mockery of democracy" by Motomby Woleta, also, Mbile: "'If the KNDP does not

cabinet of 1954 - 1959. On the whole, this could be taken simply as political verbiage deserving no serious comment.[86]

Without in anyway belabouring the fact, going through the declassified British secret documents on Southern Cameroons, very little of positive value is said about Mr. Foncha's administration and his party, the KNDP; since the British colonial officials unabashedly took sides with the CPNC. To make sense, the above criticisms should be examined within their global, historical framework beginning with political leadership generally; in Britain itself, as well as in the US, Nigeria, Republic of Cameroon and then, Southern Cameroons.

Regardless of the issue of educational qualifications, it was an acknowledged fact that Southern Cameroonian politicians were visionary leaders: intelligent, competent, simple, austere and realistic. Additionally, of the people generally and in areas as distant from Buea as Wum in the 1960s, Mr. John Percival, an Englishman and one of the twenty-five Plebiscite Officers recruited for the UN had lots of admirable things to say about the political maturity and level of reasoning of the masses. In earnest, they wanted neither integration nor unification and, he thought the British were simply escaping their responsibility by refusing to extend the Trusteeship period. It was clear to him that; "the British had negligently administered this little patch of Africa", essentially because, "it was a United Nations Trust Territory and there was no profit in it".[87] The people in general were highly evolved ethically and politically. He was critical, keen and noted how:

---

stop its mad and heedless drive …its policy may result in disintegration", see *Daily Times* DT/W/18/59.

[86] Both Mbile and Motomby Woleta were School Leavers, Ajebe Sone was a Grade II Teacher while Jeremiah Kangsen and Ando Seh were pastors while, Abel T Ngala, a Cattle Control Assistant was a First School Leaving Certificate holder as well as Vincent Lainjo with experience as a treasurer. These were cabinet members of Endeley's KNC/KPP Government but strangely defended in the interview as being better qualified than those in the KNDP. It may be added that Grade Two Teachers taught in secondary schools, which produced GCE O/L or secondary school leavers of the calibres of Mbile and Woleta. In comparison, there was no KNDP minister with a qualification below the Teacher's Grade 11 Certificate seen. Golden Age p.59.

[87] Ibid., John Percival, *The 1961 Cameroon Plebiscite, Choice or Betrayal*, (Langaa Research and Publishing CIG, Mankon, Bamenda), p. xiv. 2008.

In those days in Southern Cameroons theft was almost unknown. I left the house unlocked, even though it was stuffed with things that might have seemed highly desirable to most of the population. There were violent incidents… but anyone who overstepped the mark was likely to be hauled in front of the local court by his neighbours. Nobody starved. Nobody was alone or uncared for.[88]

Yet, Percival's was not an isolated observation. At the end of the day, Malcolm Milne himself reported even more affectionately of the people, whom he described as peace loving and trusting, and leaders whose watch words were centred on service and dedication.[89]

Qualifications and Political Leadership

The question also arises as to whether there is any direct correlation between academic qualifications, political performance and output. Cameroon and African examples indicate a very low, if not a negative correlation indeed. The governments of most countries in Africa are currently run by highly qualified technocrats and academicians, but complaints about corruption and rigging at elections are a daily occurrence.[90] What has to be said is that some education

---

[88] Ibid.

[89] Ibid., Milne, *No Telephone*, p. 447. Malcolm Milne wrote his autobiography systematically reaching a peak and making his final conclusions on p. 447. This in fact was an anticlimax to all that he had said and done.

[90] Despite appreciable efforts currently being made by President Paul Biya to bring about "transparency and good governance", Cameroon whichat one point (1998, 1999) topped the list as the most corrupt country in the world and is accused of rigging at elections is run largely by 'academics', professors and highly qualified technocrats. This is confirmed by the roll call of embezzlers and fraudsters behind bars in the Yaoundé and Douala Main Prisons. As an example, President Laurent Gbagbo, of Ivory Coast, who stuck to power after losing at elections thereby throwing his country into a bloody war until he was ignominiously overthrown, is not merely an intellectual but also a Professor of History as well. Newspaper captions without exception and the internet carry this information. The talk of the day is that of Marafa Hamidu Yaya, eg. CONAC (the National Anti-Corruption body) wants two ministers arrested for embezzlement. These are named as Bernard Messengue Avom, Minister of Public Works and Jean Kuete, Vice Prime Minister in Charge of Agriculture. See, The Post no.01297 of Monday Nov. 14,2011. Fun is made of a

especially up to High School level, which affords aspiring politicians the competence of grasping complex socio- political, economic and cultural concepts, could be an advantage but this may not be absolute. Intelligence, common sense and commitment are primordial. The biblical adage which holds that, "by their fruits we shall know them", applies in full measure to the KNDP and its leadership in disproving such unsound absolute assumptions. How could a government described so disparagingly with an assumed powerful opposition perform as brilliantly as the KNDP did from 1959-1966 despite the fact that the CPNC Opposition had the massive furtive and overt support of the British colonial administration.

In comparative terms just how much better qualified were the British political leaders themselves than their Southern Cameroonian counterparts? The question is whether the officials of the Colonial Office should have made such derogatory remarks. From all appearances it was a matter of the pot calling the kettle black.

However, there is a pertinent analytical study practically dealing with the role intellectual qualifications played in the process of decolonisation in Cameroon by David Mokam.[91] He quotes Professor Ali Mazrui, who maintains that: an intellectual is a person who has the capacity to be fascinated by ideas and has acquired the skills to handle some of these ideas effectively. He further classifies these into four categories, namely: general intellectuals, who can appreciate newspaper series, philosophies and ideas; public intellectuals, who have their own disciplines and communicate with others - interdisciplinary sort of; intellectuals specialised in ideas of governance and policy options and, finally, academic intellectuals fascinated by ideas and engaged in higher research and education. The other definition comes from Mandla Nkomfe, an African National Congress (ANC) Chief Whip in Gauteng Legislature, South Africa, who maintains that an intellectual is someone who invents ideas and helps others to analyse events. Such a

---

parallel cabinet set up in the Kondengue Maximum Prison complete with a Prime Minister, Secretary General at the Presidency, Ministers of State and others!

[91] It is entitled; "Locally and Western Trained Intellectuals Facing Decolonisationin Cameroon, 1946-1961" in, *Annals of The Faculty of Arts, Letters and Social Sciences, The (University of Ngaoundere*, Editions CLE, Yaoundé), 2011, pp. 61- 81.

one uses these skills to speak and write against injustice, shaping public opinion without affiliation to any political party.

Putting these together Mokam draws the conclusion that the concept of an intellectual should include the acquisition of good skills and expertise acquired only through long and tedious studies. This classification he does base on "long pens" (crayons) ranging from ten to 100s used in education. These are converted into: basic intellectuals (basic pens); intermediate intellectuals (long pens) and advanced intellectuals (longest pens). Taking some leaders from French and British Cameroons, a few things are clear. Chances for education beyond primary school were more limited in French Cameroon (where any education higher than CEPE (The First School Leaving Certificate) and the Minor Seminary had to be done either in Congo Brazzaville or Senegal.

The Endeley KNC / KPP Government, 1958

Dr. EML Endeley, Rev. J Ando Seh, VT Lainjo, NN Mbile, JO Field, ADH Patterson, JS Dudding and BJ Walker

In British Southern Cameroons which was integrated with Nigeria, however, the First School Leaving Certificate or better still, the highly prized "Standard Six Certificate", was a given, while most post primary technical and professional education besides, the government "Secondary/Normal Department" from the mid-1920s, which finally evolved into the Teacher's Training College(TTC)Kake took place in Nigeria.[92] The Voluntary Agencies especially the Roman Catholic Mission spearheaded post primary education in the Trust Territory, beginning with the opening of St. Joseph's College, Sasse in 1939, St. Francis' Teachers' Training College, Fiango, Kumba (female) in 1947, TTC, Baseng (later Njinikom and St. Peter's Teachers Training College, Bambui,1948) followed by Cameroon Protestant College, Bali in 1949. In other words, before the 1950s, any serious post primary education was mostly available in Nigerian institutions such as: Government College, Umuahia, Government College, Ibadan and Government College, Zaria.

Prominent Southern Cameroonian political actors engaged in the decolonization process included: Paul M Kale, Emmanuel Liffaffe Endeley, Nerius Namaso Mbile, and Motomby Ndembo Woleta, who campaigned for integration with Nigeria; and, John Ngu Foncha, Augustine Ngom Jua and Solomon Tandeng Muna, who stood for reunification with Republic of Cameroon. Of these, except Muna and Jua, who had the same post –primary qualifications at home, all the others pursued further education, "abroad" in Nigeria and, by Mokam's classification, well qualified. By all comparisons this left no room for any criticism as this was finally confirmed by no other person than Malcolm Milne, who considered them the best small cabinet he ever had the privilege to work with.[93] They were competent, intelligent, dedicated and knew exactly what to do. Interestingly this was exactly the same government described by his colleague, Foley Newn out of spite for the KNDP as "inexperienced and naïve ex-primary school teachers". This was the pattern of reporting at the colonial office.

In perspective, Endeley attended Government College Umuahia, where he trained to become a Medical Doctor but got dismissed for impropriety in 1946. However, providentially, this accorded him the opportunity to take up active political leadership in Southern Cameroons; Kale, who initially was headed for further studies at Fourah Bay College in Sierra Leone ended up as a teacher at Salvation

---

[92] Ibid., Mokam.
[93] Ibid., Milne, p. 434.

Army school, Lagos; Foncha attended St. Charles' TTC Onitsha, and continued to Moor Plantation, Ibadan for the professional specialisation in agriculture. Muna attended the Normal School, Buea and finished up at Kake, TTC as did Jua. Muna further attended the Institute of Education, University of London. Motomby Ndembo Woleta went to Baptist Boys' High School, Abeokuta, Nigeria while Nerius Namaso Mbile attended Hope Waddell Institute Calabar, Nigeria. So, by Mokam's classification these leading Southern Cameroons political leaders of the decolonisation era qualified as "Intermediate Intellectuals," while Endeley was obviously an Advanced Intellectual.[94]

On the other hand in French Cameroon: Andre-Marie Mbida after Primary School, studied in the Minor Seminary at Akono and later on at the Major Seminary, Mvolye, after which he was appointed headmaster. Reuben um Nyobe attended Presbyterian schools in; Makak and Illange in the Maritime Sanaga Region, and got the CEPE in 1929. He did Teacher Training at Foualassi, where after some difficulties and expulsion, he graduated as an external candidate. He taught as a Probationary Teacher in the Presbyterian School, passed the entrance examination for Junior Clerks and was engaged in pursuing Law through correspondence. Felix Roland Moumie, attended Protestant Primary School, Njisse near Foumban, moved to Government Primary School Bafoussam in 1935 and continued to Dschang Regional Primary School, where he passed out in 1940. He then went to Ecole Superieure, Edouard Renard, Brazzaville in 1941 before proceeding to William Ponty Higher School, Senegal from 1945-1947 for professional training and qualified as an African Physician. Ahmadou Ahidjo on the other hand, attended; Ecole Regionale Primaire, Garoua, where he failed and then moved to the Yaoundé Higher Primary School, where he got his CEPE and was recruited as an agent for Post and Telecommunications. Thus by Mokam's classification Ahmadou Ahidjo was the only person who failed to qualify as an intermediate intellectual. Paradoxically, he ended up becoming the most enduring if not the most "successful" of all the politicians put together, having ruled for close to thirty years. However, Mokam appropriately finally summarises:

---

[94] Ibid., Mokam.

The advanced intellectuals played a very small role. The greatest role was played by locally trained intellectuals who were capable of couching ideas and were realistic enough to understand some needs. Cameroon obtained independence and reunification thanks to the work of locally trained intellectuals who constituted a chain made of "basic" and "intermediate" intellectuals to spread nationalist ideas.[95]

Interestingly Ahidjo who did not qualify either by the standards expressed in the *Summit Magazine* interview or by Mokam's analysis ended up becoming the most "successful" politician in Cameroon making nonsense of the correlation between educational qualification and political performance.

A Distinct Southern Cameroons Political Culture

Given the fact that all within ten years (1951-1961), together with the plebiscite of 11 February 1961; Southern Cameroonians had been to the polls six times, this certainly had a significant impact on the political consciousness and maturity of the people. Outstanding among these was the 1959 election which led to a peaceful transfer of power from the ruling KNC/ KPP alliance to the opposition KNDP despite the fact that the former enjoyed all the rights and privileges of incumbency. The prevailing atmosphere at the handing over of power characterized by cordiality was exceptional as the leaders and their spouses shook hands and embraced each other in public. This culture continued to evolve and mature as during the plebiscite, Southern Cameroonians overwhelmingly demonstrated their political readiness by deliberately choosing what was considered by all descriptions as the 'most unpopular option' imposed on them at the UN – Reunification with Republic of Cameroon (and yet won). After the plebiscite Dr. Djalal Abdoh, the Iranian UN Plebiscite Commissioner wrote back commending the people of Southern Cameroons for the "remarkable

---

[95] Ibid., Mokam, p.79. For more on educational qualifications and political leadership, see Appendix ii.

calm which had prevailed" during the process. The elections as well as the plebiscite were generally considered free, fair and transparent.

Dr. and Mrs Endeley "Congratulate" Mr. JN Foncha

This Followed Defeat of the KNC/KPP alliance by the KNDP and Replacement of Endeley by Foncha as Premier.

Peaceful, Harmonious Transfer of Power in 1959

Considering the frequency of these elections and the fact that they were always preceded by campaigns and sensitization of the people before the electors made their choices at the polls; the average Southern Cameroonians through frequently, in fact, biennially exercising their franchise definitely were better informed about their civic rights and responsibilities than their Nigerian or French Cameroonian neighbours, or for that matter, electors anywhere at all. One of those high points in the mature political culture of Southern Cameroons that deserves special mention was the peaceful handover of power after free, fair, transparent and peaceful elections in 1959. On that occasion as indicated above, the ruling KNC/KPP alliance leader was defeated by the KNDP opposition. Without ruffles of any kind, Dr. EML Endeley, the serving Prime Minister accompanied by his spouse, calmly and even with a measure of joviality embraced and shook hands with his victorious opponent, Mr. John Ngu Foncha, Leader of the Opposition in the glare of photographers and the press.

One wonders where else such a spectacular transfer of power could have taken place. Hence, the Southern Cameroonian politicians and electorate deserve far more than the derogatory descriptions cast at them. There are no known institutions where the electorate goes to for preparation to become better "voters". Southern Cameroons, already enjoying universal free primary education through "Education Rating" under the Foncha administration with 100% trained teachers by UNESCO standards in 1970, could not be considered anything less than among the best. Adult education classes were organized throughout the Territory to great effect, not only through the agency of the government but with the collaboration of the Christian denominations. These apart, while education such as desired in the interview could be an asset in imbibing political issues and complicated concepts, it is definitely not an absolute necessity. Intelligence is not a monopoly of the literate and must be distinguished from literacy and the ability to read and write or what is derisively described as, empty "book knowledge".

The Sagacity of Traditional Rulers

Many of the so-called "illiterates" have a wonderful grasp of issues that affect their lives and society as a whole, which even the "well educated" persons may not understand. Otherwise, the question may well arise as to where sagacious rulers of the stature of Fons: Achirimbi II of Bafut, Asonganyi of Fontem, Galega I of Bali or Mbinglo of Nso and countless others like them received the education to enable them administer their large Fondoms so tactfully, diligently and successfully with highly acclaimed systems of dispensing justice in the Native Courts for ages before the arrival of the colonial masters.

His Royal Highness, Fon Achiribi II of Bafut

He was chairman of the Fon's Conference in Bamenda

Rather, it is for this reason that the British colonial administration easily adapted the much glorified and idealized policy of "Indirect Rule" (or Native Administration (NA)) using the traditional or "natural" rulers as a means of retaining the highly treasured African traditional values and customs, while adapting to modernism or what was referred to as the "Dual Mandate". In fact, it was initially the objective of British Colonial Policy in Nigeria by the Richard's Constitution of 1946, which, while dividing Nigeria into three regions was still mightily NA centred. Rather, it was envisaged that at independence power would subtly glide from the hands of the colonial masters into those of the traditional rulers, who constituted the Native Authorities. This constitution deliberately side-lined and ignored the rapidly rising vocal educated elite and provoked widespread opposition to it in Nigeria and Southern Cameroons. Thus, it instigated and fuelled the rise of nationalism since the educated elite felt marginalised, ignored and regarded as mere[96]"Verandah Boys", of little consequence. Before being fully implemented it was substituted by the Macpherson Constitution of 1951, which made provision for democratic elections into the various assemblies. While it rejected a Regional status for Southern Cameroons it, however, enabled them to come to the fore and for the first time stood for democratic elections in Eastern Nigeria and Southern Cameroons with which it was jointly administered.

As a result, Southern Cameroons intelligentsia as members of the CYL provided a ready recruiting pool for membership into the nascent NCNC of Nnamdi Azikiwe.[97] It will be recalled that led by Mr. PM Kale the early Southern Cameroons nationalists almost without exception, who began by enrolling in the CYL, were also members of the NCNC, which became a sort of nursery school for budding nationalists and political leadership in Southern Cameroons.[98]

High Calibre Political Leaders: Products of their Time

In the interview it is maintained that Southern Cameroons 'Had a Raw Deal' because of the "greed" of Southern Cameroonian politicians in general and those of the KNDP in particular.[99] It is important to note that talking about the early Southern Cameroonian political leaders is not making reference to a set of superhuman beings: saints, sinners or villains, living in a unique and perfect world. They, like political leaders the world over were ordinary mortals, products of their time, place and circumstances with their shortcomings, strengths and weaknesses. However, they were the very best that their society could produce at the time and any comparisons made outside these parameters are bound to be lame and in historical terms "anachronistic."

---

[96] JF Ade Ajayi & Michael Growder eds. *History of West Africa Vol II,* Longman, 1974; See especially "Politics of Decolonisation in Bristish West Africa"p. 622-655.

[97] Ibid., Frederick Lugard, *The Dual Mandate in British Tropical Africa,* 1926, p.193. Even up to independence, Mbile, Motomby Woleta and others continued to identify with the NCNC and Nigeria.

[98] Ibid., Malcolm Milne, *No Telephone* pp.424-427.

[99] Ibid., Epilogue; Malcolm Milne, pp7.4424-427.

Peter Ndembo Motomby Woleta Staunch KNC / KPP Member

Vocal and outspoken used Cameroon Champion extensively

The 1959 General Elections in Southern Cameroons were extremely polarised, as they introduced the worst divisions ever among the people and thus creating a very dense, contagious political atmosphere. The platforms between the KNDP and the KNC/KPP alliance were as incompatible as between "fire" and "water" and just how these parties were expected to collaborate as expressed in the interview is inconceivable. In fact, Mukong, expressly stated the view that at heart, it was not in Endeley's best interest for Foncha to succeed, although there was no clear evidence to back this view after 1961. However, in 1960, Endeley, Mbile and Motomby Woleta fiercely kept taunting Foncha and the KNDP with Endeley openly admitting that he had held three nocturnal meetings with Ahidjo behind Foncha's back that year. In fact, Endeley was desperate for inclusion after defeats at the polls and was convinced long before 1966, that:

> We can operate a one party system, which would certainly guarantee that everybody has the right to express opinions within the party. This would make the best use of the talents we have in

the country, and we could evolve a system of agreement without engendering animosity.[100]

This of course was treacherous. Even so, it did not bar Foncha involving the CPNC, the Fons and Chiefs, as well as the OK at the Bamenda All Party and Foumban Conferences, where they made constructive contributions as borne by their speeches at these meetings. The reaction here is best summarized by Dr. George Atem, who argues that accusations in the interview that the KNDP did not want to share power are untrue; he even goes further:

> The party had a mandate in the 1959 elections and was responsible to the people and not to any other political party whose politicians had been rejected at the polls. Foncha and the KNDP were even magnanimous, they took the opposition leaders to the UNO, invited all shades of opinions to The Mamfe Conference, Bamenda and Foumban Constitutional Conferences. Was it that Foncha should have formed a coalition government? Foncha did not attend the Tripartite Conference in Yaoundé alone.[101]

Perhaps, the only little addition would be that with hindsight, we now know that before the holding of the Tripartite Conference in Yaoundé, Britain had defied all the agreements and norms openly colluded with and handed over power to Ahidjo instead of to a "body representing the federal government" subscribed to by the governments of Southern Cameroons and Republic. It would have made no difference if Foncha carried with him the CPNC leadership and all the suggested lawyers. Ahidjo simply invited his "ubiquitous French advisers to privately draw up a document which he got the legislature of Republic of Cameroon to enact on 1 September 1961,

---

[100]*Cameroon Times*, Monday 28 April, 1962; also, Johnson, p.62 ;*Southern Cameroons*,(Langaa Research and Publishing, CIG, Mankon, Bamenda, 2005), p .233.
[101] George Atem. "The celebration of the 50th Anniversary of the Cameroon Unification" *Cameroons Panorama*. No. 657 of Dec. 2012. p.6.

and became the Federal Constitution including Southern Cameroons."[102]

British open subversion of the final decolonization process in Southern Cameroons had begun at the aborted Buea Tripartite Conference in mid May 1961. In fact, Her Majesty, the Queen wrote directly to Ahidjo and not to Foncha, declaring:

> On the occasion of the ending of the UK Trusteeship in Southern Cameroons, I send Your Excellency my sincere good wishes for the future of the united territories over which you now preside. I am glad that friendly cooperation between our two countries should have made it possible for Southern Cameroons to attain independence in accordance with the result of the February plebiscite. I look forward to the continuation of our cordial relations in the future.[103]

To say the least, most of these Southern Cameroons political actors were exemplary, dedicated and selfless patriots with great visions for their "beloved motherland". Nor should it be forgotten that they were pioneers, the first fruits of the land. This applies to: Paul M Kale, Emmanuel ML Endeley, John Ngu Foncha, Nerius N Mbile, Augustine N Jua, Solomon T Muna, PM Kemncha and all the others. As pioneers, they were adventurers, sacrificial lambs and explorers who plodded virgin, unknown territory in the course of which they burnt out their lives in the service of their people and their country in accordance with the visions they conceived when forming proto nationalist organizations such as the CYL and the KUNC. Naturally, with all the zeal, in the course of pursuing these objectives they made

---

[102] See, Carlson Anyangwe, *Betrayal of Too Trusting A People: The UN, The UK and the Trust Territory of Southern Cameroon*, Langaa Research and Publishing, CIG, Mankon,Bamenda. The draft of the Unity constitution of 1972 was overseen by Maurice Duverger, a Frenchman was hired to review the constitutions of 1960 and 1961 both of which had been drafted by Mr. Jaques Rousseau, Ahidjo's French Technical Adviser on administrative and institutional matters p. 120.

[103] They were forced to resort to violence by French colonial anti-nationalist measures. This was especially the case during the tenure of High Commissioner Roland Pré beginning in 1954. For more onthis; see Daniel Abwa, *Commissaires et Haut Commissaires au Cameroun*. .

their mistakes and learnt by them. It was a matter sometimes of trial and error as there were no precedents or blue prints to follow. This partially explains the apologies made by JN Foncha and ST Muna during AACI at Buea in 1993.

It cannot be over emphasized that all comparisons are lame and that is why in history they are usually made within context; juxtaposing such individuals or events with similar or dissimilar examples and never in isolation. This helps to put things in perspective and because History does not deal with absolutes, which in any case do not exist in this imperfect world of mortals. That is why a brief glance is taken of the situation with our compatriots across the border during the same period.

"Maquizzards", Rebels, Nationalists, or Freedom Fighters

It was one of the numerous positive aspects of British colonial policy in Nigeria and the Southern Cameroons that the violent and bloody conflicts described below never took place in "peace loving Southern Cameroons".[104] The point is beautifully made by Chief Obafemi Awolowo, who joked that the British did not give their colonial subjects the opportunity to practice something of nationalist martyrdom in Nigeria as was the case elsewhere. Rather, from experience in empire building, they remote-censored the desires of the nationalists which were defused constitutionally. The emphasis was on the force of argument and use of the ballot box and not argument through the barrel of the gun.

---

[104] *Eden Xtra*, pp. 19-22, Daniel Abwa, "Contributions of Francophone Cameroonians to Reunification of the Cameroons, also", Emmanuel Njoya Ibid, in Frontier Post p. 4.

Individual UPC Leaders

Reuben Um Nyobe and Family:

Assassinated(ambushed) 13 Sept 1958

Ernest Ouandji in Handcuffs

Faced firing squad 15 Jan. 1971 under Ahidjo

Dr. Felix Roland Moumie: succeeded Um Nyobe as President

Assassinated with rat poison in Geneva, Switzerland 3 Nov. 1960

Abel Kingue VicePresident

Died 16 April 1964

UPC Leaders

(L. to R.) Front row: Castor Osende Afana, Abel Kingué, Ruben Um Nyobé, Felix Moumié, and Ernest Ouandié

However, in comparison, just across the border in French Cameroun with which Southern Cameroons shared a common colonial origin and heritage, the political evolution was characteristically different. Consequently, the contemporaries of the Kales, Endeleys, Mbiles, Fonchas, Munas, Juas and countless other Southern Cameroonian politicians; their counterparts in French Cameroun sought to acquire political power and leadership mostly through the barrel of the gun by fighting against the French colonial masters in a prolonged brutal colonial war.[105] This explains why Ndeh Ntumazah, leader of the One Kamerun (OK) party, the Southern Cameroons version of the UPC, had such a contemptuous attitude towards all Southern Cameroons political leadership because he maintained, they never fought any colonial battles against the British. That was his own crude yard stick for measuring the strength of nationalism.

Most of them made the supreme sacrifice by selflessly offering their lives in the process. Such was the case with most of the early leadership of the UPC: Reuben Um Nyobe, Felix Roland Moumie, Ernest Ouandie, Abel Kingue and countless others. Some of these leaders at different times held crucial meetings with their "British" Southern Cameroonian counterparts at venues in Kumba, Buea, Tiko

---

[105] Richard Joseph, *Radical Nationalism in Cameroun*, (Oxford at the Clarendon press), 1977, pp. 349-50.

and Bamenda during the initial stages of the reunification process. There can be little doubt that these contacts helped in no small way to sharpen, blend and mould the political thought of their Southern Cameroonian counterparts one way or the other. At the time, these leaders were variously described as "terrorists", "rebels" and "maquissards"[106] by the French colonial administration. Consequently, they were hunted down and killed in the fratricidal conflict, while they justified their ferocious counter attacks against the French colonial masters and their supporters as the struggle for freedom (immediate reunification and independence) and wanted the French colonial masters expelled from Cameroun.[107]

After independence these clashes continued with the same ferocity characterized by burning, killing, looting, maiming, kidnapping and scorched earth policies under the Ahidjo Administration. This is what was responsible for the unattractive, literally dreaded "Second Option" of "Joining the Independent Republic of Cameroon" in the 1961 plebiscite. This should be borne in mind when mention is made of the 'warring' Southern Cameroonians; where there were never any open hostilities among the political parties. There were categorically no lives lost during the political wrangles that took place among and between the political parties even during the worst of times. The "wars" frequently referred to were nothing more than "verbal" tirades based on the force of argument and not muscle."[108] In fact, it deserves to be emphasized that for all its existence as a Trust Territory and throughout the dense climate running up to the plebiscite, there was no recorded fatality of any kind. That is why the people earned the distinction of being regarded by one and all, priests, pastors, visitors, administrators and above all by Malcolm Milne as the " little peace loving people" of Southern Cameroon.

---

[106] This fact deserves due emphasis.
[107] Richard Joseph, *Radical Nationalism in Cameroun*, (Oxford at the Clarendon press, 1977), pp. 349-50.
[108] This fact deserves due emphasis.

'Jocular' Not Bloody Fights

In typical Southern Cameroons style, opposing politicians were known to travel in the same convoy or even vehicles during their political campaigns. They would chat, eat and drink together and then use the roofs of the same land rovers to "attack" each other's political platforms. These were pretty often, jocular "attacks" with nothing faintly approximating what was taking place across the border. They played the game of politics which in ordinary parlance meant the force of argument and not the argument of force'. While much is made of "warring Southern Cameroonian politicians"; the most glaring example is set at the Bamenda and Foumban in 1961, where Foncha and Endeley leading the KNDP and CPNC parties travelled as a team and spoke with one voice. Endeley seized the opportunity to ask Ahidjo where his opponents were.[109]

Of course, leaders of the opposition parties in the Republic of Cameroon were all behind bars and Ahidjo came to Foumban with only his UC party. Most of the speeches and quotations in this exposition by Endeley, Foncha, Mbile, Mukong and Motomby depict these traits.[110] Mbile makes the point lucidly when he reiterates: "It is to our credit that even in the years of bitter politics; there was not a single case of extreme action like murder, violent assault or people "jumping into the bush." [i.e. Terrorism] and of the plebiscite he maintains. "We fought the plebiscite and we bowed to the will of the majority of our people right or wrong".[111] Today, these former "rebels," "terrorists" and "maquissards" of Colonial French Cameroun have been rehabilitated and are hailed as "nationalists", freedom fighters and liberators who sacrificed their lives for the freedom that Cameroon presently enjoys.[112] There were no such political martyrs in Southern Cameroons; nevertheless, it was replete with patriots and nationalists.

---

[109] See, the Foumban Conference Chapter Seven for appropriate excerpts.

[110] Ibid., Mbile, *Eyewitness,* p.322., Ndi, The *Golden Age,* pp.64-68.

[111] Ibid., p.322 it should however be remembered that he fought against the results of the plebiscite right to the UN, leading the Balundu 'Mokanya' cult; Bakossi Secret Society NAB Ref. O.36/31/35 of 25, Aug 31 st 1962..

[112] Ibid., *Eden Xtra,*pp. 19-23 Daniel Abwa, "Contributions of Francophone Cameroonians to the Reunification of the Cameroons" in the Summit Magazine and Political life does not reflect this reality.

Unfortunately, the picture painted of Southern Cameroons politicians is far from inspiring.

Political Leaders: Past, Present and Global

Current events in some African countries and in the Arab world (the so-called Arab Spring): affecting Professor Laurent Gbagbo of Ivory Coast, Ben Ali in Tunisia, Hosni Mubarak in Egypt, Muammar Qaddaffi in Libya as well as those in Yemen and Syria are instructive. These are leaders who had acquired the status of demi-gods in their countries but have crumbled and are crumbling like packs of cards in the face of "people's power". To these could be added the examples of other dictatorial and tyrannical African leaders such as: General Idi Amin Dada of Uganda, Sanni Abacha of Nigeria, Joseph Laurent Desiré Mobutu (also, called Mobutu Sassa Seko Wazabanga) of Zaire and Charles Taylor of Liberia, who trampled on the rights of their people and squandered the wealth and resources of their countries thus invoking war and misery on their own people.[113] Without exaggeration, in Southern Cameroons, the British Administration was benign and by the very nature of Indirect Rule was rather paternalistic in what Lord Lugard from the Nigerian experience described as the "paramountcy of African interests" the exact opposite of the French policy of "assimilation". In this regard, Lugard prescribed that:

> The task of the administrative officer is to clothe his principles in the garb of evolution, to make it apparent alike to the educated native, the conservative Moslem, and the primitive pagan, in his own degree, that the policy of the Government is not antagonistic but progressive-sympathetic to his aspiration and the guardian of his natural rights.[114]

---

[113] *Time Scape Magazine* Vol: 02 No. 08069 November/December 2011, article by John Akuroh on pp. 52-53, for updates on Qaddafi and Gbagbo; Jean –Emmanuel Pondi, *Life and Death of Al-Qadhafi, What Lessons for Africa?* (Editions Afric'Eveil), 2013.

[114] Lugard, The Dual Mandate in British Tropical Africa, 1926, p.193.

Muammar Qaddaffi: Late Libyan Leader

Killed in Libyan Revolution

By this definition, the African's way of life and outlook as far as it did not contravene any accepted modern norms was not to be interfered with. In other words it aimed at striking the delicate balance between change and conservatism. And, for one thing, the British administrators were too few and far in between. Come to imagine that Bamenda Division (the entire North West Region) was administered by just one Senior Divisional Officer (SDO),until1948, where we now have seven Divisions administered by SDOs with numerous assistants and a Governor.

The immediate antagonists with the approach of independence in Southern Cameroons were not the British but Nigerians or specifically the Ibos, who were hated because of their all-pervading existence, grasping and arrogant attitudes. The missionaries and even administrators were welcomed by the people. Though few in numbers most of the British colonial administrators in the field were unlike those at the headquarters at Buea or at the colonial office in London, directly involved with development in their specific areas of command. They generally wrote stimulating reports that closely reflected the local realities but these were hardly translated into action because of bottlenecks at the headquarters, by their superiors who instead transmitted politically polluted versions to London.

The Foncha KNDP Government, 1959

Hon. J.N. Foncha: Premier, Sitting left to right JO Field, Commissioner, Sir James Robertson (High Commissioner) Governor General of Nigeria, JN Foncha and Malcolm Milne (Deputy Commissioner)

Visionary Leaders: Simple, Austere, Honest and Realistic

Description of the commitment of Southern Cameroonian leadership to work, once again, is best encapsulated by Malcolm Milne who maintains that: "service was their watch word".[115] These examples clearly distinguish the high calibre of leaders who launched the political process in Southern Cameroons and whose credit should be seen in the context of their time and circumstances. Nothing in the lives of these leaders, even in the worst of them could remotely compare to the examples cited above. Put together, the early political leaders were practising Christians, a significant number of whom for that matter were Church ministers.[116] Every single one of them lived a simple austere life. True to the game of politics there was ample room for "opportunism" and the struggle to gain political power and influence, which in insignificant cases reached inordinate proportions, but

---

[115] Ibid., *No Telephone*, p. 409.
[116] Ibid., Ndi.*Golden Age*.

nothing near qualifying the majority of them as "greedy". This is the proper context which should help in evaluating these pioneer political leaders in Southern–West Cameroon, practically none of whom accumulated inordinate, wealth, exhibited traits of conspicuous consumption to the point of "greed", a description repeatedly echoed in the interview. This view is also inappropriately used by NN Mbile in qualifying the KNDP for "going it alone" when they wielded power from (1959-1962) although the KNC/KPP Alliance never shared power with the KNDP when they held the reins of government, 1954-59.[117] But even then as the boundaries between them narrowed the Jua Administration progressed into a coalition absorbing the members of the CNPC, while Mbile himself was a member of the Jua and Muna Governments.

Malcolm Milne Pays Glowing Tribute to Foncha Cabinet

Over and above all of this is the generous tribute from none other than Malcolm Milne himself. He not only extolled the exceptional quality of the political leadership but of the ordinary run of low to middle grade civil servants in Southern Cameroons as well. Here it deserves to be remarked that he had experience of service in Eden, Ghana and Nigeria before coming to Southern Cameroons. Of the top grade politicians, who, at this time, interestingly exclusively consisted of members of Foncha's KNDP Government, Malcolm Milne was keen to note and to declare his unqualified admiration for Southern Cameroonian ministers without exception. He took note maintaining that:

> The situation has changed again during the last four or five years of my service when l was operating at permanent secretary level or above. Then l was dealing with individual ministers, with cabinet committees or in the case of Southern Cameroons with a

---

[117] Part of Mbile's verbosity may be understood in the sense that he was a journalist by profession and so was Motomby Woleta. Both men were ferocious in their taunts of the KNDP.

small government. Almost without exception they were people of high intelligence who knew exactly what they wanted.[118]

What is most remarkable here is that the calibre of people referred to above are exactly members of the Foncha cabinet, elsewhere referred to by his colleague Newn as "naïve schoolmasters". The real puzzle is why of a sudden these same leaders are being denigrated. Having examined the credentials of a good sampling of political leaders it is easy to agree with Malcolm Milne that Southern Cameroonian leadership was among the best anywhere. Milne's thoughts again went to the Bamenda corps of messengers with whom he had worked closely ten years earlier, dating back to the era of the "Anlu" in Njinikom. With current reports from Mr. ED Quan, Assistant Secretary for Establishment; from this corps only one person had retired, Mr. A Dinga. Of this valiant unit in 1961, Malcolm was passionate and emotional, noting, forty years later: "I felt vaguely then, and know for certain now, that working with these men had greatly enriched my time in the colonial service. There was something very special about that corps; their service was their watch word".[119] The surprise is where the negative remarks in the Summit Magazine interview find their source. The split personality in Malcolm Milne is of great essence here and it is the role of the historian to decipher where the truth lies.

A Unique Southern Cameroons Civil Service

The KNDP are charged with "weak negotiation skills" because of low education, greed and all. Here, it should be added that the Foncha Administration was always aware especially after the vengeful mass resignations of Nigerian civil servants followed by those of British expatriates from the Southern Cameroons civil service intended to bring down the KNDP Government. This was precisely what took place on the eve of 30 September, 1961 as Omer BB Sendze, a key actor and living witness shadowing Albert Mukong, recounts:

---

[118] Ibid., *No Telephone* p.254, .
[119] Ibid., *No Telephone*, p.409.

The British after the plebiscite were very bitter and disappointed and were only interested in cutting their losses and taking off. ... On the night of the handover, the British in Buea ... really all British civil servants were evacuated to a warship which was anchored in Victoria Bay. Those who were working in the CDC were herded in areas closed by high fences. Thus in the Public Works Department the expatriate staff of 15 was reduced to two, all superintendents or technicians.[120]

He, Omer, then a young civil Engineer was one of the two Cameroonians, the other being Mr. Ndumu. Consequently what he was relating was first-hand experience at a relatively high level, much like Alert Mukong. Quickly through his Cameroonisation policy, Foncha set up a Public Service Commission that worked tirelessly to recruit, promote, train and make urgent replacements. The operation was so swift and "efficient" that in terms of the smooth functioning of the various services, the only significance was that Cameroonians found that overnight they had been catapulted to higher ranks in their various services and departments to replace their former Nigerian and British bosses. In fact, this is one of the historical contexts in which Foncha made his apology at the All Anglophone Conference 1 (AAC1) at Buea in 1993 as suddenly he had to replace these civil servants, who had deserted their posts.

This in itself was great motivation and before long, those promoted felt challenged and quickly squared up into their new positions of responsibility since it was an "on the job affair" and there was nothing so new to learn after all. This was strengthened by repatriates from Nigeria, recruits from the West Indies and young graduates coming back from studies abroad following the mass award of scholarships. In fact, this should constitute a good part of a chapter in any work dedicated to Foncha as the Southern Cameroons, later West Cameroon civil service soon became ideal and till today remains a nostalgic point of reference for those who were privileged to live its experience. This is the context in which the Colonial Office criticisms

---

[120] Ibid., Sendze, My reflections.

of the Foncha government as an administration of former primary school teachers should be understood.[121]

Cameroonisation

The Government established the Southern Cameroons Recruitment Committee on 1 May 1959 with precise instructions to eliminate foreign domination in the civil service. The Cameroonisation policy was extended to the private sector, which led to a new breed of Cameroonian functionaries and bureaucrats. The Foncha Government applied this policy systematically and methodically; recuperating Cameroonians who were working elsewhere and integrating them into the new public service while yet recruiting others afresh. Cameroonians with expertise of any form were sure to be engaged and even the untrained and unskilled got jobs as cleaners and watchmen. The idea was first to be a Cameroonian and then to train and excel on the job. Next there was a massive education crusade. This involved training programmes to meet skilled manpower needs in the long and short run. Grants–in–aid to the various religious denominations were raised and scholarships granted to Cameroonians studying in Nigeria and abroad under the ASPAU, African American Institute (AAI) and various other scholarship programmes.

The comparatively large number of Southern Cameroonians awarded scholarships by the Foncha Government in particular, then together with the CDC, the various religious denominations and other bodies testifies for itself and can be seen on record.[122] In this connection, note should be taken of the secretly plotted and executed, massive resignations of the Nigerian civil servants serving in the Southern Cameroons civil service followed by those of British expatriates all deliberately intended as vengeance against the plebiscite results that went in favour of reunification and also to embarrass, cripple and cause the collapse of the Foncha Administration. Foncha

---

[121] Ibid.., Ndi *Golden Age*, pp 6-12, also, Sendze Memories.
[122] *Cameroon Tribune Hors Serie* Octobre 2011, "Reunification One Cameroon, A Dynamic Story" pp. 126-7. Prof. Ngoh himself acknowledges the fact that most of the Cameroon students and intellectuals8s9upported Foncha and the KNDP. In fact, he was interviewed by Prof. Monekosso.

and his administration had to act without delay to fill in the gaps. All he could do in the circumstances was to deploy the best human resources at his disposal, who of course, were the school masters, whose mettle was proven in the manner in which they ran the primary schools since all of them were experienced headmasters, who as well assisted in village administration. These were people with records to show off their competence as administrators.[123] It was a question of using what was available to achieve what was desired instead of crying for pies in the sky. And in any case all worked well, in fact excellently, judged by the results.

The competence of the Southern – West Cameroon civil service remains inestimably proverbial and nostalgic to those who savoured the experience. Operating at the time without computers but manned by highly motivated, assiduous and diligent personnel, a civil servant employed on the 29th of the month was sure to be paid his due salary at month end just as those who retired had their pensions and retirement benefits paid on the spot, or on monthly basis as they quit the service without having to compile dossiers towards that objective. Retirement was an occasion to anticipate with satisfaction after a job well done marked by celebrations festooned with the award of medals, gifts and eulogies.

Mr. Emmanuel Tabi Egbe, repeatedly referred to in the interview easily was the first ever qualified Southern Cameroonian lawyer. He was not left out as insinuated but engaged immediately after graduation first by the CDC and later became the "darling" of the Foncha administration.[124] Personally, he had great respect and admiration for the "man" Foncha, whom he considered as selfless, dedicated and honest: "one whose vocation was to serve and not to be served".[125] It is an acknowledged fact that most Cameroon students and intellectuals such as Egbe supported Foncha and the KNDP. In fact, he was variously invited to address their conferences at Kumba and Yaoundé. Perhaps the other point worthy of note is the fact that the "Cameroonisation Policy" implemented by the Foncha administration

---

[123] Bernard Fonlon, *A Simple Story Simply Told or The Rise of Dr. Pavel Verkovsky, First Archbishop of Bamenda.* (Yaoundé, CEPER, 1983).

[124] Ibid., Sendze, "My Reflections".

[125] Ibid., Tributes ET Egbe.

though apparently starting with "substandard" personnel hurriedly recruited and promoted to fill in the vacuums created by the depleted civil service in time and with meticulous in-service training produced the closest to the ideal civil service anywhere along the West African coast. Equally conscious of the very limited human, material and financial resources, emphasis was placed on self-reliance and self-actualization through the introduction of intensive adult education and community development projects. This together with education rating greatly raised the level of literacy, efficiency and productivity in the territory. It is a generally acknowledged fact except by the British whose duty was to establish it but who rather expected the Foncha administration to fail.[126]

Southern Cameroonians serving in Nigeria or overseas, as well as all recruits from overseas were quickly seconded to the new Public Service. Put together, this approach yielded enormous dividends to the extent that by 1962 – 1965 there were more graduate civil servants engaged in the West Cameroon Civil Service than in East Cameroon. And for one thing, they were generally acknowledged to be efficient, diligent, assiduous, transparent and reliable. It would be a calamity that with such brilliant achievements, which have left an indelible trail on the sands of time, anything should be done to tarnish this record for posterity. Without in any way imputing triumphalism it would be much worse playing the ostrich for any reason whatsoever. This is a highly cherished patrimony, indeed, an accomplishment for which all former Southern Cameroonians deserve to be justifiably proud and which constitutes the essence of The Golden Age of Southern –West Cameroon.[127] Furthermore, it is a worthwhile challenge which budding historians and social scientists should take up for further and better investigation. This was a diligent assiduous and dedicated civil service whose watch word as coined by Malcolm Milne was "service"[128] It is regrettable that this brilliant memorable indisputable legacy of Southern Cameroons deserving rooftop showcasing for posterity missed the vigilant radar of the Summit Magazine which sets out to extol the best of Cameroon.

---

[126] Ibid.,Sendze, "My Reflections"
[127] Ibid., Ndi, The Golden Age.
[128] Ibid.

Chapter 4

The Plebiscite: Litmus Test of Political Maturity

Of all the events which occurred to actualize it and those which have happened in its wake, the plebiscite of 11 February1961 is incontestably the highest watershed in the political history of Southern Cameroons; as by it, all the political activity in that territory beginning from 1951 was epitomized. It was a momentous decision taken by 349.652 or 94.75 of the total electorate and was the most critical decision that has continued to affect the lives and times not only of the inhabitants of that part of Cameroon but that of the entire country. Internationally, certified as sacrosanct free, fair and transparent, it was supreme to all other forms of elections that took place before and after it. In a way, it constituted the essence directly or indirectly, of the substance covered by the caption of the Summit Magazine. Consequently, because of the numerous allegations that have dogged it, it deserves special attention and the statistics provided when carefully analysed speak volumes as there is a limit to the distortions and games that can be played on these figures.

There are numerous allegations in the interview targeted at the plebiscite, the worst of which is the delusion that; "There wasn't an overwhelming support for reunification per se."[129] Even more disparaging, Professor Ngoh holds that: "in the plebiscite of February 11, 1961, most voters in British Southern Cameroons did not understand what they were voting for. Some felt they were voting for a loose confederation, others for a Commonwealth ..."[130]

Besides the fact that the option of reunification with Republic of Cameroon was the "most" unattractive option because literally it was on fire, it should be understood that the campaigns were fierce and thorough; and the plebiscite was superbly well organized to the point of unanimous satisfaction as borne by the observations at the time by all the parties involved. The impression created by the UN Plebiscite

---

[129] Ibid., see Epilogue
[130] Ibid., *Time Scape Magazine*, p.18.

Commissioner himself, Dr. Abdoh Djalal, the Iranian, whose account to the UN General Assembly was lucid, speaks for itself. In it at the cost of repetition for emphasis, he reported:

> One of the outstanding aspects of the plebiscite in the Southern Cameroons was the remarkable calm, which prevailed during all its phases, despite the density of the political campaign during the last weeks preceding the polling. It is with great satisfaction that l pay tribute to the people of Southern Cameroons for the respect they showed for law and order.[131]

This amounted to a superb performance report card for the entire Southern Cameroons populace especially the electorate. It was also a manifestation of the high level of political consciousness, degree of patriotism and civic responsibility of the people of Southern Cameroons. Interestingly, John Percival, one of the twenty-five Plebiscite Officers, though a British citizen bluntly condemned British benign neglect of the territory and politicking at the UN. Yoking both together, he considered the entire exercise bogus, unnecessary and sheer eyewash by Great Britain and the UN from the angle that the electorate was deprived of the Third Option of Independence. Thus in the first place he saw:

> The whole plebiscite as a public relations exercise designed to demonstrate to the world at large that the people of Southern Cameroons were being given freedom of choice, whereas the only choice they wanted was denied to them.... arguing passionately in favour of independence.[132]

He maintains that Southern Cameroonians even as far away as Wum were very politically mature, clearly pointing out that they had been deprived by the British of their most cherished option which was independence. However, Percival still confirmed the views of Dr. Djalal Abdoh concerning the thoroughness with which the process

---

[131] Ibid., Ndi, *Golden Age* p. 79.
[132] Ibid., Percival, p.79.

was executed. He, Percival, alone hired twenty registration clerks besides other officials and for the process, he notes:

> As soon as we had corrected the typescripts, we took the finished forms back to our districts and had them posted where they could be available to everyone in each village. This was to give the opportunity for people to point out omissions on the list, or to make objections against the inclusion of any one they believed to be an unqualified voter. The time table allowed for these objections to be heard later on at specially convened magistrate's courts.[133]

However, above all that could be said about the conduct of the plebiscite and the resultant reunification, nothing surpasses the observation later made by Dr. EML Endeley himself as well as by NN Mbile his deputy in the CPNC. After five years of deep reflection the following declaration of the stand of the CPNC in that process marks Endeley as the statesman that he is in Cameroon history. In his own words, he stressed of that memorable experience; that he had sacrificed more than anybody knew in the struggle towards the plebiscite. Yet, he graciously conceded at the CPNC Convention holding at Tabenken in Nkambe Division in April 1966 courageously:

> The people of West Cameroon have very bravely and cheerfully adapted themselves to the changes that have taken place since unification with little or no visible discomfort. This is a glowing testimony to the fact that reunification was genuinely desired and accepted by the people. Even though the burden of change fell more heavily on West Cameroonians, the average West Cameroonian is as cheerful, friendly and humorous as ever.[134]

This is a superlative statement that can hardly be superseded by any armchair critics. Much earlier, NN Mbile, Vice President of the

---

[133] Ibid., Percival, p. 74
[134] *The Cameroon People's National Convention Newsletter;* Speech by the President General Dr. EML Endeley in N1ka0m3be, April 2 1966.

CPNC in July 1962 had gone even further to appreciate the virtues of the plebiscite and reunification. He paid tribute to President Ahidjo:

> Who after the 'controversial plebiscite with his Foumban Conference seems to have launched out on a brilliant key note ... he registered a signal success at this conference... giving away two mighty points, direct election for the office of president and direct election for the federal parliament. The President appears to have made the best out of material which was given him.[135]

The simple point of observation that logically follows to emphasize these facts is that these statements and conclusions were reached by the two most qualified "Generals" of the opposition CPNC party who relentlessly fought the unification war and lost. They even took an appeal against the plebiscite results right to the UNTC and lost gallantly. However, being the typical Southern Cameroons statesmen that they were, they thoughtfully and calmly accepted the results. In case of continued doubt, the declarations quoted here, it should be noted, came several years later, after mature reflection. What logic can there be without any new discoveries of further historical evidence fifty years or precisely half a century or two generations later to raise questions on issues thrashed by those who fought the battles and faced the bullets. At best these can only amount to so much pointless academic philosophizing. However, for the sake of thoroughness so that lingering doubts can be laid to rest, data relating to the plebiscite is elaborately presented here essentially targeting the criticisms that arose in the Summit Magazine interview.

Origins of the Plebiscite

In the interview, it is maintained that the plebiscite options were, "twisted to be a struggle between Grassfields (Foncha) and Forest (Endeley"). (sic) These are radical allegations which deserve to be examined in their proper global context. Consequently, the origins of the plebiscite questions are examined in the widest ramifications

---

[135] *Cameroon Champion*, Friday 6th July 1962 'Our Guest Writer' page 2.

possible with statistics to clarify any lingering doubts. This equally links up with the issue of the North-West, South-West divide. Prior to the February 1959 general election it had been agreed that the party which won would proceed to execute the platform on which it had campaigned. Consequently, with the KNDP victory over the KNC-KPP alliance, Foncha thought this was a clear mandate to take the Territory on the KNDP platform of extended Trusteeship, independence and later, negotiated reunification, but Endeley argued that greater proof was required because the margin of victory, 14:12 was too narrow. There was also the persistent problem of financial solvency. The two or more commissions set up by the Foncha Government to study the situation rendered either inconclusive or negative reports. As indicated in the evidence by Malcolm Milne, this was a deliberate manoeuvre by the colonial administration to ensure that Southern Cameroons remained stuck to Nigeria.[136] Since there was an absence of consensus on all the issues, the delegates who went to the UN were advised to return home and seek a compromise. This followed the visit of the Governor General of Nigeria, Sir James Robertson to the Southern Cameroons in July 1959 in which he sought to help strike an agreement on the impasse but failed. He however got the political leaders to resolve the issues at a scheduled meeting at Mamfe under the chairman-ship of Sir Sydney Phillipson.

The Mamfe Plebiscite Conference 10-11 August 1959

The Mamfe Plebiscite Conference was attended by a multitude of political parties and groups: KNDP, KNC, KPP, OK, KUP, Chiefs, NAs and political pressure groups. British (colonial) bias in favour of the KNC – KPP alliance was openly expressed by Malcolm Milne, Acting High Commissioner. In his address he reminded the delegates of the advice earlier given by Sir Alan Lennox Boyd, British Colonial Secretary at the London Constitutional Conference in 1957. He had remarked that; "Many of the best friends of the Cameroons do not foresee a destiny more likely to promote her happiness and prosperity than continued association with Nigeria." This was a hackneyed statement that was to be repeated *ad nauseam* by nearly all the British

---

[136] Anyangwe p.173.

officials who touched on this subject. It was obvious that Foncha and the KNDP were fighting a stiff battle on several fronts.

However, Sydney Phillipson "apparently" to facilitate discussions at the Mamfe Conference clarified and simplified the issues to be discussed. There were just two; who should vote and what questions should be asked the voters. Mr. Foncha agreed with the Chairman and made the following appeal:

> We are out to reach agreement on points on which political parties have disagreed. My delegation is therefore all out to be guided by those who have no party affiliation as such, but who nevertheless have kept the well-being of the Cameroons as a nation uppermost in their minds....Here we have some of our aged rulers rubbing shoulders with the students not up to the age of their grandsons. These are men who have a high record as devoted rulers of their people. Humble in front of you, Mr. Chairman they are ready to pass on to the youths their long experience and wisdom in the service of this territory.[137]

The debate that followed focused on three crucial areas: the nature and the status of a self-governing Southern Cameroons within an independent Federation of Nigeria; separation from Nigeria with a period under British Trusteeship; and separation from Nigeria with the opening of early negotiations with French Cameroons for reunification on acceptable terms. The National Union of Kamerun Students (NUKS) proposed "secession and ultimate reunification" and even voting by proxy. This was close to the KNDP position. Kale's KUP stood for secession and independence, while the Cameroon Society led by Mr. Nicholas Ade Ngwa advocated Association and Secession. The Chiefs took a similar stance with the sagacious Fon Achirimbi II reminding the delegates that at an earlier Conference in Bamenda they had "rejected Dr. Endeley because he wanted to take us to Nigeria. If

---

[137] Ibid., Milne

Mr. Foncha tries to take us to French Cameroon we shall also run away from him".[138]

In short, the Fons stood for the independence of Southern Cameroons or the "Third Option", which the British resolutely blocked. As Chairman of the Chief's Conference, Fon Achirimbi II had warned explicitly:

> We believed on two points during a conference in Bamenda in which Dr. Endeley and Mr. Foncha were present. I was chairman of that conference. We rejected Dr. Endeley because he wanted to take us to Nigeria. If Mr. Foncha tries to take us to the French Cameroons we shall also run away from him. To me, French Cameroons is 'fire' and Nigeria is 'water;' Sir, I support secession, without reunification.[139]

Evidently, the roles played by the assortment of fons, chiefs and the students were crucial in shaping the plebiscite trends; additionally the students unions acted as think tanks for the KNDP.

Role of Kamerun Students Unions

There is no gainsaying that the Cameroons Students Unions in Nigeria and Great Britain gave enormous support to Foncha and played a major role in the reunification struggle. In the context of the time this was very significant as they dispatched delegations who attended decolonization conferences even at the UN as was the case with Gorji Dinka, Albert Mukong and Professor Boniface Nasah[140] who were yet students at the University of Ibadan, Nigeria. In fact, these early students saw themselves already as leaders waiting on the wings and were the think-tanks for the political parties especially the KNDP. Talking about the role students, principally those in Britain

---

[138] Translation by PM Kale, quoted in Bongfen Chem.-Langhee, The Paradox of Self Determination in the Cameroons under United Kingdom Administration, (University Press of America Inc. Maryland 1975) pp.118-119.

[139] Ibid.

[140] Although broadly acknowledged in documents, he says he did not go. This came out of a discussion with him at Bamenda in 2005.

and France played in the struggle for reunification Professor Gottlieb Monekosso, maintains that as one of those who lived through the experience:

> We had no doubt in our minds as to our desire for it. I say we as a small group of Cameroonian students in the United Kingdom in the late 1940s. We were about ten or twelve. We had an association of Cameroonian students in Great Britain and Northern Ireland. ... The chairman of our group was Victor Mukete. We had Gwanulla, Anomah Ngu, Tutu Dibue, Ebai Mbiwan, ... Teresa Sona and others. Meetings were held between Anglophone and Francophone brothers alternatively in London and Paris in which we prepared documents for the politicians.[141]

The Ibadan Cameroons Students Union on the other hand sent out a circular letter to all the Southern Cameroons political parties advocating reunification, while standing fast against integration. In other words, they were staunch federalists. This was signed by TA Oben as President and JN Ekang as Secretary. However, on the overall, student union representatives at the UN were generally sponsored by the UPC and took the UPC platform of immediate reunification and independence, which went further than what the KNDP opted for.[142] Actually, the Kamerun students formed a powerful intellectual forum churning political ideas for the KNDP.

---

[141]*Cameroon Tribune Hors Serie* Octobre 2011. "Reunification One Cameroon," A Dynamic Story, pp.. 126-7 also, Prof. Daniel Abwa, in *Eden Xtra* p.22. He adds the following Francophones to the list: Ndooh Michel, Sack Joseph, Melone Thomas, Foalem Fotso who together with 8 Anglophone students from Nigeria and Great Britain attended the Yaoundé meeting. To show Ahidjo's support for reunification although he had not closed ranks with the UPC, the opening session was chaired by Michel Njine, the Vice Prime Minister in charge of national education with other ministers in attendance. The meeting held at Yaoundé from 27-30 August 1959; See the views of Mrs. Regina Mundi in the same paper.

[142] PM Kale: Foncha was invited and gave the key note address at one of the meetings in Kumba among others, also, BB Sendze, Reflections, Conferences such as the Bamenda All Party Conference were presided over by statutory British colonial officers e.g. the Bamenda All Party Conference was presided over by Mr. J Beeley, Administrative Officer with J Dixon as Secretary. It was mandatory with Britain as the administering authority and not a matter of choice as insinuated.

Plebiscite: Basic Irreconcilable Positions

These options initially had to do with: secession or integration with Nigeria, independence by integration with an independent Nigerian Federation or independence by reunification with an independent Republic of Cameroun or simply independence. Obviously, of all of these, reunification with French Cameroun was not an attractive proposition; secession from Nigeria was most popular, while association with Nigeria was just passable. In summary, the KNDP wanted "Secession or Association but avoided Reunification", while the KNC–KPP alliance preferred Reunification with Cameroun Republic or Association with Nigeria but detested Secession from Nigeria. So clearly, the delegates at the Mamfe Conference stubbornly continued to hold their ground without relent. The matter was as a result transferred to the floor of the Southern Cameroons House of Assembly for debate on 9September 1959. All through, though the most popular, the Third Option for independence was suppressed.[143]

At the Southern Cameroons House of Assembly in Buea, nothing much changed, with Motomby Woleta restating the KNC– KPP stand and Rev. Kangsen adding that Southern Cameroons could only survive by associating either with Nigeria or French Cameroon and Jua for the KNDP retorting that if Gambia with only 250.000 people could stand as a nation there was every reason for Southern Cameroons which was much bigger to be given due consideration. Foncha held the view that reunification was a domestic affair and should not be imposed externally. By this logic joining French Cameroon should not constitute any of the plebiscite questions. Arguing for the KNC-KPP Alliance, FN Ajebe Sone quipped that the KNDP was attempting to conceal the idea of reunification from the electorate. Obviously even at the level of the House of Assembly no compromise could be reached. The debate was therefore thrown back at the UN.

There, before the General Assembly with the 82–nation Trusteeship Council Foncha and Endeley, while agreeing that one of the choices should be continued association with Nigeria could not find common ground for a second question. Both parties continued to dig in their heels on their original positions, with Foncha arguing that

---

[143] Ibid., *Eyewitness*, p. 310. This was supported by the KNC/KPP Alliance.

Southern Cameroons could not carry out reunification negotiations until it had achieved its own independence. Separation from Nigeria would open the door for building up a greater Cameroon nation whereas Federation would close it. He added that it "was nothing short of treason that any one for selfish motives should want his country to be engulfed by another". Endeley's response was that he did not want Foncha and the KNDP: "to take the territory and its people on a joy ride to an unknown destination" insisting that reunification had to be indicated because it was the destination towards which Foncha's Government ultimately was taking the people after separation. During the debate:

> Mr. Foncha found himself alone espousing an intermediate step of a separate independence for Southern Cameroons and unification later. Mr. Moumie the UPC leader was very influential in the African group headed by President Nasser of Egypt and Dr. Nkrumah of Ghana. The African group under the influence of the UPC leader, Moumie took the stand that Southern Cameroons was too weak to survive as a state and would be used as a base by the British to subvert Nigeria and East Cameroon.[144]

This was Foncha's most difficult moment as he was neither understood by his political colleagues back at home neither in Cameroon nor by the various forces at the UN. Even more devastating was the fact that both the communists and capitalists were totally against independence for an economically insolvent Southern Cameroons following Sir Phillipson's report.

The UN Debate: A Catch 22 Scenario

Given the fact that this debate was taking place at the height of the "Cold War" is important because, amazingly, all alone and estranged at the UN, Foncha was faced with an extremely embarrassing paradoxical situation. This was coupled with the fact that the issue under discussion being to determine whether, Southern Cameroons should

---

[144]*Daily Times*, 15/10/60., Sendze, My Reflections.

attain independence by the Third Option of "standing on its own", directly translated as weak and feeble, or as "balkanization" by an array of Afro-Asian bloc of countries at the UN.[145] In their collective view any attempt by Southern Cameroons standing and gaining independence alone would expose it and make it an easy prey either to Capitalist West or Communist East. The options for Southern Cameroons "joining" either the Federation of Nigeria or Republic of Cameroon was understood without doubt as a move towards creating a "viable" African state and was therefore more admissible. Njeuma put the nature of increased British pressure on Foncha in a nutshell:

> Throughout 1959 British officials increased pressure on Foncha to abandon reunification. They organised several meetings in West Cameroon, Nigeria, Britain and the United Nations. Under the spell of the personalities of Endeley and Mbile, they minimised Foncha and failed to take cognisance of the soaring popularity of the KNDP after the 1959 elections, and Endeley's waning fortunes among the leading politicians. There were signs that Foncha was willing to abandon reunification provided that the British extended the period of trusteeship and stopped insisting on an even more unpopular option for West Cameroonians, the Nigerianization of Cameroon.[146]

For different reasons but reaching the same objective, the US led by McCarthy, with Britain and France wanted the Trust Territory to stay in their grasp as left alone with Ghana and Egypt it would go communist especially with the UPC lobby. One fact not generally emphasized is that the UPC joined forces with those who supported immediate independence and reunification of both Trust Territories at the UNTC debate ably led by Dr. Felix Roland Moumie, who lurked in the lobby. In this Cold War climate everything was seen as either "white" or "black" with no grey areas. Foncha was thoroughly grilled by forces which stood either for Communist Russia or Capitalist America, both of which were determined that in any case, Southern

---

[145] Ibid., Sendze. "My Reflections"
[146] Ibid., Martin Njeuma.

Cameroons could not be granted independence standing alone as it would be too weak and so become subject to absorption by either of the Cold War blocs. Of course, the British took sides with Endeley, while the Americans:

> Dominated by anti-communist forces directed by the infamous Senator McCarthy stood against an independent Southern Cameroons because they feared that such a state would be quickly taken over by the UPC which was classified as communist and would enable the Soviet Union to undermine the states of Nigeria and East Cameroon.[147]

Obviously, the Soviet Union backed the African group. This was a typical catch 22 situation and Foncha could not hope to escape from this tight situation. Alone at the UN it was impossible to get the KNDP rank and file back at home in Cameroons to understand the situation in which he was trapped. A casual glance at the declassified papers shows that the British had meticulously taken all these factors into account prior to moving to the UN for the debate. Foncha did not have much of a chance, caught as it were between the devil and the deep blue sea; communist Russia and capitalist America, neither of which wanted Southern Cameroons in the grip of the other. This was exactly the trap Britain had carefully set out of which Foncha could not wriggle free.

A glaring fact that now emerges from the declassified British secret papers is that the British colonial administrators were largely responsible for the hardened up positions taken by the parties in the search of questions to be posed during the plebiscite by ensuring that the CPNC did not relent. These were the same tactics which they used in Northern Cameroons which voted handsomely for secession from Nigeria in the 1959 plebiscite but reversed that decision massively in February 1961 for no apparent reason. In relation to this Sir Perth pointed out in no mistakable language that; "Compared to Northern Cameroons, Southern Cameroons was expendable" and that the

---

[147] Ibid.

British did not want what was happening in Southern Cameroons to influence Northern Cameroons.[148]

Long lines of people queuing to Vote On 11th February Plebiscite 1961. Note the large numbers involved

Counting the Votes

---

[148] Ibid., Appendix; Declassified British papers.

Post Plebiscite
Plebiscite Commissioner and Colleagues

Tallying the Plebiscite Votes: Dr. Abdoh Djalal

Foncha Gives Press Conference after Plebiscite

Note Fonlon Second to Foncha's Right

Plebiscite Questions: Reasons and Genesis

Still, in the interview it is alleged that the "plebiscite questions were twisted". Here an attempt is made to trace the origins of the questions and especially the tortuous, arduous and agonizing course that was undertaken in having them constructed totally against the demands of the KNDP hierarchy. Foncha naturally was frustrated and bitter, when he met Cameroonian students on his way back from the UN in London. They did their best to console him hoping that the best would happen in the circumstances.[149] The 13th Session of the UN General Assembly as a first step settled on a plebiscite, but for the questions they were still not agreed. Foncha suggested it should be separation from Nigeria or "Association with Nigeria; Reunification," he maintained could not be part of it because logically it could only come after separation from Nigeria must have been effected. Endeley rejected this proposal and suggested that it should be reunification either with an independent French Cameroon or association with an independent Nigeria. Precisely, as Ngoh himself put it:

> In the view of Foncha, Southern Cameroons could not undertake negotiations for reunification with French Cameroon until it achieved independence on its own. He felt that separation would leave 'the doors open for the building up of a greater Cameroon nation' while 'federation will close it.[150]

To further expatiate and drive home the point, Foncha thought that it was "nothing short of treason that anyone for selfish motives should want his country to be engulfed by another."[151] On the other hand, Endeley in his turn:

---

[149] Ibid., Sendze. "My Reflections" 110

[150] *Press Release* No 485 of 29/09/59 "Plebiscite Questions- Premier and Opposition Leader Disagree at UN," p.2. also, Daily Times, 14/08/59 Plebiscite, UN mediation

[151] *Press Release* no. 485 of 29/09/59 "Plebiscite Questions- Premier and Opposition Leader Disagree at UN," also, daily times, Thursday 13/8/59; "Deadlock faces talks in Cameroon; Three Ideological Blocs Emerge: Foncha, Endeley and Ntumazah".

Explained that he did not want Foncha and the KNDP, 'to take the territory and its people on a joy ride to an unknown destination' and because of that he 'insisted on the second question ... to indicate somehow that reunification is the ultimate policy towards which ...Foncha's government shall work after separation.[152]

After this, Endeley proposed the plebiscite questions to be:

1. Do you wish to continue as an autonomous or self-governing Region in an independent federation of Nigeria?

2. Do you wish to secede from Nigeria to effect reunification with the Cameroons Republic (formerly under French administration)?

Neither of the political leaders was ready to give in to the other. With the assistance of Angie Brooks, the Liberian Ambassador to the UN, working with the African delegations, Foncha and Endeley, a draft resolution was finally reached at the UN Trusteeship Council in October 1959. The plebiscite was to hold not later than March 1961, while preparations were to begin on September 30, 1960. Following further arm-twisting and cajoling and pressure from the African delegations at the UN together with Mexico and the United Arab Republic it was agreed that the plebiscite questions should be:

1. Do you wish to achieve independence by joining the independent federation of Nigeria?

2. Do you wish to achieve independence by joining the independent Republic of the Cameroons?[153]

---

[152] PRO COS54/2412 XC3343 of 12 1O1c4tober 1960.See Dispatch No. 5. .
[153] NAB V6[b] 1962]4 *Press Release* No.485 of 29/09/59;"Premier and Opposition Leader Disagree at UN".

It is reported that on receiving this devastating news, the subalterns of the KNDP craved for Foncha's immediate resignation as leader of that party.[154] No one in his correct senses at the time could opt for reunification with a French Cameroon which was blistering in the flames of terrorism. Just what manner of twisting this question could have convinced 233.571 or 70.5% of the electorate to vote in favour of reunification with an independent Republic of Cameroon as against 97.741 or 29.51% in favour of integration with Nigeria definitely requires a more serious explanation to convince any rational mind. And besides, the ability to twist such questions was not the privilege of the KNDP alone. There were campaign strategies used by the KNDP as much as by the CPNC

As regards the qualification of voters Foncha suggested that Nigerian and French Cameroonians residing in Southern Cameroons could not vote given that the plebiscite was an issue of deciding if indigenous Southern Cameroonians wanted association with Nigeria or reunification with French Cameroun. He maintained however, that those born in the territory of French Cameroonian or Nigerian parentage could be considered separately. This had been the bone of contention between Endeley and Dibongue for years. This time however, Endeley argued for the enfranchising of both French Cameroonians and Nigerians resident in Southern Cameroons conscious of the large number of Nigerians as compared to the much smaller number of French Cameroonian immigrants in the territory.[155]

Derogatory Statements about the Plebiscite

Many disturbing, confusing, sweeping statements and half-truths resonate in the interview and were simply taken as given without question or qualification by the interviewer. These include the following:

- "The KNDP made the population to believe there would be a transitional period of five years…" (Definitely, political campaign

---

[154] He quotes Victor LeVine., See, VJ Ngoh, *Constitutional Developments in Southern Cameroons 1946-1961*, (CEPER 1990), p.168.
[155] Ibid.

strategies and verbiage were not a monopoly of one political party in a contest that was considered dense.) In fact, Percival thinks there was more scarifying about the terrorism, gendarme brutality and inhuman French laws by Endeley than by Foncha and the KNDP.

- **"On the day of election most Southern Cameroons voters thought they were voting for Southern Cameroons as a separate state"**. (i.e. **Most of the 331.312 voters?**).

- "A good population of the workers on the plantations came from the **grassfields**..." (i.e. Bamenda Grasslands, a truism, which serious politicians would naturally have taken cognizance of in drawing up their political strategies, and actually had done so in previous elections) and,

- "Worst of all", it is maintained: "There wasn't an overwhelming support for reunification per se ..." (to consider the KNDP surplus over CPNC of 135.830 votes or 2.4 times the total CPNC score of 97.741 as not being overwhelming is certainly the strangest computation!)

- **The 'KNDP played on the fears** to get the voters' (and in the same breadth own up that reunification was the least acceptable option).[156]

---

[156] The figures, words and phrases in bold represent .

The Plebiscite in Context: Statistical Analysis

Plebiscite Results Pasted up at Buea

To be realistic and to put things in their proper perspective, whenever referring to the plebiscite of 11 February 1961 in Southern Cameroons the statistics should always be borne in mind. These are by all comparisons colossal in terms of the total population of the Trust Territory of Southern Cameroons relative to those who went to the polls, those who voted either for integration with Nigeria or reunification with the Republic of Cameroun and even the demographic distribution of those votes. Consider the fact that:

- **331.312 or, an imponderable 95% of the electorate** in total throughout Southern Cameroons of their free will and under all odds undertook to go to the polls to exercise their civic duty, an indication in the first place of their political maturity, commitment and patriotic spirit. After counting the votes:

- **The KNDP and Reunification with Cameroun Republic** polled 233.571 or 70.5% of those votes,

- **The CPNC and Integration with Nigeria, polled 97.741 or 29.51% votes**

- "A majority of the population': i.e. 135.830 voters, or a ratio of 1:2.4 (approximately1:2+);" in other words, for every one person who voted for integration with Nigeria, 2.4 persons and more voted for reunification with the Republic of Cameroon. Yet in the interview it is maintained: "Worst of all, there wasn't an overwhelming support for reunification per se ..." How could these statistics be said to have been played down?

In context, it means that for every one person who voted for integration with Nigeria, 2.4+ people voted for reunification with Cameroun Republic, which was acknowledged as the least attractive option. With or without the seemingly insurmountable odds that were faced by the "re-unificationists", it is mindboggling to picture how phrases such as those used in the interview could apply in describing these relatively colossal figures.[157]

Invisible Hand of British Colonial Administration

In the course of the Fourth and last UN Visiting Mission to the Southern Cameroons in November 1958, they were inundated with both petitions and requests from the various political parties and political pressure groups on the future of the UN Trust Territory. The OK party urged the UN to unilaterally reunify French and British Cameroons; the KNDP asked for the secession of the territory from Nigeria and its ultimate reunification with French Cameroon on mutually acceptable terms, while the KNC-KPP alliance requested for a fully self–governing region for Southern Cameroons in association with the Federation of Nigeria. The Traditional Rulers on the other hand, demanded secession of Southern Cameroons from Nigeria; and ultimately for it to achieve independence as a separate entity within the Commonwealth insisting that they were not prepared to integrate with Nigeria nor was French Cameroun a welcome alternative. In all of this as in subsequent debates on the topic there was practically nothing

---

[157] These statements paint a picture of the Southern Cameroonians who massively and freely exercised their franchise as: zombies, fools and idiots, who were either massively nose led, misled or hypnotized. How such declarations could have been admitted by the interviewer without asking for clarifications is puzzling.

new. As a matter of fact, the battle lines had already been defined at the 1956 Bamenda Conference and at the London Constitutional Conferences of 1957 and 1958 at which the KNC-KPP alliance consistently called for the granting of full regional status to Southern Cameroons within Nigeria.

Consistent Voting Patterns in Favour of Secession

What is equally obvious is the fact that integration with Nigeria had consistently been rejected at the polls during the elections of: 1953, 1957 and even more so in 1959. For example in the 1957 election Endeley's KNC won only 06/13 seats, the KNDP of Foncha 05/13 seats and the KPP of Mbile 02/13 seats. Endeley tenaciously clung to the reins of power only by forging an alliance with his erstwhile adversary and rival, Mbile with their combined seats totalling only 08/13. Prior to going to the polls in January 1959 it had been agreed that the party which won in those elections would decide which direction Southern Cameroons would attain its independence whether by secession or integration with Nigeria. As Njeuma lucidly explains:

> In West Cameroon, the political leadership was under great pressure to define reunification in concrete terms since reunification was at the top of the political agenda. However, this instead led to much tension and political polarisation. The dominant issues were on the one hand, association with Nigeria, advocated by Endeley's party with the tacit approval of the British authorities, and on the other hand, secession from Nigeria and reunification with East Cameroon advocated by Foncha's party. It was generally understood that the victor in the elections would proceed to negotiate the terms of union with either Nigerian or East Cameroonian leaders.[158]

However, after the KNDP, Foncha's party won the election by 14 to 12 seats, receiving over half the popular votes, immediately several

---

[158] Martin Njeuma., ; also Joseph Lon Nfi, "Ethnic Tensions . During the 1961 Plebiscite and Reunification in the Southern Cameroons." In *Cameroon Journal on Democracy and Human Rights (CJDHR) (http://www.cjdhr.org) 07/07/13*

basic problems arose. Firstly, the victory gave the West Cameroon government the constitutional power to pursue reunification. Secondly, Endeley (and the British) seized moves towards the further integration of Southern Cameroons into Nigeria. Indeed, reunification became for the first time a State to State affair. Foncha had fought the elections on the platform of secession from Nigeria and reunification with East Cameroon outside both the French Community and the British Commonwealth.[159] However, what generally is hardly ever taken into consideration is the analysis of the statistics and the polling pattern. While emphasis was placed on the members of parliament elected, the number of electors was side-lined.

The voting pattern stood as follows: KNDP, 73.304; the KNC: 35.327 and the KPP, 16.027. Put together, the KNC/KPP alliance totalled 51.354 votes to the KNDP's 73.304. In other words, the KNDP's 14 seats won significantly more in terms of the overall number of votes cast because of the skewed and unequal geographical distribution of seats. In short, statistically, the KNC/ KPP Alliance with 53.354 votes got only 41.2 % of the votes but won 12/26 of the seats, which was 46.2%, while the KNDP which polled 73.304 votes scored 59% but won only 14/26 seats, which was only 54%. This was a pattern that became overwhelming in the ensuing plebiscite of 11 February 1961 and could easily with a little analysis have been forecast in the elections of January1959; where emphasis was placed more on seats from unevenly distributed constituencies than on the weight of votes as became the case in 1961.

To plead the existence of ethnic cleavages during the plebiscite as a reason why Endeley (Forest) and integration lost is largely lame, because in the first place, in formulating any political strategies such issues should have been factored into their prognosis. Besides, these cut across the political divide, and affected all the political parties though to different degrees. Even more important is the fact that the ethnic imbalances had always been there right from when Endeley enjoyed ubiquitous popularity, held unrivalled political power and

---

[159] Ibid.

leadership throughout the territory from, 1954 -1957.[160] At the time there were no North West and South West arguments. These complaints only erupted after Foncha succeeded him in 1959. It should also be noted that throughout this period there was an unwritten convention that was closely observed in the distribution of political offices between the regions. This principle transcended political divides and was evident in the Endeley, Foncha, Jua and Muna Governments throughout the existence of the State of Southern-West Cameroon from, 1954 - 1972. Consequently, the landslide reunification victory, though the "most" detested and unpopular option could well have been foreseen by seasoned politicians with a clear vision. The trends with a little analysis were discernible and not an abrupt introduction.

British Support: Remarkable Suggestive Trends

That Southern Cameroonians were consistently opposed to any form of collaboration with Nigeria; whether "integration" or "association" was crystal clear. Interestingly, the first step had been taken by Endeley himself when on the floor of parliament in Lagos in 1953; he declared "Benevolent Neutrality" by the Southern Cameroons bloc in Nigerian politics. Thereafter he initiated the process which led to the creation of the "Quasi Federal" status for Southern Cameroons with its own House of Assembly with himself as the first Leader of Government Business and later, first Premier. There was actually no logic in fighting tooth and nail to tear off from Nigeria in 1953, only at great cost and with enormous bitterness that wrenched the territory into shreds in 1959-61 for integration with the same Nigeria. Endeley and Mbile who had been bitter opponents, the reason for creating two opposing political parties in 1953 found common ground in 1957 barely four years later. This enigma in KNC/KPP turncoat politics could be found in the ambiguous British policy in the territory.[161]

One strong and strange observation is that made by John Percival, an Englishman who was employed and seconded to the UN as

---

[160] It would indeed make a good research topic investigating why Endeley's popularity slumped so suddenly given that already by 1957; he had required an alliance with Mbile's KPP to stay afloat in power till 1958.

[161] This could equally constitute a good research topic.

Plebiscite Officer. His stand like that of Malcolm Milne turned out radically against British action in Southern Cameroons. He was very critical of British neglect of the territory clearly stating:

> I felt continuously disenchanted with the whole progress, because 1 still felt that the British government had neglected its responsibilities, forcing the people to make a difficult decision, with far reaching consequences without preparation. Many Southern Cameroonians continued to plead for the colonial administration to be prolonged for a little longer, to give them a chance to make informed decisions about the future, but both the UN and colonial authorities had refused to countenance this option.[162]

After thoroughly and elaborately examining this situation he was led to logically conclude that the plebiscite was a wholly unnecessary exercise. He continues:

> By this time 1 saw the whole plebiscite as a cynical public relations exercise designed to demonstrate stubborn in backing the Reunification Option fell sick with the declaration of the plebiscite results in which integration with Nigeria had lost by an imponderable to the world at large that the people of Southern Cameroons were being given freedom of choice, whereas the only choice they really wanted was denied to them. I held strangely the rose tinted view that of a benign British Administration ... arguing passionately in favour of independence [for Southern Cameroons].[163]

As a matter of fact, Mr. K Lees, the Plebiscite Supervisory Officer for Bamenda, another Englishman like Percival repeated questions he was confronted with in the field by the population who were perplexed

---

[162] Ibid., Percival p.77, Also, declassified documents No.3 in Appendix II, K Lee's Report on the first plebiscite enlightenment campaign of 28thOctober 1960, to the Deputy Plebiscite Administrator, Buea.

[163] Ibid, p. 79.

with the attitudes of the British and the UN over the omission of the Third Option in the plebiscite. In his report Lees noted: "One question was always asked. This was, "Why have we not had a third choice? Why can we not stand alone? Why should a poor man sell his independence to join with bigger and richer men?" In other words, the views of Percival about the people in far flung Wum were precisely matched those of the people in Bamenda as reported by Lees, which says a lot about the political consciousness of the people as a whole.

Spree of Resignations from Endeley's KNC

In perspective there was a serious decline in the fortunes of the KNC of Endeley beginning in 1955, when it was forced into an alliance with its erstwhile bitter adversary the KPP of Mbile. This was followed by a stream of resignations from the KNC which all along had received the unanimous support and loyalty of the inhabitants of the present day North and Southwest Regions of Cameroon (Southern Cameroons). This had been the case during the elections of 26 October 1953, when Endeley's KNC campaigned against Mbile's pro-Nigerian KPP branding them as an annex of the Ibo dominated NCNC of Nnamdi Azikiwe. On this ticket, the KNC won massively, taking 12/13 seats, with one independent member and 0/13 for the KPP. At the time under Endeley's leadership Southern Camcroons was close to becoming truly united and monolithic. He had demonstrated that good and effective political leadership is about galvanizing popular support, predicting, directing and guiding the expectations of the electorate towards a common goal. This was until he turned round and began to favour integration with the same Nigeria most likely with British enticement.

Strangely, with the KNC Government firmly established, Endeley as Leader of Government Business astonished the party stalwarts by striking a rather bizarre political alliance with the Action Group of the Western Region of Nigeria. Next he invited its leader, Chief Obafemi Awolowo as his guest to Buea. This was the last straw, because by this act he had veered 3600 round thus leaving his followers in total confusion.¹⁶⁴ The kick start to the resignations began with Foncha and Jua in 1955, who formed the KNDP to oppose and later seize power from him. Explaining why he denounced the KNC, in the Southern Cameroon House of Assembly (SCHA) on 3 March 1955, Foncha says he did so because:

> The party had fallen into wrong hands. That this statement is true can be judged from what is now taking place in the KNC. During my pronouncement, l deplored the fact that l could not after several attempts get the faults of the leaders of that party straightened, while l was the opposition within: and knowing that l was elected to serve the people of the Cameroons and not personnel or the party, the only alternative left for me was to resign.¹⁶⁵

This was Foncha in his element. This statement precisely reflected the substance of the letter he had earlier written to Kale in1953 asking him to join Endeley and the other nine in support of "Benevolent Neutrality". Of course, Endeley had changed his mind dramatically by 1955. He further complained that members of the KNC executive were gullible, courting the favour of their master for personal gain. The meetings were dull because they were centred on one man, the "chairman" (Endeley), the dictator, who would not disclose the agenda, while the executive could not influence Government policy, surrendering all their powers to him.¹⁶⁶

Two years later, they were joined by Muna, who left the KNC for the same reason. Chief Victor K Mukete decamped in1959 protesting that Endeley had turned his back on reunification. The resignation of PM Kale in that same crucial year from the KPP, which was in alliance with Endeley's KNC, dealt even a greater blow because he formed the

---

¹⁶⁴ *Daily Times*, 17/02/59, Mukete Victor; 'My expulsion from the KNC is Ultra Vires. As if to fully declare how far he meant to go, Endeley further married a Yoruba lady.

¹⁶⁵*Daily Times*, Actually, the resignations came in fast: The Resignation of Kale and expulsion of Mukete, 11/02/59; Foncha's letter of 3 March 1955 in his own handwriting (in the family archives).

¹⁶⁶ Ibid.

Kamerun United Party (KUP) which stood not only for secession but for independence for Southern Cameroons, the exact opposite of the KNC/KPPP platform. All of these were "big names" who carried with them large numbers of followers that eventually took shape in the plebiscite polls of 11 February 1961.

These moves were clear enough proof and indications to Endeley that the policy of the KNC-KPP Alliance of integration with Nigeria was very unpopular and that he had backed the wrong horse the reason why many of his able lieutenants were jumping ship. There is enough inferred proof that Endeley's persistence on integration with Nigeria was largely masterminded by the officials of the British Colonial Office. This is buttressed by the massive evidence of British opposition to the "Third Question" for independence for Southern Cameroons and their schemes for carpet crossings in the Southern Cameroons House of Assembly (SCHA) so that Foncha's Government could crumble as became clear in the declassified papers.[167] With a little analysis, farsighted politicians with an ear to the ground for grassroots sensitivities these trends could have been detected- that in the prevailing circumstances integration with Nigeria did not have a chance. Also, this should have better prepared their minds to accept the massive intimidating plebiscite results. The obstinacy displayed by Endeley and Mbile in accepting the results is largely attributable to British guile.[168]

Best Solution Obstructed by Britain

Once the intricacies are exposed, Britain clearly becomes accountable for the expensive, nerve-racking, pointless, movements and protracted negotiations that engulfed all of Southern Cameroons intensely from 1958-1961, sowing destructive seeds of discord among an otherwise, erstwhile friendly, peace loving and united people. All attempts by the protagonists in the plebiscite to reach a consensus that

---

[167] NAB ; see, the Burke Commission Reports.
[168] Malcolm Milne who all along had maintained that Foncha was blind and stubborn in backing the Reunification Option fell sick with the declaration of the Plebiscite results in which integration with Nigeria had lost by an imponderable margin.

touched on "independence" were sure to be frustrated by British opposition. One notable offer was that made by the UN Secretary General, Mr. Dag Hammarskjöld, who to avoid a "contest between two independent states" suggested a round table discussion in March1960 involving all the protagonists: Ahidjo, Foncha, Endeley and representatives from Nigeria. It was one of the closest to such a Delegations Return from London to such resolution but it too was quashed by the British out of hand.[169]

However, inexplicably by some act of divine intervention, Cameroonians regardless of political leanings unanimously on the eve of the plebiscite reached a consensus to have it cancelled. In reaching this agreement BJ Greenhill reported that:

> The government and opposition in Southern Cameroons were getting together to urge HMG and the United Nations that the plebiscite should be abandoned and Southern Cameroons given immediate independence on its own leaving the question of union with its neighbours for settlement later.[170]

Prior to that, the campaigns had resulted in unknown bitterness, hatred and divisions among the political leaders in particular and people in general. But in a spirit typical of Southern Cameroons political ethos, these differences were overcome and replaced by points of convergence. As reported by JO Field, the Commissioner, these points constituted:

1. "The realization by Endeley and his supporters that the vote is most unlikely for Nigeria.

---

[169] Ibid., Appendix II, Declassified docs. No. 25.
[170] Ibid., DT: Feb. 6 1959; Foncha and Endeley to See Sir James Robertson: Foncha saw no need for a plebiscite while Endeley saw grave need for one; Johnson reports on visit by Southern Cameroons delegates to London – without comment; Also, BJ Greenhill to JO Field (?) London Nig 40/47/1 of 19/10/60; also, DT: Feb. 6 1959; Foncha and Endeley to See Sir James Robertson: Foncha saw no need for a need for a plebiscite while Endeley saw grave need for one.

2. Doubts by all parties as to the capacity of the Republic to replace Nigerian federal services and provide financial and economic support.

3. Instability of Ahidjo's government and fear that Moumie may get into power".[171]

However, among others, Cohen's response from New York was sharp and crisp to: "Strongly advise that …we should stick to our original plan and pursue the plebiscite as arranged."[172]This was the best chance to have had the Southern Cameroons conundrum amicably resolved without any bones. In fact, the more any attempt was made to find out how a consensus could have been reached so easily over such a thorny divisive issue, the more mysterious the British made it. This indicated that Southern Cameroonians at heart wanted the Third Option of independence, which of course, the British Colonial Government protested with "swords and daggers".

Foncha Addressing Crowd at Tiko after Aborted London Talks

---

[171] Ibid.
[172] Ibid.

By this arrangement, all the political and para-political forces in Southern Cameroons including the colonial administration were to meet in London in November 1960 to seek the approval of the British Government to have the whole saga of the plebiscite annulled in favour of an independent Southern Cameroons.[173] Indeed, attendants at the conference did assemble and the conference held but ended up in a tower of Babel with the British Government raising all sorts of flimsy arguments and finally, tactically throwing back the problem to the UN.

Thus, it was not clear what had happened and who was responsible but one thing was clear, people like Mbile, put the blame squarely on Foncha. He was alleged to have side-tracked the discussion and was asking for a parting handshake of fourteen million pounds[174] from the British Government. As in many such accusations, Foncha bore the blame until the disclosures in the declassified British secret papers. These are the sort of allegations that have over the years contributed to the pool of conspiracy theories surrounding Foncha.[175] Ultimately, the delegation returned to the Cameroons and the politicians picked up their campaigns even more fiercely divided than ever before towards the impending plebiscite of 11 February1961. Increasingly, it became obvious why everything pertaining to the plebiscite and independence for Southern Cameroons was so intractable and mystical. All the same, it was clear to Professor Njeuma that:

> Mbile and Endeley, as leaders of the Cameroon People's National Congress (CPNC), continued to fight a losing battle based on the earlier conception of reunification as an extremist and vague notion. The consequence of Endeley's weak campaign showing was that Foncha, as Premier of West Cameroon, now felt confident to negotiate reunification, or the specifics of federation, with Ahidjo single-handed, without first seeking general consensus in his party, the KNDP, let alone amongst the population of West Cameroon.[176]

---

[173] See *Eye witness* for attendants also, Ngoh p.195.
[174] Ibid., Mbile, Eyewitness.
[175] Ibid.
[176] Ibid., Martin Njeuma." ".

Of course, they were massively backed by Britain which garnered the support of the powers and the international community against the re-unificationists. Able to see through the charade, Njeuma from a historical perspective notes that:

> It was certainly not in Foncha's political interest to involve Endeley's party closely in the process of federalising the union between East and West Cameroon. Foncha feared that the opposition in West Cameroon would put a wedge between him and Ahidjo. Accordingly, Foncha restricted the joint East and West Cameroon constitutional discussions to the two governing parties.[177]

This clearly flies in the face of all the accusations that Foncha adopted a do it alone policy in his dealings with Ahidjo.

Conclusion

At the 1957 London Constitutional Conference, Mr. Allan Lennox Boyd, Secretary of State for Colonies stated unequivocally that the options for Southern Cameroons were either for continued British trusteeship or independence with Nigeria. This was the view sustained by the KNDP. However, with the approach of elections in 1959, the stand of the KNC/KPP alliance in Mbile's words was to: "Let Southern Cameroons make a clear choice for independence either with Nigeria or with the Republic of Cameroun" so generally, it was understood that with such conflicting requests, "the January 1959 elections would be won by the party which best tailored its platform to suit the wishes of the electorate."[178] But when the time came and the KNDP won the elections, the KNC-KPP alliance refused to concede defeat with the strong backing of the British Government arguing that the margin of victory, 14-12 was too narrow and indecisive for a verdict that would be binding for posterity. What is most bewildering is that when that victory was overwhelmingly delivered through the

---

[177] Ibid.
[178] Ibid., Mbile, Eyewitness, pp.112-113.

polls in the plebiscite of 11 February 1961 as requested in favour of reunification it was hotly contested by the same CPNC leadership.

These, comprised: Endeley, Mbile and Andoh Seh, lead a delegation at great expense to the poor peasants, who bore the cost right to the United Nations demanding the mutilation of the country along tribal voting lines in the ratio of: 29.51% (or97.741voters) for integration with Nigeria, to 70.5% (or 233.571 voters), who chose Republic of Cameroon. Of course, as can be imagined, this was not only an unreasonable demand but it was wholly impractical to implement. At the back of this confusion and division remotely lurked the invidious British shadow. This situation clearly illustrated the catch 22 paradox in that the KNC/ KPP alliance (CPNC) who had rejected the results of the January1959 election and fought so valiantly for a "plebiscite" as the best solution, rejected it when the results went overwhelmingly in favour of the KNDP and reunification. Majority votes and democracy were thrown to the winds demonstrating consistent prevarication and opportunism by the top leadership of the CPNC.

Foncha Opens Bamenda All Party Conference26 June 1961

Note Cabinet Jua, Muna and Kemncha to His Right

Participants at Bamenda All Party Conference 26 June 1961

Group Picture Bamenda All Party Conference

Chapter 5

The Constitutional Marathon, From Bamenda to Foumban

The Bamenda All Party Conference: 26-28 June 1961

The Foumban Constitutional Conference of 16-21 July,1961incontestablymarksthe peak of Cameroon history; the political confluence of Southern Cameroons and Cameroon Republic, which forged a common identity and took concrete shape in the Federal Republic of Cameroon. It could also be said that the Bamenda All Party Conference, which preceded it was a dress rehearsal and direct prelude to this all important conference since it was the same Southern Cameroonian delegates who proceeded from there to Foumban about a month later. Foncha's objective in calling the Bamenda All Party Conference specifically was to ensure that they went to Foumban speaking with one voice, which would also strengthen their position in the face of the East Cameroon delegation led by Ahidjo.

Ideologically the KNDP was particularly sensitive, conscious and jealous of the identity and autonomous status of Southern Cameroons within the new dispensation. Towards this objective it proposed fourteen entrenched clauses drawn from the Nigerian Constitution for inclusion in the Federal Constitution. These aimed at safeguarding the identity and inviolability of the "State" in the emergence of an overpowerful "centre". This made their amendment exceedingly difficult if not impossible without the concurrence of two-thirds of the members of each State Parliament, or a majority of votes cast in a referendum in each State. No powers were to be exercised "concurrently" by Federal and State Governments.[179] These proposals were finally condensed and implanted as the famous, indelible Article 47 (1) of the Federal Constitution. It stated:

---

[179] Ibid., Johnson, p. 172.

No bill to amend the constitution may be introduced if it tends to impair the unity [the writers had a union in mind] and integrity of the federation.(3) The amendment may be passed by a simple majority of the membership of the federal assembly, provided that such majority include a majority from each federated state. [180]

However, Article 59 in part stated that: "The constitution was to come into force on the 1stOctober 1961 and shall be published in its new form in French and in English, the French text being authentic"[181] thus imputing some ulterior motive. Nevertheless, all being equal, there was enough security inscribed into this constitution together with the veto powers contained in the "simple majority plus one vote" provision for the representatives of either state in the Federal National Assembly when major decisions had to be taken. This safeguarded the interests of the minority in parliament. In short, it was the "equality veto" clause, which brought the two states of Southern Cameroons and the Republic of Cameroon together on 1 October 1961 at par, as co-equals. However, the extent to which it was effectively implemented is another question. Further elucidated, Article 47 of the Federal Constitution to all intents and purposes was designed to be bounding:

> Auto –limitative to the sovereignty of the Federal Republic of Cameroon in the legal sense that the people decided in advance under that constitution never to do anything or to act in any manner whatsoever to impair the unity and integrity of the Federation they had set out to create, and to accept that any such impairment would be legally inadmissible.[182]

Furthermore,

---

[180] *Post News Watch*, October 2007, p.10. Federal Constitution, Part X Amendment.
[181] Ibid.
[182] "Memorandum Relative to Constitutional Reform, Cameroon Anglophone Movement: a Cultural Association", Douala, 5 December 1991.

It is a fundamental principle of law, whether municipal or international, that a sovereign can accept to be bound by legal enactments which would limit its sovereign action and that is precisely what the sovereign people of Cameroon did under article 47 of the Federal Constitution and the introduction of the so-called constitution of 2nd June 1972 should have respected that legal norm of auto-limitation.[183]

Mr. François Sengat Kuo, an eminent writer, former minister and political secretary of the Cameroon People's Democratic Movement (CPDM) identified himself as a mentor (author) of the Unitary State constitution.[184] In drawing up the resolutions the delegates at the Bamenda All Party Conference were assisted legally by Mr. BG Smith, the Attorney General, who made substantial contributions to its formulation especially in connection with sovereignty for the transitional government, which he maintained should at all times belong somewhere.[185] At the time the nascent legal community of Southern Cameroons with only twelve of the thirty-five members being Cameroonian was not yet formally created. What existed was the Nigerian Bar Association led by prominent Nigerian lawyers like OA Alakaja, Otu and others.

The Southern Cameroons Bar Association was formed on 6 June1961, with the Attorney General as Chairperson and Lawyer SML Endeley as Vice Chairperson while, ET Egbe who was secretary was engaged with the CDC. In fact, the West Cameroon Bar Association was only authorized by Federal Law no. 63//LF/37 of 5November 1963 and could therefore not have rendered legal advice before its authorization as repeatedly asserted in the Summit Magazine interview.

However, after that its advice was continuously solicited on a number of unresolved questions as indicated by Willard Johnson: "The

---

[183] Ibid.

[184]*Cameroon Post* No. 004 of October 14 1991, pp. 2-3. Though, Article 2 of the Federal Constitution stipulates that national sovereignty is vested in the Cameroonian people, who shall exercise it by way of a referendum it does not in any way contradict or impair the application of the express provisions of Article 47.

[185] However, it was Mr. J Dixon (Attorney General) who accompanied the delegates to Foumban as conference secretary unlike the allegation in the Summit Magazine interview; Albert Mukong, Southern Cameroons.

newly organized Bar Association rendered opinions and suggestions on almost the entire range of the KNDP constitutional proposals"[186] with Egbe very close to the Prime Minister. (Foncha)

Endeley Refrained from Attending Bamenda Conference

Another significant point that emerges in this account is the fact that "Endeley deliberately refrained from attending the Bamenda All Party Conference lest his presence impede progress toward a common program."[187] Mbile who attended pledged the cooperation of the CPNC since they had finally reconciled with the Foncha Government on reunification. Nevertheless, he continued to argue for the CPNC that "Southern Cameroons should not forever be incapacitated by the results of the plebiscite."[188] By refraining from attendance at the Bamenda All Party Conference coupled with his attitude later at the Foumban Constitutional Conference, Endeley displayed exceptional traits of nobility of character and statesmanship that mark him out as the great politician that he was and continues to be recorded in the annals of Cameroon history.

Ndeh Ntumazah: Opponent and Critic

The other relevant view is that of Mr. Ndeh Ntumazah, who was an unrelenting critic of all Southern Cameroonian politicians because as he maintained, they did not like their UPC counterparts in French Cameroon face any "baptism of fire" against their British colonial master. He was also a direct opponent to Foncha in his Bamenda electoral constituency, where neither he as an individual, nor his One Kamerun party ever won a parliamentary or Municipal Council seat. However, on the flip side, the UPC was banned by the Endeley Government in Southern Cameroons in 1957 for their pro-communist and radical ideology. They were very vocal critics of practically every government action. The One Kamerun (OK) was created to replace the banned UPC and practically pursued its ideology.

---

[186] Ibid., Johnson, p. 180.
[187] Ibid., p. 171.
[188] Idem.

Ndeh Ntumazah

OK Leader

On Foncha 'holding the Ahidjo draft Constitution to himself', Mr. Ndeh Ntumazah the OK leader affirmed without a doubt that Foncha "certainly" had it (although he was far away in Guinea Conakry when Johnson put this question to him) pointing out that Foncha's only thought was on Dr. Endeley.[189] Foncha, in Ntumazah's estimate saw the Foumban Conference not as the occasion to prepare the future of his people but only as an opportunity to defeat or settle scores with Endeley. He was further disdainful of Foncha because he thought that he was unequal to the forces mounted against him by President Ahidjo and his French henchmen. He went as far as comparing Foncha to Joseph II of Austria! Above all, he blamed Foncha for not standing up against Ahidjo but rather became subservient to him and dismissed all excuses of Foncha: wanting peace, fear of safety for his family or of his

---

[189] Ibid., Johnson ,171.

own life, maintaining that as a leader, Foncha should have been ready to make supreme sacrifices.[190]

Interestingly, what Ndeh Ntumazah prescribed for Foncha, he did not apply to himself. This critic declined from attending the Foumban Constitutional Conference precisely because he had been warned by his mentor in the UPC that Ahidjo would assassinate him. Above all, he totally ruled out the Third Option of independence for Southern Cameroons because: "when the Kamerun people opted for reunification, it was complete and entire... there was never a condition attached thereto". Of course, this has to be understood in the context of the UPC's stand on "immediate independence and reunification."[191]

"Unanimous Endorsement at Bamenda"

Nevertheless, unanimous endorsement was accorded to the KNDP proposals at the Bamenda All Party Conference by the combination of the CPNC, the One Kamerun party, the Fons and all the delegates, although the CPNC further expressed the reservation that federalism was not the ideal constitutional format for the country. In fact, Motomby Woleta specifically advocated a "Unitary State" system as the CPNC platform[192] far removed from the "Confederal" State advocated by the majority of the delegates. Mbile as Deputy Leader of the CPNC, while pledging the cooperation of his party with the KNDP, added that "nobody has ever been asked to give cooperation in the dark." This was because it was felt that Foncha had been conducting discussions with the Republic of Cameroon in secret; to the exclusion of the CPNC. [193]

---

[190] The OK exhibited extreme radicali1sm41and never won a seat at any level even Municipal ones; Ntumazah thought Foncha should have questioned Ahidjo why he came to Foumban without his own opposition colleagues; see Ntumanzah's Autobiography pp.169-173.

[191] Ibid., Johnson, Reports, p.171. Although acknowledged as founder and leader of the One Kamerun party, Ntumazah remained a UPCist at heart to the end. At his funeral attended by the entire UPC party leadership from all over Cameroon, his coffin was draped in UPC colours and so were the other burial rights and eulogies. The author was present.

[192] This was later emphasized by Mbile at the Foumban Conference.

[193] *The Cameroon Champion* of July 4 1961.He did this through the auspices of the CPNC mouth- piece.

Of equal significance is the fact that despite exaggerated reporting by the British colonial officials about the "fireworks" that were expected to wreck the Bamenda All Party Conference no such thing happened, leaving a huge question mark on all the wild talk of a "secret deal" and a "hidden draft constitution". By the same token, still of greater historical relevance is the fact that they had no effect whatsoever on the Foumban Constitution but have suddenly become recurrent topical anachronistic issues in Southern Cameroons History. At best this is stuff for pseudo history as it cannot stand the test of simple logic let alone critical history, and thus makes a strong case for a careful study and analysis of what transpired at Foumban through all the stages from a historical perspective. (This is extensively examined in Chapters Seven and Eight).

Foumban Constitutional Conference: 16-21 July 1961

Since most of the criticisms with reference to Foncha and the KNDP sprout from the events leading up to, during and after the Foumban Constitutional Conference and not from the "bad faith", greed and insincerity that beguiled the discussions and resolutions; the addresses and proceedings at that momentous conference are rendered here in extensor to obviate misinterpretations. The proclamations, speeches and resolutions of the main actors at Foumban: President Ahmadou Ahidjo, Dr. John Ngu Foncha, Dr. Emmanuel ML Endeley, Messrs Nerius N Mbile and Albert Womah Mukong, who led the various political parties to the Foumban Constitutional Conference of 16-21 July 1961, were largely without blemish.

The defects came later and should be sought elsewhere. Ahidjo, Foncha and Endeley said as much in different words in their concluding remarks. Mr. Emmanuel Tabi Egbe given his legal standing made many pertinent remarks on the constitution and consequently his views on Foumban are included here. However, with the providence of hindsight, and proper analysis many of the speeches made by Ahidjo were mere pious declarations and playing to the gallery but at the time there were no crystal balls which people could use to predict the future. There were certainly suspicions in some quarters and veiled criticisms by people like Albert Mukong, who had an idea or two about

President Ahidjo and reliance on his French Technical Advisers but hardly loud enough to attract any serious attention. At the time the truth lay in the future, when the tiger fully released his claws and exposed his fangs, displayed his black spots; perhaps too late for his victims to reverse the harm done.

Departure for Foumban

Dr. EML Endeley, Mrs. Endeley and NN Mbile at Tiko Airport

Anglophone Delegates arrive at Koutaba Military Airport

Prominent, Left to Right Muna, Endeley, Foncha and Kemncha; The Police Constable is Yakumtaw

Representation at the Conference

Southern Cameroonian representatives at the Foumban constitutional Conference comprised politicians from all the political parties, traditional rulers and officials. In detail, they included the following:

- The KNDP Government: Premier JN Foncha, AN Jua, ST Muna and PM Kemcha.

- Others: Messrs Binkar Michael Fontem, Kimi, P Kome, Peter Tamfu and Lifio Carr.

- The House of Chiefs: The Fons of Nso, Bali, Bafut, Mankon and Chiefs Kumbongsi, Buh, Oben, Ebanja and Dipoko.

- The CPNC: Dr. EML Endeley, Messrs Nerius N Mbile, Peter N Motomby Woleta and Rev. S Andoseh

-One Kamerun: Messrs Ndeh Ntumazah and Albert W Mukong. Though scheduled, Mr. Ndeh Ntumazah finally did not turn up. He maintained that he did not shy away from the conference but had been forewarned by his 'senior' in the party (UPC) hierarchy, Mr. Ernest Ouandie that Ahidjo planned to eliminate him. However, he sent Albert Mukong and George Mbarga to represent OK.[194]

- The Southern Cameroons Officials at Foumban included: The Attorney General, Mr. J Dixon (Conference Secretary), Dr. Bernard N Fonlon, the translator and the official photographer.

In all, and in terms of accredited delegates, the KNDP and CPNC each fielded four delegates and five others; the House of Chiefs, nine delegates and One Kamerun, two delegates. In addition, the CPNC took along a press team with Mr. Wem Muambo in charge of the CPNC mouthpiece, the Champion Newspaper, which reported elaborately on the proceedings. Consequently, beginning from the Bamenda All Party Conference and even more so at Foumban; Messrs Mbile, Motomby Woleta and Endeley (absent at Bamenda) were pretty vocal on record. The other outspoken attendant was Albert Mukong of the OK party. Nothing much is recorded of the KNDP delegates other than the speeches by Foncha as its leader.

To balance this large contingent of 25 delegates from Southern Cameroons, Ahidjo turned up with only twelve delegates from the Republic of Cameroon at the Foumban Constitutional Conference. For the Anglophones, this was very much the same team that had participated at the Bamenda All Party Conference. The Prime Minister, his ministers and the delegations from Victoria and Kumba flew in by air to Foumban. The rest of the delegations travelled by road and from the boundary post at Matazem (Santa) were escorted by security forces through the terrorist infested areas of the Bamboutous and Mifi Divisions to Foumban.

---

[194] Ibid., Johnson, p. 170. It is interesting that although he formed the One Kamerun party in Southern Cameroons, Ndeh Ntumazah himself retained his UPC identity and adherence till his death. It could also have been because one was contained in the other as the OK was the flip side of the UPC.

Reception at Foumban

With dozens of banners and thousands of cheering crowds lining the entire twenty kilometre stretch of road from the Koutaba Military Airport to Foumban Town, Sultan Njoya Seidou Njimouluh and his kinsman Arouna Njoya gave Prime Minister Foncha and the Southern Cameroons delegation an astounding reception with banners some of which read: "Welcome to Premier Foncha", "Long live Unified Cameroon", "Together we shall build Cameroon", "Our Union will give us strength" and "Long live the Premier of Southern Cameroons".[195] This hectic reception which concluded with a ballroom dance on the evening of Sunday 16July 1961 set the tone for the serious business commencing the following day.[196] Opening the deliberations, President Ahmadou Ahidjo, the Chairman, virtually repeated himself. Whatever the pitfalls in the Federal Constitution drafted at Foumban may be, those defects are unlikely to be found in the impeccable addresses and procedures that comprised the Foumban Conference.

Foumban Constitutional Conference

---

[195] NAB, *Press Release No.1465*.
[196] Criticisms based on the profuse supply of wine and women to sedate delegates; *Cameroon Champion* was there reporting for the CPNC led by Motomby Woleta and Wem Mwambo, who talked about the Fou1mban beauties or "long necks". Interview with Mr. Wilfred Nkwenti..

Ahidjo and East Cameroon Delegation

Crowd at Foumban

President Ahidjo Opens the Conference

Ahidjo maintained that the purpose was not to propound abstract theories of government or to construct an ideal state but to work out institutions that would "answer our needs". Consequently, only a "Federal System would be appropriate in the light of the linguistic, administrative, economic and cultural differences between the two regions. In a way summarizing what he had said in his previous addresses to the crowds at Tiko, Buea and Victoria in 1960. He reiterated with marvellous eloquence:

> Whatever may be our desire to sweep aside all obstacles, many technical difficulties remain to be overcome as we shall see as the work goes on… We approach all these questions with total goodwill, with neither regret nor bitterness. The majority has already taken their stand and there is no other clear thing to do today than to respect the will of the people by building for them a future framework that they have fixed… You know that even before the referendum and since then during our talks with Mr. Foncha, we chose a federal framework. It was so because linguistic, administrative and economic differences do not permit us to envisage seriously and reasonably a state of the unitary and centralized type. It was because a confederal system on the other hand being too loose would not favour the close coming together and the intimate connections we desire. A federal structure would be the only one which suits our particular situation, for I want to emphasize here very strongly that it was not our purpose to build, in the absolute an ideal state cut off from its roots, neither is it to prepare a constitution based on abstract theories.[197]

Seen in perspective, to those who knew him as a person, whoever wrote his speeches did a superb job but above all, Ahidjo was a matchless orator, regardless of whether his audience understood what he said or not. This was a feature which rendered his speeches memorable and paralyzing especially because of their duration. Generally, however, because his was the only voice the population heard and recognized for decades, the nation tended to anticipate his addresses, which despite their lengthy and boring nature at times received real and make-believe enthusiasm animated by party stalwarts even when people slept through or did not understand what he was saying. Grand Camarade as Ahidjo widely came to be known, called and addressed, through the choreographing by the Cameroon National

---

[197] NAB, *Press Release No, 1467*; . Note should be taken of his emphasis on federalism.

Union party (CNU) further enhanced by the national security, eventually commanded a mixture of reverence and adulation coupled with fear and trepidation rather than genuine love and respect from the masses.

Mukong a fearless, outspoken political activist, and intellectual who suffered untold torture at the hands of the Ahidjo Regime, points out that: "The "Conseiller Techniques" became the effective policy makers in the ministries and throughout the hierarchy of government. The French military presence was very heavy and sufficiently loud to cow and repress any opposition." And, as to how sycophancy came to be enshrined as a manner of approbation and political support as propounded by UC stalwarts, he notes:

> Cameroon, once a nation of dynamic, intelligent and brave patriots, was through repression converted into a nation of hand clapping alleluia boys who could not distinguish their left from their right and their French masters receded behind the screen and from there carried out a more thorough exploitative policy than previously in colonial times.[198]

For the most part his high sounding, lengthy, rambling speeches sometimes lasting four or five hours were carefully interlaced with "doublespeak" tactics that were hardly ever realized by the audience. Thus the population as if in a trance would cheer and applaud thunderously, using wooden clappers when he paused, coughed, gesticulated or made a point to which their attention was tactically drawn for that purpose. His public appearances were always solemn, given the visible presence of heavily armed police and fierce looking gendarmes besides the plain clothes security men who mixed up with the masses. Nonetheless, it was sheer drama. Generally, under Ahidjo, even the walls had ears and no one trusted his neighbour.

---

[198] Albert W Mukong, *What is to be Done?*, (Bamenda, July 1985), p.4.

Mr. Albert Womah Mukong

Leader of One Kamerun (OK)

As a result, Ahidjo's speeches were subject to being interpreted variously. This is the only possible context and interpretation that can explain how in his opening address at the Foumban Conference focused on anything ranging from a confederation to a federation, totally denouncing a centralized system as the basis for the union of the two states he could turn round in the course of the same session to present a highly centralized version for the Federal Republic of Cameroon constitution for discussion to the Anglophone delegates. It deserves to be added that even then, he had earlier co-signed with Foncha and Charles Assale, two vastly federal draft constitutions. At the time it was not seen as a virus in his style of leadership that was to destroy the foundation they were struggling to erect, possibly because the delegates were still in a state of stupor from the excessive revelry.[199]

---

[199]*Le President Parlent.*

Foncha Speaks for Southern Cameroons Delegation

Foncha Addresses Opening Conference at Foumban

Note Anglophone Delegation; Jua, Muna, Kemncha

The atmosphere at Foumban was more cordial, welcoming and relaxed than is generally depicted, such that the best was elicited from the participants. Thus Foncha could say: "I do not at this stage want to claim that we are perfect in our recommendations. But I want to assure you that what we suggest is not far from being perfect.... I want to remark this: that the recommendations we made stem out of the brotherly feeling we have toward the Republic of Cameroon". Literally, Endeley who followed him repeated the same words. Continuing, Foncha placed the constitutional talks in their precise historical perspective referring to the forty-four years of separation under different colonial masters and systems. He thought the passionate desire to reunite would provide sufficient steam to overcome any obstacles that might arise. Not only Cameroonians but other divided peoples were looking up to the Cameroon example. As if singing from the same song sheet like Ahidjo he recalled:

> In our previous discussions with ....Ahidjo, we have kept in mind that in our desire to rebuild the Kamerun nation, we must not however forget the existence of the two cultures. We have

therefore proposed a form of government which will keep the two cultures in the areas where they now operate, and to blend them in the centre. The centre therefore deliberately has only very limited subjects, while the states are left to continue largely as they are now….. Our main task is therefore to produce a constitution for a federal form of government, taking into consideration the peculiar circumstances in which we have found ourselves.[200]

The idea, he continued was not to produce a perfect constitution within the limited period they had but one good enough for unity by 1 October 1961 and which could serve as the basis for further development. It was a Cameroonian job for Cameroons. The third significant address was that made by Dr. EML Endeley, Leader of the Opposition. He maintained that although; "a constitution was an instrument for guiding the rights and privileges of the people…. It was not an exclusive right of the government of the day; all parties should contribute their share so that they could be associated with the decision taken".[201] His presence was proof enough and by this statement he was either affirming or applauding the act.

On behalf of the opposition he pledged open-mindedness and readiness to work for the success of the conference. He however regretted that some of the delegates were receiving the document with the draft revision of the Federal constitution only that morning, and requested for additional time to study it, still promising their goodwill, sincerity, determination and hope for a satisfactory formula.

Not tired of driving home the point, Ahidjo appreciated Endeley's desire for more time to study the draft constitution and agreed with Foncha that there is no such thing as a perfect constitution. What matters is the goodwill of the people who apply the text of a constitution: that is more important than the constitution itself. Unfortunately this stock of goodwill ran totally dry by May 1972.

---

[200] Ibid.
[201] Ibid.; Also *The Post* No 01149 Monday July 22, 2013 P4

Endeley for Reconciliation

There could not have been any better way of kick starting the discussions. In this connection, referring to the rebels, Dr. Endeley seized the opportunity to make a momentous appeal to the terrorists, as well as to President Ahidjo himself for reconciliation. This was Dr. Endeley in his best element. Addressing himself to President Ahidjo and the delegates, he declared:

> If I, as Opposition Leader, and my colleagues can reconcile with Foncha, I cannot see why those who are the opposition and gone wild in the bush cannot reconcile with your government. I have had great reason to feel that Mr. Foncha is an enemy to me and I would not work together with him, as the terrorists have felt against President Ahidjo. We have come to set an example- I have come to set an example-that by working together, we can make a better country. If, by this example which I have set with my colleagues we cannot produce a peaceful Cameroon, then we will be a laughing stock to the country.[202]

In retrospect, Endeley's address bore by far greater significance than was attributed to it at the conference. Statistically, how justifiable was it that whereas Southern Cameroons mustered 25 delegates with only about 20% of the total population of the Cameroon, Republic of Cameroun fielded only a twelve man delegation absolutely without opposition representation. For whatever can be said, the Southern Cameroons delegation to Foumban did so as one unit including both the CPNC opposition and the ruling KNDP led by Foncha together with Endeley, Mbile and Albert Womah Mukong of the OK party in tow; while on the other hand, for the Republic of Cameroun only Ahidjo's UC was represented.

---

[202] *Press Release No. 1468.* .

Fuelling Conspiracy Theories: "Endeley Exclusions"

That the entire CPNC leadership was present at Foumban led by Dr. EML Endeley himself is a documented fact of history. Yet, this in itself is not as solid as the powerful eloquent statements he evoked establishing the facts as indicated above. These historic statements made on the floor of the Constitutional Conference at Foumban, precisely just before 4.00 pm on 21 July 1961 are among several momentous interventions by Endeley, which go back to over fifty-two years. At the time owing to their significance they made headline news captured by the public and private press, as well as constituted the subject matter for common discussions and, therefore should be found in the files of the great leader's family archives.

In context, and on record, the KNDP ruling party and the CPNC opposition party contributed an equal number of accredited delegates (four each), first to the Bamenda All Party Conference(Endeley declined to attend for personal reasons) and later to the Foumban Constitutional Conference. In addition, the CPNC took along a vocal press the crew of the Champion Newspaper, which reported on both conferences in detail, especially by Wem Muambo, the CPNC Press Officer. This was in spite of the fact that on the side of Republic of Cameroun led by President Ahidjo himself there was not a single opposition member as Endeley was careful to point out. Even more striking is the fact that beginning at the Bamenda All Party Conference, the CPNC unlike their KNDP counterparts had been outspoken on all the topics as can be found in here. Statements made by Mbile and Motomby Woleta besides the topical ones made by Endeley himself, largely constituted the reports at the Foumban Constitutional Conference. On the other hand, other than Foncha, none of the KNDP delegates is on record as having made any significant contributions either at Bamenda or at Foumban.

The bewilderment however, is that a recent glamorous publication carries the biography of Mrs. Gladys Silo Ramatou Endeley, among others. It audaciously maintains that though she was a political figure in her own right and ought to have been invited to the Foumban Constitutional Conference, she was left out because she belonged to the CPNC, which was excluded from the Conference. The author goes beyond that and unequivocally declares that:

> Gladys was not invited to go to Foumban and she did not go to Foumban and with the politics of the time it is easy to extrapolate why. The winners of the 1961 plebiscite, the Foncha faction did not want any of the losers to go with them and the Endeleys were definitely in the opposite faction. This is one of the reasons why when things went wrong, when there was misunderstanding about the terms of agreement of the federation or when those terms were changed or not respected, the CPNC insisted that the Foncha faction accept full responsibility.[203]

All of this is an entirely false and baseless allegation, which starkly contradicts the spirit and content of Endeley's declarations on the floor of the Foumban Constitutional Conference as indicated above. However, to many readers of the book, this of course becomes gospel truth on which they would vouch their lives.

It becomes an incorrigible distortion of the facts of history that continue to be peddled, contaminate fertile minds and further polarize and deepen the gulf especially between the North and South West Regions of Cameroon. This reservoir of conspiracy theories is fed and, in turn reinforced by erstwhile diehard critics of the KNDP Government of Foncha and the Foumban Constitutional Conference faulting both for the present tribulations of Southern Cameroonians. It reflects the ethos of the *Summit Magazine* interview and further demonstrates the ease and degree of gullibility on which "conspiracy

---

[203] See, Tricia Efange Oben, *Women of the Reunification*, (The Media Com, 201). p.55. Mrs. Gladys Endeley was also Assistant Director of Education to AD Mengot. As Secretary of the Scholarship Board, both people were accused of switching scholarships won by Grass-Landers to Banyangi and Bakweri candidates. However, in a brilliant, balanced and solid Preface to: Choves Loh, *Ugly Journalism*, nd,. 2013, she pays glowing tribute to Anglophone role models of journalism, who would; "dig deep and unveil what is hidden that made us famous such as: the late Tataw Obenson, Jerome Gwellem, Epsi Ngum, Akwanka Joe Ndifor, AdolfDipoko, Victor Epie Ngome, Charly Ndi Chia, Eric Chinje, Boh Herbert, Ntemfack Ofegue among others." p. 8.

theories" have festered and continue to thrive, blossom and become near impossible to rectify since they are "published" in history books.

Observations regarding the fact that Ahidjo fielded only half the number of delegates brought in by Foncha from Southern Cameroons at the Foumban Conference, and for that matter, all from his (Ahidjo's) own Union Camerounaise (UC) party, were an indication that something was radically wrong with the Ahidjo team. This, as observed by Endeley in his opening statement, deserved examination. In fact, with hindsight, it was portentous of what the future held in store for the union. Even during the dissolution of the political parties in 1966, it was again the same four Anglophone parties, which got fused into Ahidjo's UC party without the Francophone opposition, whose leaders were still behind bars. Ahidjo's egomaniac and megalomaniac attributes were already dimly visible at Foumban but the typical trusting attitude of the Anglophone delegates, who together with their leadership were blinded from suspecting any dark deeds especially given the superb hospitality and sweet speeches with which they were entertained. In this spirit, Endeley reassured Ahidjo at the conclusion of the talks and, directly addressing himself to the President and his delegation, reiterated:

> I do not at this stage, want to claim that we are perfect.... but I want to assure you that what we suggest is not far from perfect ... I want to remark this- that the recommendations we made stem out of the brotherly feeling we have towards the Republic of Cameroon.[204]

Endeley took a most reconciliatory tone literally repeating the stand Foncha had taken and even going further. These were splinters of true statesmanship and the Anglophone ethos.

---

[204] NAB, *Southern Cameroons Information Service, (SCIS)* Buea, *Press Release No. 1468* of 24 July 1961. The lurking reality was that what had happened to the gander sooner or later would happen to the goose, barely ten short years away.

Time Extended for Anglophone Delegates

At the request of the Anglophone delegates, some of whom including Endeley complained they were seeing the documents submitted for discussion for the first time that morning, they were allowed 'ample time' by President Ahidjo from Monday 17– Thursday 20 July to study the draft constitutional proposals to their satisfaction, a task which amazingly they were able to finish before time. This was by any means an arduous assignment but it was made light by the relaxed, festive atmosphere that interspersed the tedious sessions with good food, wine, music and cocktail parties every night. No one was rushed, no further complaints were registered and so after four days actually three and half days instead of the five they were given, the Anglophones handed in their proposals. By Friday afternoon of 21 July 1961, the Francophone delegation had completed their examination of the Anglophone proposals and the two delegations met in plenary session at 4 pm. Ahidjo laid bare all proposals for discussion on the table with no reasons to complain about " concealed" documents and shortage of time. Evidently beaming with satisfaction Ahidjo repeated on 17 July:

> We have, therefore, proposed a form of government which will keep the two cultures in the areas where they now operate and to blend them at the centre. The centre is, therefore, deliberately given only very limited subjects, while the states are left to continue largely as they are now'.[205]

In essence, this was a verbatim repetition of Foncha's iteration earlier. However, this was evidence that any lingering worries on the part of the Southern Cameroons delegates were laid to rest. Malcolm Milne's rabble rousing about "secret deals" and "hidden documents" strangely found no palpable room either at the Bamenda All Party Conference or at the Foumban Constitutional Conference. The surprise logically should be where the complaints raised in the

---

[205] NAB, *Information Press No. 54*. Note should be taken of these declarations when later, the same Ahidjo springs up a highly centralized version.

interview came from.[206] Not only were the accusations wholly unsubstantiated and without effect on the discussions at both conferences, any such allegations are in historical terms anachronistic. This is the sense that with the demands of the Southern Cameroons delegates having been fully met and resolutions taken in total agreement, the bridge had been crossed with the Bamenda All Party Conference and even the Foumban Constitutional Conference now as part of accomplished history were only awaiting the Yaoundé Tripartite Conference to tidy things up.

Thoroughness and Harmony

Systematically, to ensure that no one was left in any doubt, President Ahidjo, the Chairman gave the floor first to Foncha and then to Endeley to express their feelings. On behalf of the Southern Cameroons delegation Foncha emphasized the spirit which engendered their discussions. They had gone through every single clause many of which were "quite agreeable" and others which required minor amendments. But on the whole, he continued:

> We had heated debates on some of the points and I can assure you that that stemmed from the fact that we wished to produce the best for our country. Our recommendation therefore has nothing inimical but something which we feel the future federation of Cameroon will be proud of, if we take the points to reason and put down just what is practicable.[207]

Foncha thought much had been achieved so far but he still envisaged a further meeting principally to thrash terminology which was differently understood by either of the delegations. Endeley, who next took up the floor again agreed with Foncha. He noted with delight, and precisely in his own words declared:

---

[206] However, in a recent interview by Cameroon Tribune, Fon Angwafor III of Mankon who attended the Foumban Conference averred that Foncha "hid" the draft constitution. But it must also be understood that politically, he generally did not agree with Foncha.

[207] Ibid.

> I have great pleasure in associating myself with my colleagues the Premier of the Southern Cameroons. I must say that in my last talk, I said we were here with an open heart and to work as a team. We have succeeded in working as a team in looking through the proposals which were placed by your government before the Southern Cameroons delegates.[208]

Like Foncha, he did not presume that they had found a panacea to all the problems of reunification of the two Cameroons but they had given an indication of their thoughts and feelings, in short of their "goodwill". Visibly emotional and passionately touched, Dr. Endeley graphically concluded:

> It is like a young brother who is anxious to live with an elder brother. If the elder brother receives him very coldly and does not give him any encouragement he may feel very discouraged. Much of the desire for the people of Southern Cameroons to unite with their brothers will depend on the attitude of the Republic of Cameroon and the manner in which they treat these proposals.[209]

He added that the delegates of Southern Cameroons had come as a team, and he hoped they would return as a team. He extended his gratitude to the Sultan of Foumban and his people for the warm welcome they had accorded to the delegates and thought it was a pleasure to discuss Cameroons affairs on Cameroon soil. He felt that if conferences of this nature had been held earlier, no difficulty would have arisen about drawing up a suitable constitution for reunification.[210] By all definitions this was an exposition of unblemished faith, hope and confidence by well-meaning and trustful Anglophone leaders.

---

[208] Ibid., *Southern Cameroons Press Release* No.1462.
[209] *Press Release No.1467* of 20 July 1961.
[210] Ibid.

Closing the Conference

In his concluding remarks, President Ahidjo appreciated the marvellous work that had been done by the Southern Cameroons team. He was wholly conciliatory. Here he referred to the principal amendments the Southern Cameroons delegation had proposed in the draft, which he classified into two: "those which concerned questions of detail and those which concerned questions of principle". Referring to the second category he promised: "The Cameroun Republic delegation is in agreement with the greater part of your views". He singled out seven of these, the second of which: "In order to avoid a certain confusion that might arise from the word "indivisible", we admit that it should purely and simply be omitted".[211] In conclusion he declared:

> We appreciate these dispositions and address to you our sincere congratulations. We are all the more happy to see that in the main outlines of our views are identical. It only remains for us to put into appropriate legal form the observations returned – a task we propose to undertake as soon as we return to Yaoundé and in which the Prime Minister and his colleagues will participate at the end of the month.[212]

No palpable discord of any sort had been expressed during the plenary session. What is more; everybody was so elated that they unanimously gave President Ahidjo a rousing, standing ovation and a blank cheque to put the constitution into legal form. It was essentially of his own volition that he pointed out that Foncha and his ministerial colleagues would participate in the process. Perhaps out of excitement or ignorance, nothing was said about having the constitution ratified by the West Cameroon Parliament, which in any case would not have made any difference since everything was done in good faith. Of course Ahidjo seized the opportunity to have it sanctioned by the East Cameroon Parliament.

---

[211] Ibid., *Press Release No. 1467*: "All Party Conference Opens on 20 July 1961".
[212] Ibid.

Finally, in summarizing all that had taken place from the arrival of the Southern Cameroons delegation to the conclusion of the deliberations, he happily recounted the numerous working sessions he had with Prime Minister, Foncha insinuating that the Foumban Constitutional Conference had given birth to a healthy bouncing baby. He reaffirmed his appreciation for the dispositions taken and emphasized that:

> The value of a constitution is not measured by the length of its articles but it's well thought out and reasonable application by men animated by the same patriotic spirit and by the same desire to build a national community, in the bosom of which all strive to work for the common good, prosperity, peace and putting aside all partisan ideas. Our legislature will supply by ordinary laws the deficiencies which experience shall have pointed out to us.[213]

The substance of the contributions made by Foncha, Endeley, Mbile and others demonstrates how thoughtful and constructive the contributions of the Anglophone delegates were. They certainly knew what they were at Foumban for as declared by Mbile.

"Foumban Conference in Complete Agreement"!

This was the befitting caption of the Press Release of 24 July1961, which aptly captured the spirit of the concluding moments of the historic Foumban Constitutional Conference declaring that the conference had ended up in complete agreement.[214] With this pungent take home message, Ahidjo declared the Foumban Constitutional Conference closed. The speech received a thunderous standing ovation in a euphoric atmosphere of gaiety and jubilation both within and outside the hall with delegates passionately embracing and hugging one another as brothers, following the example of President Ahidjo and Premier Foncha.[215]

---

[213] Ibid.
[214] Ibid., *Press Release No 1468* of 24 July 1961.
[215] Pius Soh, *Dr.John Ngu Foncha, The Cameroonian Statesman*, (Centre ForSocial Sciences, Bamenda}, pp,.25-156.

Fonlon Facilitates Serene Procedure

On reflection, the Southern Cameroons delegation met alone under Foncha examining the proposals scrupulously line by line and clause by clause. Thereafter they met with Ahidjo before finally meeting in the plenary session. Dr. Bernard Fonlon meticulously interpreted the draft constitution so that everybody was able to understand. He equally facilitated communication between the Anglophone and Francophone delegations during plenary sessions. The procedure at Foumban was surrealistic; transparent and simple. This was all far too good to be factual. Practically re-examining the presentations, it is obvious that all the major proposals raised by the Anglophone delegation and even more were admitted by Ahidjo with distinct hilarity and magnanimity.

Thus to turn round and blame the failure of the Federal Republic of Cameroon and the woes of Anglophone, or Southern Cameroonians on Foumban would be a total misrepresentation of the historical facts. Almost all of what went wrong with the FRC and the Anglophone woes arose after Foumban. That offspring is to be found in the style of administration unleashed by President Ahidjo soon after that and in subsequent years.

Chapter 6

Foumban: Beyond The Constitutional Conference

Contemporary Observations on Foumban Accord

In retrospect, it is doubtful if indeed, there were better alternatives to what took place at Foumban after all that had transpired in Southern Cameroons leading to the referendum. Foumban was taking place with a "French Cameroon" that had already attained its independence with a solidly centralized presidential type constitution already approved in a "referendum", while Southern Cameroons was plainly still in political limbo. All along, Foncha had declared his desire for a maximal situation in which Southern Cameroons was allowed an extended period of trusteeship by Britain and reunification achieved only after its sovereignty so that it could negotiate reunification with the Republic of Cameroon at par but Endeley backed by Britain dug in his heels against it. In other words, what the CPNC pushed for, reunification and independence paradoxically was what the KNDP finally delivered in full measure.

Regrettably the goodwill desired by Dr. Endeley on behalf of the Southern Cameroonian delegation was much sooner than expected matched by "bad faith" and lack of political will by Ahidjo. Therein is to be found the genesis of the demise of the Federal Republic of Cameroon and the onset of the Anglophone woes centred primarily on marginalization. All of this is far removed from the contents of the Foumban Constitution.

Mukong: Critical of Britain and the UN

Albert Womah Mukong who led the One Kamerun (OK) party delegation to Foumban as one of the main actors put it this way: "Mr. John Ngu Foncha, Premier of Anglophone or Southern Cameroons did not see unification in the way it was carried out". To him what happened was an imposition on Mr. Foncha and his KNDP government. He put it succinctly:

The UN Trusteeship Council operating with double standards backed out; Britain was not even present at Foumban and was in the process of withdrawing its administrative and technical personnel together with its defence forces out of the territory. The British cut off financial links and technical support at a time when the French were reinforcing their financial, technical and defence assistance to Ahidjo's Republic of Cameroon through numerous agreements between Paris and Yaoundé.[216]

This terse comment encapsulates the double faced attitude of the British colonial administration. At the time, it was merely deduced but it became clearer with the declassified British documents. Foncha had very limited options and was, if anything at all, at the mercy of President Ahidjo. Actually, given the constrictions imposed on Foncha by the British colonial Administration he had pretty limited options at Foumban and Ahidjo deserves to be congratulated for the agreements struck at the Conference. In-fighting prior to the plebiscite remote controlled by British colonial officials and later at the Buea Tripartite Conference had thoroughly undermined the KNDP's negotiating options but Foncha on this part made the best of what was available.

President Ahidjo's Magnanimity

Ahidjo held trump cards, which for the time being he used very judiciously, quite unlike the manner in which he had handled his opponents in French Cameroon. Comparatively, his patience and magnanimity in dealing with Southern Cameroonians cannot be underrated. So that no one was left in doubt, Ahidjo ensured that areas of convergence were carefully recapitulated, doubts clarified and those of divergence reserved to be handled at subsequent meetings. It was agreed to have a federal system of government with two States; East Cameroon with headquarters in Yaoundé and West Cameroon with headquarters in Buea. Subjects fell into two, those under Federal authority and those under State competence. A provisional Government was set up pending the completion of the constitution

---

[216] Ibid., NN Mbile, *Eye-Witness*.

and the holding of elections. The proposal by Southern Cameroons for separate and direct elections to the National Assembly was accepted, while elections to the National Assembly were to be separate and distinct from those into the State Assemblies. So far, this was transparency at best and in action.

Equality Clause: Reunification a Political Decision

As requested by the Southern Cameroons delegation, an idea generated at the Bamenda All Party Conference: The "Executive" National President was to be elected by the entire nation and not by members of the National Assembly alone. In the Federal Assembly a law had to receive 50% of the votes of the members of each State to pass, i.e. of the 40 East Cameroon Deputies and the 10West Cameroon Members of the Federal Assembly. This together with Article 47 (1) of the Federal Constitution was an important safeguard and check providing veto powers and a sort of "equality clause" for the Southern Cameroons minority. One fact generally ignored or not properly emphasised is that "reunification was a political decision arising from the will of the people." The idea of majority and minority therefore should not have been a matter of any great debate. In the circumstances, as far as political maturity was concerned, Southern Cameroons which had begun enjoying a considerable measure of Internal Self-Government as far back as October 1954, was five years more experienced than French Cameroun which practically only achieved that status in 1959. Over the years, track has been lost of this reality, while examples such as Québec and Ottawa that constitute Canada could be cited.

Devolution in Point of Law

Clearly it was never envisaged that power should be transferred to the Republic of Cameroon in between the plebiscite and independence for Southern Cameroons. This had been a serious issue at the Buea Tripartite Conference when Ahidjo wanted everything to be centred on his person. In the plebiscite negotiations, Nigeria had earlier opted to grant Southern Cameroons the status of a full self-governing region. Consequently, it was submitted that:

> It is clear beyond peradventure that the Republic of Cameroon has contracted to receive the Southern Cameroons as an equal sovereign state and at one and the same time to form with it a federation of two equal sovereign states.[217]

In another communiqué it was reiterated that:

> The Republic of Cameroon has agreed in the second communiqué that the sovereign powers shall be transferred to an organization representing the future federation. Since the state of the southern Cameroons will be a sovereign, independent state equal in all respects to the republic it is necessary that the organization representing the future federation shall be composed of equal elements representing the Republic of Cameroon and the state of southern Cameroons. It is not compatible with the dignity of the southern Cameroons that the organization should be the President of the Republic acting in association with the head of state of Southern Cameroons.[218]

Nevertheless, it was again later reported that Ahidjo was determined that on 1st October the Southern Cameroons:

> Shall join the Cameroon republic and that there is to be no nonsense about the federation actually being arranged on that date although they have not repudiated the idea that a federation will be established at an early date thereafter.[219]

So far it was obvious that Ahidjo had always been dictatorial and impervious to federalism as he was averse to sharing power with

---

[217] PRO CO554/2188 XC 3406
[218] Ibid., See also Jacques Benjamin, p. 60.
[219] PRO CO554/2258 XC 3911, Burr to Emmanuel of 11 July 1961. This was after the Buea Tripartite Conference. .

anybody. It is also clear, that he was not a man of his word, having already signed two broadly federal draft constitutions and made public declarations in favour of federalism, and shared power at independence; he now reneged on these promises as it suited him.

On Equality, the Communiqué continued:

> In order that the people of the Southern Cameroons may achieve independence by joining the Republic of Cameroon it is necessary that the federation should come into existence at midnight of 1stOctober. At one and the same moment there will be born the independent state of the southern Cameroons and the federation of the United Kamerun Republic. The federation would be a free association of independent and equal sovereign states.[220]

On the issue of the West Cameroon judiciary, it was agreed for the opinion of the West Cameroon Bar Association to be sought first.[221] The idea of the entrenchment of fundamental Human Rights into the Constitution was accepted in principle but modified by President Ahidjo; to be included in the Preamble instead. Whether deliberately or not, he never implemented this promise and probably because of its absence, he was able less than a year later to tamper with the judiciary. In other words, with hindsight, the bad faith and absence of good will was remotely discernible even at Foumban.

Pertinent, Sober Reflections with Hindsight

Details of the discussions may be found in the reports, while acknowledging that there is no such thing as a "perfect constitution". What happened at Foumban was essentially agreeing on a proper framework the satisfaction of which was expressed by all the key speakers; namely Ahidjo, Foncha and Endeley. It would be presumptuous expecting that all the proposals and desires expressed in the resolutions of the Bamenda All Party Constitutional Conference had to be accepted and adopted at Foumban as given in their original

---

[220] PRO CO554/2188 XC 3406, Conference.
[221] However, formally, this was only p1u7t 1into form in 1963 as the structure that existed had more foreigners than nationals.

form. Then of course there would have been no reason for a conference at all. It involved the exchange of ideas: discussions, dialogue, giving, taking and striving at consensus. There is a world of difference between philosophizing, idle academic or political criticism and practical reality. Nor was there a question of winners and losers at Foumban or anywhere else. The delegates did not go there for a battle or for any sort of competition. The welcome banners said it all; the Foumban Constitutional Conference was supposed to be a first meeting of long lost 'brothers'. The target was consensus, good will and the determination to build available FRC.

Albert Mukong: Pertinent View

In retrospect, the views of Albert Mukong, who in the absence of Ndeh Ntumazah, actually led the delegation of the One Kamerun [OK] party at Foumban, reasonably captured the strength of mind of some of the Anglophone delegates. In fact, his observations touched on those later raised by Emmanuel Njoya. Unlike Ndeh Ntumazah who had developed cold feet at the last moment, Mukong had sound background knowledge of Ahidjo's torture chambers and prisons.[222] He observed that from the time of the commencement of the conference the Anglophone leaders were already overtaken with fear. Given his UPCist intuition and his normal critical manner of thinking, he was led to comment on Ahidjo and his French backers, British undermining of Foncha and Endeley's attitude:

> I must here observe that even from this time the Anglophone leaders were already gripped with fear. The fact that Ahidjo had the backing of the French and French military might lay at his disposal; while the British were packing out bag and baggage, the British in our civil service were resigning and even those in the CDC were packing back home, as they said, in fear of the guerrilla war that was going to overrun the entire territory. This fact greatly weakened Dr. Foncha and his men. On his part Dr. Endeley did not seem to care much what fate befell those who had voted

---

[222] Albert W Mukong, *Prisoner without a Crime*, (London: Edition Nubia), 1990.

against his option and of course even his supporters. It appeared he would love to see us sink into the deep and so prove right the fears he had expressed at the campaigns.[223]

As one who lived the reality of the moment and suffered torture at Ahidjo's hands, Mukong's observation coming several years later after further reflection carry enormous significance.

Nerius N Mbile Favours Centralisation

Nerius N Mbile, another prominent personality, actually the deputy leader of the CPNC, and therefore a principal actor, like Mukong, had been bitter and critical of Foncha for the proceedings leading up to the Foumban Constitutional Conference. However, reflecting on the Foumban Constitution some time later though initially in favour of a more centralised system, Mbile now maintained "We may not have done more if we had spent five months instead of five days in writing our constitution at Foumban". Then he continues:

> Our Bamenda ideas were not without their own hazards, as a loose union might easily have snapped at the slightest friction resulting either in a separate West Cameroon, or the eruption of a civil war if the Easterners were tempted to resist the severance. No one can say for sure that a separate West Cameroon nation may not have produced another Marcias Nguema for us. We can see dangers and grave peril of a loose federation that was naively conceived at Mankon....[224]

Very clearly Mbile by this statement endorsed the fact that the Foumban constitution could not have been surpassed even with additional time. Over time, with mellowed passions and better counsel, Mbile became equally appreciative and was even boastful of the plebiscite experience placing that event in historical perspective he noted that:

---

[223] Ibid., p. 26.
[224] Ibid., Mbile, *Eyewitness*

> February 11, 1961 was our finest day for while most African States and their limits were chosen for them by powers they never even saw in far off Berlin in 1884–85; we, the one million Southern Cameroonians must thank destiny that we did exercise the sacred right to choose our future on plebiscite day.[225]

Such declarations coming from a person who could easily be described as one of Foncha's greatest detractors and one who had never wavered from his attachment to Nigeria, amounts to the maximum compliment and endorsement that could ever be rendered to Foncha as the "Architect of Reunification". For example, contrasted to a statement to the Daily Times in Lagos barely a year to the plebiscite, Mbile had sternly warned;

> If the KNDP does not stop its mad and heedless drive for secession, the disintegration of the Southern Cameroons will become inevitable' and went ahead to name several tribes including the Bakweris of Victoria division, the Balondos and the Bakossis of Kumba division, the Ejagams of Mamfe division and the tribes of Wum Central as well as all the tribes of Nkambe division were determined to stay with the federation of Nigeria.'[226]

He even went on to declare that; "If a plebiscite is decided upon at the UN as the method of ascertaining the wishes of the people, the KNC/KPP alliance would insist on the vote being counted according to tribal units ..." and in fact, this was a threat he and Endeley executed though without success. That Mbile finally paid such glowing tribute to the success of the Foumban constitution and even the plebiscite itself is therefore of enormous significance and renders critics of that "Act" idle arm chair gossips and rabble-rousers.

---

[225] Ibid.
[226] Ibid.

Emmanuel Tabi Egbe: Reflections on Foumban

Emmanuel Tabi Egbe

First Southern Cameroons Lawyer

Much is made in the interview about Hon. Emmanuel Tabi Egbe as an "indispensable lawyer", who together with the Southern Cameroons Bar Council and advice of the British Colonial Masters would have changed the face and fate of Southern Cameroons. It is important therefore to see him in the context of the time relating to the KNDP, Foncha and his views on the crucial Foumban Constitutional Conference. It should also be emphasised that the Southern Cameroons Bar Association was in its nascent stage at the time, largely dominated by non-Cameroonians. Southern Cameroonian constituted only twelve of its thirty-five members. As indicated, it was only formally approved in 1963. Indeed, Hon. Emmanuel Tabi Egbe, easily the earliest Southern Cameroonian law graduate was a consummate lawyer and was able to make observations on the processes surrounding the Foumban Constitutional Conference as well as on the federal constitution. He maintains that: "The Foumban Constitutional Conference could not be judged on the basis of victory for the Republic of Cameroon and defeat for Southern Cameroons because the paramount interest was reunification and all decisions to achieve it were taken in good faith." Thus he shared in full, the views, hopes and fears of Foncha and Endeley that the success of Foumban depended on the "goodwill" and good faith of "our Francophone brothers", massively led by President Ahidjo.[227]

He further drove home the point, holding that; "If the Foumban constitutional arrangement is under criticism today, it is precisely because bad faith has crept into the Francophone – Anglophone relationship" and concludes that: "There is nothing as a good or bad constitution rather those who interpret and apply the law are to be blamed for bad government if it occurred".[228] Here he hit the nail squarely on the head because critics of the constitution generally miss this point and instead pick holes in phrases, processes and procedures surrounding the constitution.

Foncha: Star of Foumban, Awards, Tributes, Decorations

To most outside observers and even some of the delegates, what was most unforgettable about the Foumban Constitutional Conference was the fact that Foncha was singled out and honoured successively by the Sultan of Foumban, the people and the municipality. And, indeed, it was to mark the historic occasion and in recognition of John N Foncha as "The one man who had made it happen", that led to his being honoured in a huge public decoration ceremony. This took place in front of: President Ahidjo, Mr. Charles Assale, Prime Minister of the Republic of Cameroon[229] together with the ministers, dignitaries, the Fons of Bafut, Bali, Mankon, other traditional rulers, Dr. Endeley and in short, all the delegates at the Conference. It was a popular expression of the sentiments of the people, an upwelling of gratitude and happiness coming from deep down within their hearts as demonstrated by the huge crowds who turned out for these ceremonies.

---

[227] Ibid., *Press Release*, No.1468.
[228] Sylvester Ngemasong, "Crises within the KNDP, 1959-66: An Historical Analysis", MA Dissertation, University of Buea, 2004, p. 79.
[229] Also decorated at this stage but interestingly Ahidjo was left out. One wonders what must have been going through his m1in7d6as he ceased to be the centre of focus.

Yet at a strictly personal level, it is amply demonstrated that Sultan Seidou Njoya Njimoulouh, whose Bamoun Sultanate is coterminous with the vast Fondom of Nso in the North-West Region was innately dedicated to reunification and trusted even before the plebiscite, that Foncha would be able to achieve it. This was a feeling shared with the Bamilekes to whom reunification was an "Act of faith".[230] He had been at Bamenda to receive Foncha, when he came back from the UN and again at Yaoundé Airport on 3 March 1961 to welcome him, when he came to brief Ahidjo on the outcome of the plebiscite.[231] The ceremony comprised dressing the laureate with an intricately embroidered metal necklace with brass miniature human heads and a sword in a scabbard, the highest honour in the Bamoun sultanate reserved for victorious warriors returning from battle. Other than the historic significance of the occasion, the items of the decoration were the best of the best in the context of the fact that Foumban art is unbeatable by all standards. Accompanied by the same dignitaries, Foncha was taken in procession through a mounted contingent of the Sultan's bodyguards and warriors amidst thunderous gun-firing, chanting of war songs and ululations into the inner court, where he was received by the Sultan and his courtiers. To crown it all, the ancestral traditional gong was sounded for the first time in fifty years. So, the bonds between the two men, Foncha and Sultan Seidou Njoya Njimoulouh went further than met the eye[232]

---

[230] These included people like Kamdem Ninyem, Ministers in Ahidjo's cabinet.
[231] Ibid., *Frontier Telegraph* p.4.
[232] Ibid., Frontier Post.

Sultan Seidou Njoya Njimoulouh Decorates Foncha and Charles Assale

Foncha: Civil and Municipal Decorations

Sultan Njoya Seidou Njimouluh and his courtiers had performed what could be termed the royal decorations but the "Bamoun people" outside the royalty were anxious to take their turn. This took place the following night at a farewell dinner party, where they presented Foncha with a bronze statue of a mounted warrior on horseback in full battle regalia. Together with this was a carved plaque of Foncha himself, proof of the fact that plans for this occasion had been on course for a considerable length of time. The special significance of this ceremony and the fact that it was taking place in the presence of the new Cameroon Head of State, President Ahidjo, deserves to be taken note of as well as the choice of the ancient city of Foumban as the venue for the momentous conference. Put together they definitely left indelible impressions on the delegates.

President Ahidjo and Premier Foncha had already paid tributes to Sultan Njoya Seidou Njimouluh in their opening addresses. At a glance the presence of mounted and foot warriors, carrying arms, firing (Dane) guns and beating war drums would convey the impression of a state, within a state but powerful as the Bamouns had been in the past, these paraphernalia were now no more than ceremonial symbols.

Domesticated by colonial experience, his father was sent on exile by the French colonial masters in 1931 the supremacy of the state was fundamental. In fact, like other Sultanates in Northern Cameroon and powerful Fondoms in the Bamenda Grasslands they were currently little more than tourist sites and shadows of a glorious past. Traditionally they continued to wield enormous influence over their subjects.

The Setting: Significance

However, Foumban remains a famous Moslem traditional town and capital of Bamoun (the country) which is unique for its spectacular geographical setting with volcanic lakes, rolling hills and mountains, fertile volcanic soils; it is the bread basket of the entire region and beyond Cameroon, supplying various foodstuffs to Gabon, Central African Republic and Equatorial Guinea. Its art especially cast in bronze and metal are unsurpassed and so is the hospitality of its people. The father of Sultan Seidou Njimouluh, Sultan Ibrahim Njoya had been a renowned ruler and an inventor of repute having instituted his own writing, language and religion. Foumban has throughout the ages attracted tourists and researchers in and out of season.

No location other than Foumban would have suited the reunification conference better at the time.[233] It is also within the reunification celebration that the honour done to Premier Foncha can better be appreciated. He was the equivalent of a warrior or a reputable hunter who had single-handedly, more or less killed and brought home a fierce game such as a lion or a tiger. In this instance, Foncha had brought home the greatest game, the reunification of the two Cameroons. The impact and emotions this ceremony evoked among his colleagues, rivals, detractors and admirers can be interpreted variously with feelings ranging from admiration through inspiration to utter jealousy and even rancour by those who had expected him to fail.[234] However, to Foncha, himself a prince from the Nkwen Fondom and one who held tradition in great esteem, these activities actually,

---

[233] However, this is contested on security grounds by Mr. Emmanuel Njoya as will be seen presently.
[234] Such were the expectation of Malcolm Milne and JO Field.

traditional "initiation rites" were highly treasured.[235] As a sign of this attachment even before this occasion, Foncha was always to be seen on official occasions wearing his traditional gown which incidentally has outgrown its "Bamenda Grassland" origins and assumed the significance of national Cameroon outfit.

Other Awards, Tributes and Decorations

To say the least, Foncha was the "man of the hour" and Foumban was his best moment. Two years earlier he had been decorated with the title of "Commandeur de l'ordre de la valeur". Later on in the course of a tour of Europe, he was conferred the Great Cross of the "Ordine Pia" in a papal decoration by Pope Paul VI. It is among the highest equestrian orders. This was in recognition of his distinguished services to humanity. In the USA, he was accorded an Honorary Doctorate of Laws (LLD) by St. John's University, Long Island, N.Y. by Very Rev. Edward J Birth, President of the University as a distinguished statesman and diplomatist who had shown rare qualities of leadership and dedication in helping to guide Cameroon into the international comity of states. It is amazing in this connection that he was never considered for any British decoration or award.

However, as a traditionalist to the core and within the context of all that had taken place at Foumban, Foncha treasured these moments profoundly. Above all, it marked him out as the undisputed "Architect of the Reunification of Cameroon". The Sultan of Foumban and his people who had lived the reality chose to crown him within that process and in the full glare and presence of President Ahmadou Ahidjo, his cabinet and the conference participants. The arguments that were concocted later as to who is the real Father and Architect of Reunification are therefore, basically academic exercise. As an aside, one wonders what must have been running through President Ahidjo's mind as he stood by and watched Foncha being repeatedly honoured and publicly decorated with so much fanfare; encomiums which were not extended to him even though he himself was an acclaimed friend of the Sultan as of Arouna Njoya, a prince and member of Ahidjo's

---

[235] His attire and administrative reforms depicted amply this attitude of his.

cabinet.²³⁶ Certainly these must have been sore moments for J.O. Field and Malcolm Milne who had prescribed cataclysmic failure for him.(Foncha)

Penultimate Conclusion

So far without belabouring the point to cite the views of many more participants especially as there were no contrary Anglophone observations, it is clear that the Foumban talks ended on a harmonious and near perfect note. The document that was finally approved was dynamic, providing room for necessary amendments to make up for any shortcomings. This was found in its articles 47 (2, 3&4) with the threshold and safeguards entrenched in Article 47(1) which simply and unequivocally stated: "No bill to amend the Constitution may be introduced if it tends to impair the unity and integrity of the federation". It is easy to see that "federalism was intended by the framers of the constitution to be kept intact under the provision of Article 47 of the Federal constitution just as the framers of: the US Federal Constitution, the German Federal Constitution, the Canadian Federal Constitution, the Indian Federal Constitution and the Australian Federal Constitution had enacted theirs."²³⁷

Consequently, if those who prepared this broth, pronounced it "excellent" and delicious for consumption, all that can be said about those finding fault with the Foumban Constitution now are either armchair academic critics picking needles in a haystack or outright destructive critics struggling to reinvent the wheel. There can be no question about the failure or destruction of the federation that resulted from it. Evidently, the failure of the Federation lies far, far away from the conclusions reached at Foumban, the processes leading to it or in the contents of that famous document which with all its "alleged" defects is still so much sought after till today.²³⁸ It is in this connection that the absence of the 'Ahidjo Factor 'in the Summit Magazine interview gravely faults its merits. So much of the reporting on the Foumban Constitutional Conference paints a near harmonious and

---

[236] Ibid., *Frontier Telegraph*.
[237] See Cameroon Anglophone Movement, p.11.
[238] Ibid., proposals at the all Anglophone Conference (AAC1), Buea 1993.

perfect story. Even with all the praises just like any human endeavour, it was not impeccable and could still have been better. Thus, for a better and more balanced understanding it is interesting to see the flip side of the Foumban Conference.[239]

Beyond the "Glamour and Glitter of Foumban"

Much like the release of the declassified British secret papers in 1998 revolutionized knowledge and concepts of the activities of the British colonial office during the period leading up to the plebiscite in 1961; providentially, fresh historical insight on the famous Foumban Constitutional Conference, some fifty years after, erupted precisely in July 2008. Again, very much like the declassified British secret papers, this information largely brings to light, what was apparently what eluded the official and popular press, especially the Anglophone press. This probably might have been due to mature self-censorship by journalists at the time who excised exposure of such excessive revelry which would certainly have been received in bad taste by the Southern Cameroons society, where public morality by those in leadership positions was still highly valued.

There are all prospects that this information could radicalize some concepts so far held as sacrosanct on Foumban. Significantly, therefore, these fresh rather, untoward revelations originate from a French language journal. It records the passionate and unmitigated confession of an octogenarian insider administrator, who after deep reflection decided to make a clean breast of the sinister plans and deeds that took place under his watch behind the glitter and glamour that characterized the famous Foumban Constitutional Conference of 16-21 July 1961. This in no way passes any verdict on the agreement that was reached at Foumban, which might have been better but was as good as it could possibly be under the prevailing circumstances.

Doubts Cast about Security

As indicated, it emerges as a "one off" account, interestingly by a Francophone journalist, whose report had to be rendered into

---

[239] Ibid., See *Frontier Telegraph*.

English.²⁴⁰ For one thing, the views expressed are logical, pertinent and akin to those of Professor Willard Johnson, who wrote broadly on the Foumban Conference and therefore lend credibility to the report the insinuations raised by Albert Mukong and the general observation made by NN Mbile in his autobiography added to the fact that he attended the Foumban conference in the double competence of delegate and journalist. Entitled "la Duperie de Foumban17-21 Julliet, 1961" and rendered in English as "the Deception of Foumban, the article by Xavier Deuchua"²⁴¹gives a first-hand account of an octogenarian administrator, who with his boss was directly involved in the intimate and detailed organization of the event, charged with" the "tedious problems of accommodation, transport and feeding of the delegates as well as the animation of Foumban during the six days of the conference". In short, it meant that he, Mr. Emmanuel Njoya as the "Sous Prefect" or Assistant Senior Divisional Officer (ADO) with Mr. Jean-Marcel Mengueme, the "Prefect" or Senior Divisional Officer (SDO), were at the heart of all that transpired at Foumban.

However, in the initial analysis, examining the choice of Foumban as the venue for the conference, Les Cahiers de Mutations, conceded that "Foumban is a calm, sunny and beautiful town, where Ahidjo went for relaxation because of his "twin friendship with Sultan Seidou and Arouna Njoya" but the description according to some eyewitnesses, that it was, "an island of peace in the midst of an armed rebellion was false." The paper pointed out that in the fortnight preceding the conference more than 100 people had been killed by terrorists in the towns of Loum, Bafang, Ndom and Douala. Echoes of these killings rapidly spread across the Mungo and seriously worried large numbers of unification advocates there, reason why Foncha on July 3, 1961 at Douala appealed to those killing to stop and return to legality. "Ahidjo was very worried about how to reassure the leaders to the conference of the security of Foumban mindful of the fact that Dr. Felix Roland Moumie was a son of the soil". The UPC was daring and

---

²⁴⁰ This was done by Mr. Germanus Dounge.
²⁴¹ Ibid., *the Frontier Telegraph, Vol. II no. 0007* of Jan. 16, 2008, p.4.The article is culled from: Les Cahiers de Mutations, Vol. 018 of Jan. 2004, a Monthly French language newspaper. The translation is byGermanus Dounge (Fotabong Village, Nweh Mundane LGA, Southern Cameroons). Finally the article is reproduced in: a Special Edition of the Frontier Telegraph.

despite the existence of the military post at Koutaba they had recently assassinated the SDO, Mr. Albert Khong. To curb the infiltration of terrorists, curfews were reinforced in all administrative units around Foumban beginning from 3 July 1961, at Mbouda, Bafang, Dschang and Bangante.

Mme Njoya née Nyimbe Jeanne (Aged 77 in 2011)

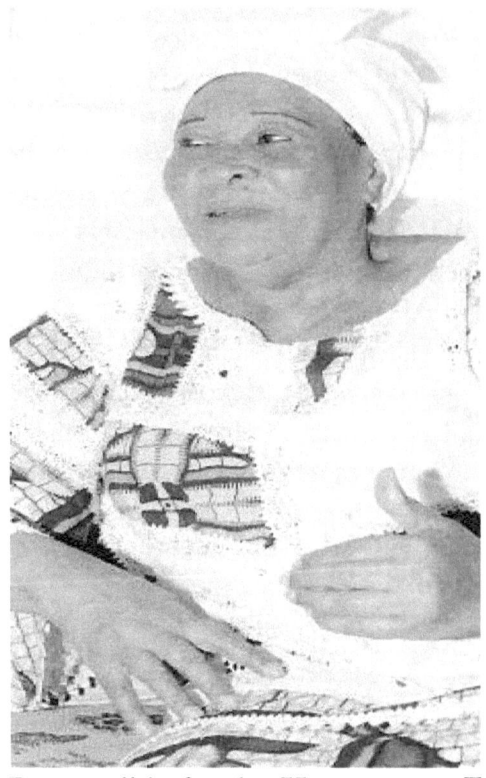

Responsible for the Hostesses at Foumban and Maintains they were good girls and did an excellent job

Choice of Foumban: A Contrary View

Consequently, according to the paper, "the much publicized tranquillity, serenity and paradisiacal locality of Foumban was all fake, the National Liberation Army (NLA) of the UPC proved too formidable for the Cameroon army".[242] The paper then concentrates

---

[242] Special Edition of the *Frontier Telegraph, Vol. II no. 0007* of Jan. 16, 2008, p.4.

on the dark plots and deeds of the conference as seen through the eyes of the 92 year old Sous Prefect. As a sort of link, his account is grounded in some of what were generally light heartedly referred to in some fairy tale manner as: Foumban "beauties", "long necks", ballroom dances and parties but that the depravity that took place there was of such gigantic proportions would have been inconceivable to ordinary Southern Cameroonian mentality of the time.

Alleged Massive "Corruption" and Deceit"

At the ripe age of 92 in 2008, with gratitude to God Almighty for a long life Emmanuel Njoya reflected deeply and meditated on the dark deeds and plots that had been set afoot to dupe and ensnare the Anglophone delegates at the Foumban Conference on "instructions from above" through his instrumentality. Now, some fifty years later, worried and ready to unburden his soul, he courageously volunteered some of the most sordid things that were done to unsuspecting Anglophones, who honestly regarded the Francophones as "our brothers". He proceeded as follows:

> as I must speak the truth, we cajoled, lured and enticed the Anglophones by our way of welcoming them; we were given so many things to prepare for the conference – with all these things at our disposal we lured the Anglophones. …we were given special instructions to blindfold them: so each delegate had a refrigerator in his room, which was always full of champagnes and other assorted drinks; each big one among them had two refrigerators in his room, had a well-made bed with the most beautiful and expensive mattress and bedding.[243]

So far this might sound strange, awful and detestable to decent minds but it was not sufficiently debilitating for the purpose of the authorities. Thus:

---

[243] Ibid., *Frontier Telegraph*, The original version in French was not available for attachment. .

In addition there were two beautiful girls who were assigned to permanently take care of him. These are things which normally should not be told- these girls were instructed to permanently take care of our guest – that was real corruption- corruption has always existed- it has not started today… but at that time, it was not corruption for selfish interests as it is today … at the time it was good corruption to build the country.[244]

To ensure that the Southern Cameroonian delegates were thoroughly done with, they were further enticed with cocktails followed by ballroom dancers every single evening of the weeklong event, at Auberge de Foumban and in several other locations in the town. Emmanuel Njoya then concludes: 'These were the logistics put in place from when the delegations set foot on the soil of Foumban on 16 July till 21 July1961, when they left.[245] Such information would have been received back at home in Southern Cameroons in very bad taste. Consequently, Messrs Motomby Ndembo Woleta (also an accredited delegate) and Wem Mwambo, who attended the conference as journalists with the CPNC Champion Newspaper reported the goings on at Foumban in terms of extreme hospitality and "Foumban long necks", referring to the beautiful women for which the town is famous.[246] Justice Nyo'wakai, an actor on the Southern Cameroons scene as a civil servant in the Judiciary equally maintains, perhaps with the wisdom of hindsight, that "Foumban" was a "masquerade."[247] In this light the entire process was a thoroughly choreographed charade intended to inflict maximum psychological, socio-cultural, mental, emotional, moral and physical damage on the negotiating skills and abilities of the Anglophone delegates invited to the talks. The attractive girls recruited would certainly have been those of easy virtue, whores, capable of going to great lengths to earn a living. Actually, some of them were certified spies.[248] Taking 'permanent care' of their guests,

---

[244] Ibid.
[245] Ibid.
[246] Interview with Wilfred Nkwenti, an insider, as KNDP Press Officer of the time.
[247] Ibid., Nyo'wakai, *Under the Broken Scale*, p. xvii
[248] Discussion with Mr. James Tangiri Ndi, over 80 years old, Feb 2012.

would in the first place have entailed sapping up their energies emotionally, physically and mentally to the extent of rendering them largely impotent and unproductive during the ensuing deliberations.

The impact and toll this took would certainly have stretched far beyond the normal threshold of average male endurance especially for those weak in matters of the flesh. In fact, comparatively, the expected psycho-mental torture would have been much like the physical version administered on Ahidjo's political prisoners in the special maximum jails of Tchollire, Mantoum, Yoko and Nkondengui.[249] What Ahidjo expected from his "honoured" guests, who were overfed, overdosed, sedated, seduced, deprived of sleep, rest, mentally and psychologically sapped of all vigour is a matter of conjecture but the majority of them could not have been anything better than lethargic zombies and drunks.

Anglophone Delegates Opportunely Undeceived!

A possible reason, why these stories were not widely broadcast in detail is that they were characterized by extreme moral depravity. This would have been revolting and imponderable to the ordinary Southern Cameroonians, where public and private decency and morality held high premium. Rather, the stories would have been told in more acceptable terms of the insuperable hospitality, kindness, care and generosity accorded the delegates at the conference; thanks to President Ahidjo, the Sultan and people of Foumban.

---

[249] See Albert Mukong. *Prisoner without a Crime*; Boh Herbert and Ntemfac Ofege, *The Story of Cameroon Calling: Prison Graduate*, (Calabar, Nigeria, 1991).

Some Anglophone Delegates at Foumban

Note: Merssrs, Jua, Kale and Foncha

How much of what resulted from the Foumban Conference was affected by such a travesty of hospitality should constitute good material for research by budding historians. However, like in the Ibo proverb, that: "since the hunters learnt to shoot without missing, the birds learnt to fly without perching".[250] Mbile reports that Southern Cameroonian delegates at the Foumban conference smelt a rat and went to bed with one eye wide open. He independently took note:

> For at no time did we lose thought that we were engaged in a most tricky encounter with "untested brothers" who could use music and wine to lure us into complaisance, even as had happened to brave Ulysses of ancient Greek mythology. ... We went on hastily through the job arguing and quarrelling along from Monday afternoon to Thursday evening. We took three and half days to discuss the entire proposals. On Friday of July 21st. our views were ready. President Ahidjo acknowledged the comments we had made to their proposals indicating his acceptance of our views.[251]

---

[250] Chinua Achebe's *Things Fall Apart*, (London, Heinemann, 1958).
[251] Ibid., Mbile, *Eyewitness*. p. 170. "They slept with one eye open." .

Yet over and above everything, this conference was supposed to be the launching pad for national unity through national dialogue that would constitute the springboard for future stepping stones and bridges aimed at confidence building between the parties: Ahidjo and Foncha, Anglophones and Francophones, "two brothers" coming together in trust, and self-assurance at future venues such as this. Thus, as Foncha and Endeley pointed out in their addresses during the conference, they were coming together with trust and equal claim to the paternity of Cameroon as brothers torn apart by factors of history beyond their control. It is instructive that this was the stance of the Anglophone delegation at the talks and ever afterwards. It is strange that snares and vipers had carefully been laid out to emasculate whatever contributions they had come prepared to make towards constructing a powerful union. There were yet more surprises for the Southern Cameroons delegates and in Emmanuel Njoya's words; this happened:

> Soon after the speech (by Ahidjo), the trust and confidence of the Southern Cameroons was rudely shattered by Ahidjo to the surprise of the Southern Cameroons delegates. Ahidjo rudely requested them to make their observations on the draft constitution. Which constitution, the Southern Cameroons delegates shouted! They had thought that they had come to Foumban with Ahidjo's delegation in order to jointly draft a constitution for the future federal united state. They were very embarrassed to learn that the draft constitution had been given to Foncha long ago for screening and studying long ago: but Foncha kept the document secret.[252]

This had been intended for discussion at the All Party Conference at Bamenda Mbile reaction was typical. He quipped:

> We have the feeling that we have wasted our time coming to Foumban for the draft constitution to be tabled to us for our observation this way. This is in total contradiction to our

---

[252] Ibid., *Frontier Post*.

expectations: instead of a draft çonfederal constitution, we are being requested to make observations on a draft highly centralized constitution with unlimited powers.[253]

Bitter words erupted from all around with the protesting Southern Cameroons delegation demanding that they should be given three more weeks to study the draft. Interestingly this was the draft constitution the Foncha cabinet is supposed to have to have examined without expert assistance at Buea. They recalled the constitutional conferences of London in: 1953, 1957 and 1958 each of them having lasted at least three weeks. Endeley warned, "too much haste would have far reaching consequences on the people of the Southern Cameroons." Ngom Jua screamed: "I have never seen people expected to write a constitution in two days'.[254]

The question can now be asked as to what Ahidjo expected at Foumban? How much was he to be trusted after this experience? Just what nature of ruler and human being was he? Had these facts been known then, there would have been fewer questions to ask about the character of this leader in the dreadful things he continued to unleash until 1982.

Fon Angwafo III of Mankon, a highly enlightened traditional ruler and political heavy weight holding the post of Vice Chairman, to President Biya of the ruling Cameroon People's Democratic Movement (CPDM) is one of the few surviving personalities who participated in the Foumban Constitutional Conference. Looking back, fifty years later, he thinks things did not work out as envisaged and now suggests that unity should be built on cultures that keep us together. Interviewed, he had this to say:

> I think the constitution of la Republique du Cameroun was amended. We went there with the hope of having a new constitution to create a new federation but that did not work. Rather, some amendments were made on the constitution of

---

[253] Ibid.
[254] Ibid.

independent French Cameroun in order to integrate us into it. It was not a new constitution.[255]

Fon SA Angwafo III of Mankon

An Enlightened Fon, who was consistently member of the WCHC, WCHA, CNU and CPDM, where he is Vice President and Member of the Political Bureau. He attended the Bamenda and Foumban Constitutional Conferences

This aptly summarises what President Ahidjo did after Foumban and not at Foumban. For the way forward he argues that Cameroon is neither French nor British; Cameroon is Cameroon. As people with cultures, we should examine the cultures that hold us together; seeing ourselves as Africans with kingdoms before the coming of the whites. He further advises that we can amend our procedures and processes of what is more African and indigenous to avoid the question of division. However, for a country with over 280 ethnic groups with as many or more cultural systems, this is something of a pie in the sky.

---

[255] Ibid., See *Cameroon Tribune, Hors Serie*, pp. 106/7.

A Ramified Conclusion

In conclusion, granted that this story told from the perspective of Mr. Emmanuel Njoya was rendered through an interview in French and further had to be translated into English; there would certainly have been lapses. But on the whole it sounds coherent, credible, logical and of historical value. However, reconciling this version with those of the Anglophone private and official press calls for circumspection and one question begging to be clarified is why Mr. Njoya harboured this sordid story for fifty years. What of a sudden triggered this action that led to it being divulged? What were his religious, cultural social and political leanings in the highly charged political climate of the time, when it was not possible to handle the important position of a Divisional Officer (DO) without first belonging and devoting absolute allegiance to the party in power? And finally, what were his likes and dislikes and what did he stand to benefit after going public; simple altruism and peace of mind. This can only be accepted with a heavy pinch of salt. These and other considerations need to be examined to give the story the importance it deserves especially the extent to which it affects the facts on hand, which it will be used to qualify.

Foumban Group Photograph

In front of the Sultan's Palace

There can be no doubt however that the information released by Njoya has done much to broaden public vision of the sinister dimensions of the famous Foumban Constitutional Conference especially about ensnaring Anglophone delegates. This was similar to the traps, planted by British administrators against Foncha, but which in this case, were organized by his kinsmen with "instructions from above". From what transpired soon after the conference and has worsened ever afterwards as regards the non-implementation of the Foumban accord; this information is enormously useful in reinterpreting the socio-economic and political developments and their impact on Cameroon history in general and Anglophone Cameroonians in particular.as well it highlights the disparities between the two cultures: Anglophone and francophone.

From it answers can now be derived to such questions as: precisely what objectives and expectations President Ahidjo had in mind when convening the conference. How honest, committed and dedicated he and his cabinet were to the cause of reunification given the wide disparity between his pious declarations on the floor of the Conference Hall and the rapid demolition of the Federal Republic of Cameroon ascribed to him. How much could he be taken for his word, since apparently he broke every single promise he made? Equally, it sheds incandescent light on the sources of Anglophone marginalisation in all its ramifications.

However, relating to the resolutions reached at the Foumban Constitutional Conference, it can be said with a certain amount of confidence that the plots had little or no effect. Taking solace from Mbile's observations the snares had impalpable effect on the business at hand given the fact that instead of the five days allotted, these Anglophones took barely three and half days to accomplish their task. This largely resulted from their spirit of dedication, focus and experience from attending several highly placed constitutional conferences. But above all it was the cumulative effect of their Anglo-Saxon roots buttressed by a rich political culture after seven years of internal self-government. Consequently, in the hands of critical and analytical historians and political scientists much could be construed from that squalid past in the sense that those who do not know where they are coming from cannot adequately chart the way forward.

Chapter 7

Foncha's Waterloo: "Secret Deals and Hidden Constitution"

Nursing Smear Campaigns and Conspiracy Theories

In the context of the pungent and persistent stigmatization that Foncha "hid" the draft highly centralized federal constitution because of a deal he had struck with President Ahidjo for positions (his cabinet) in the Government of the Republic of Cameroon, recourse is sought to the original verbatim records bearing on the facts. However, it should immediately be clarified that the real issue is not about Foncha knowing or possessing the copy of the highly centralized draft federal constitution from President Ahidjo because in any case it was a document available to members of Foncha's cabinet but that he "hid" it because of secret deals he had struck with Ahidjo. For a better understanding, the accusation is placed in the plurality of British attitude toward Foncha. As a result, the approach in this Chapter is more analytical, comparative and emphatic than chronological.

A significant positive outcome of the effort in seeking explanations to this accusation is the fact that some of the interlocking factors and hideous back drop issues of Southern Cameroons political life are brought to light, which otherwise might have lain dormant[256]. On record some of these facts were elaborately dealt with at the famous but little known Buea Tripartite Conference of 15-17 May 1961 at which the contents of the highly centralized draft federal constitution from President Ahmadou Ahidjo were discussed. In fact, it was in the course of the general correspondence on issues surrounding the Foncha Cabinet building up to the Buea Tripartite Conference that

---

[256] This confusion of dates was rampant, to which were added apprehensions of security by the CPNC opposition, e.g. *The Cameroon Times* of 3/6/61 announced; "The United Kamerun Constitutional Conference opens July 2 in Yaoundé," and continued: There is reference made to another meeting that held at Yaoundé between that women from 22-24 May1961 but the dates unfortunately are mismatched with others and thereby further complicated he problem. See Abwa in *Eden Xtra*.

mention was made of the alleged "deals" involving Muna, Ahidjo, Foncha and Okala[1] Nevertheless, the Buea Tripartite Conference was significant even if only for the disagreements and confusions it registered.[257]

Therefore, it is not enough merely to paraphrase what transpired as in the *Summit Magazine* interview, which in all probability was drawn from Malcolm Milne's allegations deliberately meant to discredit Foncha, Professor Ngoh proceeds to declare with absolute certainty that:

> Foncha decided to hide this draft constitution from Southern Cameroonian politicians because he had already made a deal with Ahidjo to the effect that should the federal constitution go through, he would be made Vice President.[258]

As will further unfold in the course of this Chapter, the Ahidjo document was officially received and discussed by the entire Foncha cabinet in the presence and with the advice of Mr.BG Smith, the Attorney General of Southern Cameroons. This stands to reason that each of these gentlemen possessed at least a copy of the said draft constitution. In simple logic it is puerile to imagine that Foncha would have been "hiding" a document which at the most minimum was common property to all the members of this team. Even more absurd is the fact that in content it was largely the existing constitution of the Republic of Cameroon! Therefore, it was a common document available to inquisitive and Knowledgeable Francophones. As can be imagined, no "oath" was taken to maintain sealed lips especially as finally there was total disagreement over its preposterous contents; likely the reason, as Willard Johnson and others suggest, why Foncha did not deem it fit to be presented at the Bamenda All Party Conference.

Therefore, it is easy to conclude that all what has been taking place to which has been added the so-called "Bamenda Bag," are aspects of the smear campaigns and propagation of "conspiracy theories" about

---

[257] *The Cameroon Times* of 3/6/61
[258] Epilogue, .

Foncha[259] In perspective, the accusations fly in the face not only of Foncha's character as an individual but against the essence in which the KNDP was founded; namely to fight "falsehood." Here it should be recalled that the party was created in March1955 with the prime objective of bringing together the three Trust Territories of former German Kamerun: French Cameroon, Southern Cameroons and Northern Cameroons, three full years ahead of Ahidjo's UC which only saw the light of day in 1958 and, even then, basically borrowed or more appropriately, wrenched the ideology of "unification" from the UPC to capture power.

Confirming this reality in his own words, Foncha pointed out that before the creation of the KNDP, no political party in either British or French Cameroon had set out a "clear agenda and strategy" on the way and manner in which reunification was to be achieved.[260] To this effect he averred:

> It was not until we set unification as the ultimate aim of the KNDP that we thought of the best ways and means to overcome the many difficulties to achieve it. Hence, the following motto, policies and purpose among others were the pillars on which the KNDP stood in order to focus the attention of the advocates of unification and the welfare of the people of the Federal Republic of Cameroon.[261]

Other than the declaration by Foncha about the KNDP's founding principles, nowhere else is it alleged or proven that Foncha was a liar or cheat. The motto of his KNDP was: "That Truth Shall Prevail", its Policy also was: "Truth and Justice to Our People as the only Means to Combat Falsehood", while the ultimate purpose of the party was: "The Welfare of the People of the Federal Republic of Kamerun." Harping on truth and justice, he further explained these tenets of his party in his Open Letter to the people of Cameroon in which he unequivocally declared:

---

[259]See, Chapter Six for concrete examples
[260] Foncha's Open Letter p. 5. "Foncha Proceeds"
[261]Ibid.

My tenacious stand for truth and justice with all political parties in the Southern Cameroons and later in the Republic of Cameroons was the reason why those who believed in my stand in those days were designated 'the Foncha men'. I wish to call on all the people of this country who knew what happened to stand up and speak out now because it is falsehood that is beclouding the face of the Republic of Cameroon.[262]

During his political life Foncha was faced with several accusations but lying was not one of them.

KNDP- UC Joint Committee

Referring to the secret deals, at first sight, this apparently is such a common sense situation that needs no comment whatsoever. This is because even before the formal "Unity Group" agreement, in 1962 the KNDP as the Ruling Party in Southern Cameroons with Ahidjo's UC as the main party in Republic of Cameroon had begun subscribing delegates to a central committee, who were charged with producing a federal constitution. The first committee comprising all the top KNDP leadership was set up immediately following Ahidjo's maiden visit to Southern Cameroons from 14-17 July 1960. These comprised: Mr. S T Muna, Minister of Commerce and Industries; Mr. A N Jua, Minister of Social Services and Mr. PM Kemcha, Minister of Natural Resources. This ministerial delegation was accompanied by: Mr. P T Fombo, Private Secretary to the PM; S A Njotsa, reporter from the Southern Cameroons Information Service; Mr. E M Mbwaye, photographer; Mr. T A Abanda, Press representative and three advisers.[263] They took off for Yaoundé, on 10 August 1960 and immediately started working with their UC counterparts.

After this the joint teams met on a regular basis and between August and October 1960, they had consulted thrice and produced two draft federal constitutions that were co-signed by: Ahidjo, Foncha and Assale. They agreed to respect each other's territorial sovereignty,

---

[262]Ibid., Foncha, Open Letter,p.6.
[263]*Press Release* No.906, (16?)July 1960. This team took off from Tiko International Airport on 10 August 1960 for Yaoundé.

understanding that they would contribute to leadership at the centre. That Foncha, Jua, Muna, Kemcha and the others roughly in that order in KNDP-ranking constituted that party's hierarchy was beyond question; equally of course acknowledging the fact that like in any political set-up there would forever be jostling for positions.

It therefore did not require any sorcery and secret deals to decipher what was so obvious as even then, that line up would always be maintained as nobody from the Opposition CPNC could have replaced the KNDP leaders in Ahidjo's UC cabinet were that to have been the case. Finally, both in the transitional government and that of the Federal Republic of Cameroon that eventually emerged, the *status quo ante* came to pass. Absolutely, nothing changed in the setting placing Foncha, Jua, Muna and Kemcha in that order. However, it deserves to be stressed that even then this alleged projected Ahidjo cabinet supposed to include Foncha and Muna was never realized in any shape or form but amazingly this has continued to find ample space in the endless conspiracy theories and fantasies.

Concerted Determination to Teach Foncha a Lesson

In the ultimate analysis, before and well after independence and reunification the positioning as indicated above was exactly the same. J O Field and Malcolm Milne in their desperation could be excused for stirring up hatred and discord in the KNDP enemy camp as they were wont to do, but there can hardly be any excuse for further promotion of these infantile accusations especially after Malcolm Milne's regrets, apologies and confession.

However, for the record, it is necessary to see these accusations in their proper perspectives, considering the fact that these spurious "conspiracy theories" have gained currency and are fast becoming "facts of history." An attempt is made here to unveil the intrigues and blackmail underlying their origins and proliferation. Notably, these plots were located in the determination of officials of the Colonial Office, in Malcolm Milne's words: to trap Foncha and have him nailed. This was especially because he refused to abide by the advice from Sir James Roberson, Governor of Nigeria in December 1959 to integrate Southern Cameroons with Nigeria. On this account there were directives from HMG, which instructed J O Field to make Foncha's task as difficult as possible[264].

This sinister plot can variously be interpreted, but above all was an expression of the revulsion Malcolm Milne as an individual and JO Field had for Foncha. Having already lost the crucial battle with Foncha over the plebiscite, the only chances left for vengeance were with the Buea Tripartite Conference, the Bamenda All Party Conference and the Foumban Constitutional Conference.

Therefore, this was Malcolm Milne's last chance to do Foncha in the eye at the Bamenda All Party Conference and thereafter at the Foumban Constitutional Conference but the ground work was laid at the Buea Tripartite Conference.

These strategies were meticulously arranged and began with the Commissioner JO Field loudly making the awful declaration for the withdrawal of British Defence Forces after having been told point blank by President Ahidjo that he could not accept responsibility for Southern Cameroons defence or economic sustenance. The timing for this announcement was plotted to coincide with the opening of the Bamenda All Party Conference in late June 1961 so as to have maximum devastating effect in demonstrating the consequences of Foncha's grave "miscalculations" in having chosen reunification with the Republic of Cameroon instead of integration with Nigeria.

The Alleged Hidden draft constitution

The facts come from a letter to the Secretary of State for Colonies on June 26 1961 by Johnson Field, the Commissioner in which he reported that Ahidjo had left a copy of the highly centralized draft federal constitution for observation by the Foncha cabinet. Precisely in his words, he noted:

> Foncha and his ministers have studied constitutional proposals left here by Ahidjo last Sunday and have, in consultation with Mr. Smith proposed counter proposals which adhere very closely to the

---

[264]Malcolm Milne, *No Telephone*, p.434; after this he gloated at the prospects for the further disintegration that could take place in Southern Cameroons after 1st October 1961 in Newn's view. My 8 emphasis.

form of Federal Constitution published by Foncha immediately prior to the plebiscite, but law and order and internal defence being reserved to the states.[15]

This is the simple report that has been blown out of context. In the first place, the document was submitted to the Foncha cabinet and not to Foncha alone and even more, the Attorney General, Mr. BG smith was in attendance. Here it is copiously established that the Foncha cabinet did not accept the highly centralized Republic of Cameroon constitution drawn up by Ahidjo ignoring the broadly federal draft proposals earlier agreed upon and co-signed by himself, Foncha and Charles Assale but rather suggested the proposals made by Foncha prior to the plebiscite. That the Foncha cabinet turned down the Ahidjo proposal was only logical: in the first place, it was an altogether new and strange document and above all it was presented in French. It will be recalled that even with the expert assistance of Fonlon at Foumban it took the delegates nearly four days of hard work to work on the document yet Foncha was expected to present it as an item on the agenda at the less than two day Bamenda all party conference.

Consequently, for the Bamenda All Party Conference Foncha did the one unsurpassed thing in the circumstances. He got the Attorney General Mr. BJ Smith to polish up the KNDP manifest to earlier used for the plebiscite together with the other federal draft constitutions co-signed by Ahidjo Foncha and Assale. This was what he presented at the Bamenda All Party Conference. In content and context it was a document he knew and identified with, and which he could defend as contrasted to the imposition from Ahidjo. There was therefore no formally signed document agreed with Ahidjo which he hid or failed to present at the Bamenda Conference as alleged. That finally, at Foumban Ahidjo personally introduced his highly centralized draft version of the Federal constitution was right and proper rather than using Foncha as proxy.

The So-Called 'Secret Deal': Sources

The first notion of a "Secret deal" came up in Commissioner JO Field's report to the Colonial Office. Rather cryptically and without any logical excuse, he proffered the following: "All is not well in the KNDP; Jua's influence in the party has been increasing lately at the expense of Muna. There is a clash between those who are strongly for reunification (Muna) and those who are not (Jua). At a recent party congress, Jua was elected First Vice President and Muna failed to secure any office at all."[265] Then, he proceeds to elaborate on the secret talks between Muna and Okala merely "guessing" that:

> It came to light during the Foncha and Muna's recent visit to Yaoundé; Okala had secret talks with Muna and persuaded him to agree that the police and the army should be federal subjects on the understanding that Muna would be Minister of Defence. This was firmly rejected by the party executive. We have of course, no firm confirmation of all this but it may well be that there was such agreement between Muna and Okala and this is the origin of Ahidjo's claim that it was agreed that the army and police should be federal and put under the Cameroon ministry of defence for training[266].

It is fascinating to imagine that this entire report so far was not backed by any firm confirmation and actually did not initially include Foncha, but all the same he went onto report with "confidence" so as to implicate Foncha in one way or the other. To do this, J O Field pointed out initially, tentatively:

> If Foncha had anything to do with it he has now swung away from it and is firm with Jua in demanding that the police shall not be federal, that no forces of the Republic shall be permitted to enter the Southern Cameroons without the Southern Cameroons government's consent and that the new security force, if it materializes, shall be under Southern Cameroons control to start with. The main reason for this is Foncha's practice of shifting his ground so as to be with whatever faction at any given time is in the ascendance.[267]

---

[265] PRO CO5542247/2247XC 3343, Milne to Geoffrey of 1 July1962
[266] *Ibid.*
[267] ibid.

So far there was nothing absolutely certain about any secret talks that had taken place between Ahidjo and Foncha as such in the Commissioner's incoherent report, but at all costs Foncha's name was slotted in. The same improbable information from Mr. Field spiced with interjections from the failed Buea Tripartite Conference in Malcolm Milne's own dispatch to the Colonial Office of 1 July 1961, was given a more emphatic, cocksure flair. He turned out even more definite than his boss and advanced with enormous confidence:

> We believe, on very good in formation, that Foncha has already done a private deal with Ahidjo, the idea being that the present government of the Republic will become the government of the federation on 1st October, and that the sovereignty will be transferred to it and defence and national security will become federal matters. In return for bringing the Southern Cameroons on these terms Foncha has been promised the vice Presidency of the Federal Republic and Muna has been promised a post in the federal cabinet[268].

Here it should categorically be noted that the reference is to a "promise" and not to any finite secret deal.

Nevertheless, after spilling the beans, Malcolm Milne and J O Field had expected a show down or the worst possible fate to befall Foncha at the impending Bamenda All Party Conference. However, at that Conference the participants were more upset by the declaration of Commissioner, J O Field that British Defence Forces would be withdrawn on 1 October 1961 without any alternative arrangements for the protection of the territory they had administered for forty years. Malcolm Milne was however most upset that the rage against Foncha over the "secret deals" had not come to pass. There were no recorded eruptions of questions by the CPNC and OKP as he had expected. He was most disappointed and lousily regretted:

But all that has happened is that Foncha has trotted out his pre-plebiscite constitutional proposals and invited comments on them. The CPNC and OKP–and indeed the chiefs also-have demanded an

---

[268]Ibid., Milne to Geoffrey of 1 July 1962. .

account of what went during the last Foncha/Ahidjo talks, but Foncha strongly pressed by Muna, has kept mum.[269]

With the unanimous endorsement of the KNDP proposals at the Bamenda All Party Conference, a highly disappointed Malcolm Milne returned to his traditional invective on Foncha hoping that something ominous would happen to him in his talks with Ahidjo at Foumban. Consequently, he prospected:

> He will presumably once again test Ahidjo's attitude. If the latter is firm, Foncha, will think, give in to him and take refuge in the secret deals arrangement. I am sure that the little wretched man is moved very largely by considerations of what is best for him; the interests of the southern Cameroons will come a poor second. However, he will need more than his usual luck and the ability to avoid a moment of truth should be [he] return from Bamum having accepted Ahidjo's terms.[270]

What is remarkable with this report is the despicable description of Foncha which clearly bears Malcolm Milne's trademark of his deep negative personal perceptions of him. Furthermore, as with most of the other reports which touched on Foncha, this at best represented only Malcolm Milne's own wishes, hopes and expectations and not the realities on the ground. Unfortunately, for both men; Johnson Field and Malcolm Milne, the Foumban Conference like the Bamenda All Party Conference before it turned out as another "resounding" success story, as widely reported in the press despite their predictions of doom and gloom. In fact, one of the most notable events at Foumban comprised the multiple decorations conferred on Foncha; such that he indisputably emerged as: "The Star of Foumban" and remains on record as such.[271] The regret is that these isolated half-truths and distorted pieces of information have continued to be peddled under the guise of Southern Cameroons history.

---

[269]Ibid.
[270]Ibid.
[271]*Southern Cameroons Press Release* No.1468 of 24 July 1961.

However, it is most interesting to observe that, Malcolm Milne turns out a lot milder in his autobiography, largely cleansed of the allusions, found in his reports earlier submitted to the Colonial Office some forty years earlier, which were on the whole; "brash" and provocative. For example, reporting about Foncha trading "posts" and concealing the document he got from President Ahidjo, Malcolm Milne now simply maintains that:

> On 26th June Field was able to report that Foncha and his ministers had studied the constitutional proposals left behind by Ahidjo. Field had on good information that Foncha had already accepted Ahidjo's offer to amend the constitution of the R of C (Republic of Cameroon) leaving a place for him as Vice President. It was said on less good authority that Muna could expect office and that Jua on Foncha's elevation to Vice President, could be assured of the premiership of SC (Southern Cameroons)[272]

In the same vein he continues with a dramatic change intone:

> We had been sure that Foncha had received a copy of Ahidjo's proposal for a federal form of constitution before the Bamenda All Party Conference held earlier in June, but Foncha hadn't distributed them to most of the delegates on the grounds that members of the opposition, taking exception of them might sabotage the conference.[273]

This is a straight forward benign account stripped of the innuendos of "hiding" the constitution and "secret position deals" with Ahidjo. This clearly makes the point about the *Dr. Jerkyll and Mr. Hyde* (split personality) in Malcolm Milne: The same person reporting the same incident vastly differently. However, it is the role of historians to interpret such ambiguities to the public.

---

[272]Malcolm Milne, *No telephone,*
[273]Ibid., p. 437.

Buea Tripartite Conference: Proceedings and Impact

Actually, what poisoned the minds of the people as can clearly be deciphered in the discussions and disagreements that took place at the Buea Tripartite Conference was not simply the content of the discussions as much as it was in the partisan manner in which JO Field, the Chairman ran that meeting and interpreted its proceedings. When further taken up by Malcolm Milne, there port was carefully manoeuvred and totally blown out of context in a bid to incite members of Foncha's Government and rouse the tempers of the delegates against him. Even worse, he tried to present him as a liar and fraud to the wider public.

The Tripartite Conference holding at Buea from 15-17 May 1961 was attended by a significantly high profiled number of delegates representing: the Republic of Cameroon with French advisers, Southern Cameroons and Great Britain. It was presided over by JO Field, CMG the Commissioner of Southern Cameroons and appropriately took place in the House of Assembly. In his opening address, he declared that the purpose broadly was to try to ensure peace, progress and well-being for a United Cameroon. It would not be possible in the present round of discussions to settle all the problems connected with unification. He then invited President Ahidjo to express his views.[274]

President Ahidjo agreed that unification should be on a federal basis and that he intended to revise the Republican constitution accordingly. But at the UC Congress holding at Ebolowa from July 4-8, 1962, one year later, Ahidjo argued vastly differently. Instead, he maintained:

> It being unthinkable to temper with the Republican form of the regime, it was the Republic which had to transform itself in to a federation, taking into account there turn to it of a part of its territory, possessing certain special characteristics. The question therefore was not one of the birth of a new Republic with federal form.[275]

---

[274] O554/2258XC 4122 of 15 June 1961
[275] *As told by Ahidjo*, 1958-68,(Paul Bory Publishing Monaco, February1968), p34.

Ahidjo's address here went wholly against the grain of all the discussions he had had with Foncha prior to the plebiscite and the pronouncements, he had auspiciously made at Tiko, Buea and Victoria in 1960. The declarations he made at the Tripartite Conference in Buea and above all the exuberant public assertions he repeatedly chanted at Foumban in July 1961 apparently were cast into the dustbin.

As Ahidjo further remarked at Foumban the draft proposals were to be submitted to the National Assembly in Yaoundé in a few weeks. However, it would not be possible for federal institutions and in particular for the Federal Government to be brought into being by 1 October 1961. That day sovereignty over there unified Cameroon was to be invested in the Republican Government, and until such a time as federal institutions were established, the authorities of the Southern Cameroons would be associated in the exercise of power. Modalities were to be explained later.[276]

So far it was becoming difficult to rationally track the President's record. Though, a late and apparently, reluctant convert to the concept of reunification, Ahidjo's attitude towards Southern Cameroons continued to be mercurial and cynical. With regard to defence his stand up to late October 1960 as reported by JO Field himself was: "that the Cameroun Republic cannot undertake the defence of the Southern Cameroons, nor provide the financial and technical assistance necessary for the replacement of the agency services and the development of the territory's economy." Reporting to the Rt. Honlain Macleod, MP on the inconclusive or indeed the failed discussions between Ahidjo and the Foncha cabinet, Johnson noted:

> Immediate re-unification is demonstrably impracticable and a separate existence must, therefore intervene. Now, however, they feel greatly strengthened by President Ahidjo's statement that it is "essentially necessary for the territory's government to have an indigenous military defence of its own..." and the implications inherent in the letter addressed to you, Sir that the Cameroun Republic cannot undertake the defence of Southern Cameroons,

---

[276]CO554/2258XC4122 15 June 1961. These were certainly the promises
Tripartite Conference holding at Buea from 15-17 he made to Muna and Foncha.

nor provide the financial and technical assistance necessary for the placement of the agency services and development of the territory's economy.[277]

It is unthinkable that the Commissioner JO Field fully aware of this stance taken by Ahidjo proceeded to announce the withdrawal of British Defence Forces as well as the civil servants from Southern Cameroons, and even worse, the dastardly bias manner in which he chaired the Tripartite Conference. But it was typical of British attitude towards the Foncha Administration of setting inescapable traps for them.

Ahidjo in the meantime, acknowledged that his government would undertake the establishment of a joint committee to study the problems of reunification; an idea that he and Foncha had endorsed at a recent meeting in Yaoundé. It was to act only in an advisory capacity.

However, he unilaterally emphasized that from First October until the creation of a federal setup, power would lie with himself concurrently with a Southern Cameroons representative. Agreement had been reached with the Southern Cameroons government that all internal services would be transferred to the latter. The greatest disagreements at the Buea Tripartite Conference arose over the question of defence and the attribution of power.

Foncha argued that the British had used Southern Cameroonian soldiers in the Nigerian army who should have formed the nucleus of a home defence base and asked that they be brought back immediately. He did not appreciate the fact that Johnson Field the Commissioner and Chairman of the conference had single-handedly agreed with Ahidjo for the Republic of Cameroon soldiers to enter Southern Cameroons for training without consulting him. Had they been briefed earlier about the withdrawal of British Defence Forces his government would have made alternative arrangements as they were against French speaking instructors. In fact, by this not only were the British escaping their responsibility for adequate defence arrangements for Southern Cameroons on their departure, but they were actually abandoning Foncha and his people to the terrorists marauding the borders. This

---

[277]Ibid., CO554/2258XC4122."At the meeting the Republic of Cameroon Defence Force was generally referred to as Republican"

was sheer irresponsibility mindful that up to this point Ahidjo had rejected responsibility for the security and economic sustenance of Southern Cameroons. It is little wonder that not long after this the famous Ebubu Massacre took place in the CDC Camp near Tombel.

Paradoxically, while the British were loudly announcing their withdrawal, actually abandoning Southern Cameroons, Ahidjo's relations with his French Colonial Masters were getting much closer and stronger. Consequently, the treatment he had from them bordered on "preferential" and, were the exact opposite of what the British were meting out to Foncha and Southern Cameroons. This is clearly illustrated by Professor Njeuma, who points out that:

> Ahidjo had signed secret military and intelligence pacts with France which would increase ... Cameroon's dependence on France. France subsidized the Republic's budget by over 70% and for the most part ran the educational system. Hence, it was unthinkable for the ruling East Cameroonians to cut the umbilical cord with France so soon after independence, no matter how much pressure was brought from West Cameroon and anti-imperialist elements in the country.[278]

Remarkably, this was happening when the Buea Tripartite Conference was holding and at a very low point in the history of Southern Cameroons. Actually, it could be said to have been the "nadir" at which time, Foncha and his cabinet were being crushed between the callous weights of the British delegation led by the Chairman of the Conference, JO Field, who apparently had the pleasure of seeing Foncha being grilled and, Ahidjo, who demanded everything for himself and his own way. Practically, this is the point, where the theme of this exposition is amply dramatized – exposing the two powerful predators: the British colonial authorities manifesting their long desired sadistic vengeance of having Foncha absolutely crushed in collaboration with Ahidjo's insatiable megalomaniac ambitions.

---

[278]"Reunification and Political Opportunism in the Making of Cameroon's Independence", Martin Njeuma. My Emphasis.

In this scenario, the picture that emerges is one in which the victims were being tortured as if in a gladiatorial arena a to the pleasure and gratification of the predators; especially JO Field and Malcolm Milne, the British and French colonial authorities in collaboration with Ahidjo.

Embarrassing Disagreements

Ahidjo stressed that after 1 October1961, the Cameroon Republic would no longer have any armed forces of its own, and just the same way the Southern Cameroons had none of their own at the moment. What would happen, however, was that they would put 5.000 armed men at the disposal of the federal authorities and the Southern Cameroons would provide perhaps 500-1000. The combined forces would be bilingual but he thought that the training should be modelled on the present Republic of Cameroon pattern. This was precisely what the Southern Cameroons delegation had rejected as it would constitute a sort of Tower of Babel. Less than a decade later (1970) the Cameroon armed forces numbered 15.000 strong, were rated the largest military establishment in ex-French Africa and consuming a colossal 19.6% of the national budget besides the huge French subvention. The Minister of Armed Forces was Ahidjo's fellow northerner and trusted confederate, Saoudou Daoudou with French advisers included throughout the entire military hierarchy as well as technical advisers to the President. Foncha considered them uncouth and ill-bred and argued that they should not be hurriedly introduced in Southern Cameroons.[279] On the whole, Foncha was disenchanted with the status that Ahidjo was ready to offer him. Rather, he wanted Southern Cameroons if it joined the Republic of Cameroon:

> To be in effect autonomous over a very large part of the field (including for instance, postal matters, to which for some reason he appeared to attach importance) leaving only a few things to be dealt with by the central government or the republic. Ahidjo on the other hand was prepared to offer something which amounted to

---

[279] Richard Joseph Gaullist Africa: Cameroon Under Ahidjo, (Fourth Dimension Publishers 1978), pp192-3, Also; CO554/2258 XC 4122 of 15 June 1961

little more than complete integration of Southern Cameroons with the rest of the country, with only a few special subjects retained by the Southern Cameroons[280].

It was precisely because of this unfolding dangerous state of affairs that could arise between Nigeria and the Republic of Cameroon in the nature of a contest between these two independent states over Southern Cameroon that Dag Hammarskjöld, the Secretary General of the UN had suggested Round Table Conference involving Foncha, Endeley and representatives of Nigeria and Republic of Cameroun.ThishadbeenbilledforMarch1960butitwasrejected out of hand by the British Government and so it never held.

President Ahidjo said that he did not want to quarrel with the Southern Cameroonian delegation in the presence of the British; however, he was surprised that Mr. Foncha should have insisted that no federal troops should be allowed to cross the frontier between the two territories. After unification it would be absurd to have two armies or two separate authorities for law and order.[281]

Embroiled in this acrimonious atmosphere, Ahidjo absented himself on the second day of the meeting and Okala presented excuses on his behalf and thereafter was to speak for him. As generally agreed by his biographers and those who knew him closely, Ahidjo avoided public displays of piety, maintained a grave and humourless demeanour, as well as studiously cultivated an air of imperturbability and impenetrability, which heightened whatever fears people had of him. In this connection, he rarely laughed in public and personally admitted to Victor Le Vine that: "He disliked public debate and argumentation".[282]

In attempting to offer explanations for the fact that Ahidjo had "absconded", Charles Okala pointed out that a cloud had developed yesterday between the two Cameroonian delegations. The main difference being that Foncha insisted on Southern Cameroons having its own police force and in any case in future the Southern Cameroons element would not retain a separate identity. Okala spent the rest of

---

[280]CO554/2258XC 4122 of 15 June 1961.
[281]Ibid.CO554/2258XC 4122 of 15 June 1961
[282]*Press Release No. 906*,(16?) 1960. This team took off from Tiko

the time at the Meeting pleading that Ahidjo should be allowed to exercise full powers between October 1 and the creation of the federal structures. Interestingly, neither Okala, nor the British delegation saw the need for a final communiqué to be issued probably because of the fact that the conference had not reached any tangible resolutions. In fact it was a dismal failure. Despite the fact that Charles Rene Guy Okala served Ahidjo with unqualified dedication and loyalty as Minister of Foreign Affairs especially over the loss of Northern British Cameroons in the plebiscite, he was sacked without compunction by Ahidjo in March 1962 for daring to question the manner in which political parties were forced to join his UC.

With the prospects of mounting disagreements between Ahidjo and Foncha, Johnson Field became apprehensive and hysterical. There was fear that with such an impasse, things would backfire creating the possibility of "Foncha and Jua" as a last resort proceeding to the UN to demand for independence for Southern Cameroons. Everything had to be done to bring Ahidjo and Foncha together to forestall this happening. It was finally dawning on Field that the British policy, especially of bringing excessive pressure to bear on Foncha, which had reached its nadir at the Buea Tripartite Conference was becoming counterproductive.

Independence for Southern Cameroons was the one thing the British Government would not countenance. It was for this reason and at this point that JO Field wrote to Sir Christopher Eastwood, afraid that with the continued impasse between Foncha and Ahidjo, Foncha and Jua could proceed to the UN demanding for outright independence for Southern Cameroons. However, instead of softening their stance, the British finally threw in all their weight behind Ahidjo; by passed the UN resolution, which prescribed that at independence, power should be transferred to a body representing the two states. Rather, on 1 October 1961, Sir Hugh Fraser, British Under Secretary of State for Colonies informed the House of Commons that Southern Cameroons had been transferred to Ahidjo.[283]

---

[283]Carlson Anyangwe, *Betrayal of Too Trusting A People-The UN, The UK and the Trust Territory of Southern Cameroons,* (Langaa Research and Publishing CIG, Mankon, Bamenda 2009), p. 54.

Even more amazing, Her Royal Majesty the Queen wrote directly to President Ahidjo. This was precisely what Ahidjo arrogated at the Buea Tripartite Conference and was protested by Foncha who charged the British and Republic of Cameroon delegations with collusion. Nevertheless the queen declared:

> On the occasion of the ending of the UK Trusteeship in the Southern Cameroons, I send Your Excellency my sincere good wishes for the future of the united territories over which you now preside. I am glad that friendly cooperation between our two countries should have made it possible for the Southern Cameroons to attain independence in accordance with the results of the February plebiscite. I look forward to the continuation of our cordial relations in the future[284]

On the same day, the British Secretary of State for the Colonies, Mr. Iain Macleod, addressed a rather subdued message of "Best wishes" to Mr. JN Foncha, the PM of Southern Cameroons. This was rendered by CE King, the British Ambassador to Cameroon at Buea Mountain Hotel on the eve of Southern Cameroons Independence and Reunification. It read as follows:

> As the period of our trusteeship comes to an end and your country takes its place with the Republic of Cameroon in the new federation, I should like to send my best wishes for the future to yourself and your countrymen. We look forward to maintain with the Federal Republic of Cameroon the happy ties of friendship which have linked us with Southern Cameroons for over 40 years[285].

In sequence, Malcolm Milne, the Acting Commissioner concluded his farewell address to the one million Southern Cameroonians

---

[284]Ibid., Anyangwe, p. 233.
[285] Ibid., p. 234. This was rendered by CE King, the British Ambassador to Cameroon.

declaring: "our task is done; the Southern Cameroons emerges into nationhood".[286]

Foncha: Suspected of Communist Sympathies

The Cold War at the heart of which was the bogey of communism came to be factored into the process for the reunification struggle. As Percival an insider points out: "The only reason for hesitancy in handing over power was connected with the Cold War. In all their colonies the British tried to ensure that the incoming African administration was not too left wing and therefore likely to fall into the Russian sphere of influence"[287] Furthermore, it was strongly argued that:

> Southern Cameroons is a frontier exposed ...to communist inspired influence which can become a danger of serious magnitude. This reason is not to speak of its great potentialities makes the Southern Cameroons an area of serious concern for the United States..... The logical conclusion would seem to be that the Southern Cameroons with its remoteness from Lagos, its complexities and its vulnerability, deserves increased attention on the part of the United States.[288]

These theses clearly pointed out to two grave options; firstly, that Southern Cameroons could not be allowed to become independent alone and secondly, that Foncha was a Communist suspect and had to be checked.

---

[286] *Press Release* No.1562, *West Cameroon Information Service*, Buea, 9 October 1961, p.3. This was delivered by Mr. Malcolm Milne, the Deputy Commissioner

[287] Percival, P 78. Also, Emmanuel Sobseh, Global Conflicts and International Relation (Global Press Bamenda) 2011 PP.206-207)

[288] See Appendix 1 No. 25.

Open Collusion: British and Republic of Cameroon Delegations

However, returning to the Buea Tripartite Conference, there were certainly behind the curtain discussions and deals between the French and British officials, who concluded that Foncha unlike Ahidjo in the Cold War interpretation of all international events at the time belonged to the "left" and had to be treated with caution. In fact, between them Ahidjo the conservative and malleable Moslem Northerner was preferable. As to the suspicion of Foncha, this had rootsgoingasfarbackasto1959, when in seeking for an expert to evaluate the economic viability of Southern Cameroons in the event of independence, his cabinet had seriously contemplated turning to President Kwame Nkrumah for assistance, following his recent visit to the territory in February 1959. Foncha was openly Pan-Africanist with sympathies for Patrice Lumumba. This is raised as one reason why Ahidjo was reluctant for reunification[289].

Alarming and ominous to the British, and even worse to President Ahidjo was the fact that Foncha consistently offered to mediate between Dr. Felix Roland Moumie, the arch-UPC rebel leader and the Ahidjo Government. Foncha had accommodated him in1957,when contemplating a KNDP-UPC coalition of sorts and recently had met him in Conakry and probably had overtures with him.

To Foncha's mind, the occasion for independence and reunification between Southern Cameroons and the Republic of Cameroon, the vision for which the UPC had fought so valiantly was the appropriate moment to bring these antagonistic compatriots together. But to Ahidjo, the French and the British the interpretation was much different, he was obviously too leftist and, Moumie was *persona non grata*. This was at a boo classification in the Cold War context, which brought about the gory memories of Patrice Lumumba and the Congo. Foncha was considered something of a Leftist.[10] Recent murders in Douala were held against him and he would immediately be arrested if he dared enter Cameroon territory.

What is more, with the impending withdrawal of British Defence Forces, Foncha had openly voiced his intention to seek assistance from

---

[289]CO554/2249XC3406 of 19 July 1960,PatrickJohnst onto Commissioner of Southern Cameroons

friendly countries elsewhere, since he was averse to the introduction of the uncouth Republican (i.e. Republic of Cameroun) forces into Southern Cameroons territory. This was immediately translated to be Czechoslovakia next door to Communist Russia since in their minds he was pro-communist[290]. Here therefore was the junction combining the British, French and Republican (Republic of Cameroun) minds on the floor of the Southern Cameroons House of Assembly in Buea. To Ahidjo's Government, reconciliation with Moumie was anathema and his Government declared they would not grant him safe passage if he set foot on Cameroun soil.[291] As a matter of fact, Foncha's apparent "socialist" links unknown to the trio went even further. Prior to striking a deal with Ahidjo's UC for political collaboration over the question of reunification between the two Trust Territories of British and French Cameroons, Foncha and his party had in this instance first approached the UPC with which from a far, they seemed to share certain principles on reunification. As he put it himself:

> Earlier, we had received the UPC and hosted them as the partner to the KNDP in the struggle for reunification. It was unfortunate that we disagreed on the procedure of achieving it. We were pleased to cooperate with *Action Nationale* before it was dissolved. The tribal organizations of Dschang for the Bamileke and the *Ngondo* of Douala played the role of animators in reunification.[292]

So indeed, Foncha's Socialist leanings though far from "Communist", radical and extremist, as suspected were nevertheless real.

Consequently, all of these considerations were brought to bear and made manifest around the Buea Tripartite Conference discussions and even beyond. Nor could Ahidjo's distrust for Foncha have been

---

[290] This was a taboo classification which brought about the glory memories of Patrice Lumumba and the Congo. Foncha was considered something of a Leftist; Comment by Patrick Johnson, PRO 0554/2249 XC 240

[291] Recent murders in Douala were held against him and he would immediately be arrested if he dared enter Cameroon territory.

[292] Foncha" Open Letter Addressed to the Government of the Republic of Cameroon the Operation of Unification. P.6.

improved by these moves on his part, further given that the Bamilekes saw Foncha as their likely liberator from Ahidjo's claws. Pressure from the Bamileke ministers even in the Ahidjo Government for reunification was enormous. In the words of Ninyem Kamdem, Minister of the Armed Forces "reunification was an act of faith".[293] It may be remarked that Ahidjo's sluggish conversion to reunification may have resulted from this reality.[294] So; Foncha's charge of collusion between the British and the Republican delegations was not farfetched.

Foncha Cabinet Disappointed

Foncha and the Southern Cameroons delegation were disappointed that they would not have even a small striking force in being before the British Battalion left the territory. He openly suspected that the British delegation had made secret contacts with the Republic of Cameroon delegation and felt the former had not taken account of the needs of the Southern Cameroons. The creation of a local force should be set in hand at once. If the United Kingdom delegation had agreed to let the Battalion remain there would have been no reason for disagreement between the two Cameroonian delegations. The degree of collusion between the British and Republic of Cameroon delegations to Foncha was so obvious that:

> Foncha said he did not wish his remarks to be interpreted to mean that he was accusing the United Kingdom and the Republican delegations of collusion. Nevertheless, it was a coincidence that the British position corresponded exactly with that outlined by Ahidjo. His delegation insisted that there should be a separate Southern Cameroons Defence Force…It had never been his idea that Southern Cameroons should utterly be dependent on the Republic for its security. This he had promised during the plebiscite and if he did not get it he would have deceived the people. Muna agreed with Foncha on the collusion between the British and Republican delegations.[295]

---

[293] CO554/2249 XC3406 of 19 July 1960
[294] See Patrick Johnston to Commissioner, CO554/2249XC3406 of July 19, 1960.
[295] Ibid. CO554/2258XC 4122 of 15 June 1961

However, despite Mr. Okala's disavowal of collusion, he is reported by Mr. Johnston, the British Ambassador in Yaoundé to have made approaches to him at a recent send-off party pleading for increased powers for Ahidjo and that the Anglophones should not be allowed to get too much of their way. Among themselves, the officials at the Colonial Office indicated their displeasure that the French were rendering too much support to Ahidjo, while in their case they were bent on driving nails into Foncha's coffin for obscure reasons. It is only proper that the Secretary of State for Colonies was held seriously to account for the shameless manner in which they had abandoned Foncha and Southern Cameroons at the time of their gravest need. Apologies, explanations and promises were made on the floor of the British Parliament at the hands of Hon. GM Thomson, MP for Dundee. He interrogated Hon. Fraser, the Under Secretary of State demanding explanations for the shabby manner in which the Premier and people of Southern Cameroons had been treated and promises for rectification extracted although it was all too late. There was yet another probing of Hon. Fraser at the hands of Mr. Creech Jones on the form of government that had been put in place for Southern Cameroons prior to departure by the British.

Buea Tripartite Conference: Lamentable Failure

In every sense of the word, the Southern Cameroons delegation at the Buea Tripartite Conference became a veritable punch bag in between the British and Republic of Cameroon delegations. Perhaps, the most remarkable thing about the Buea Tripartite Conference attended by a large number of high profiled delegates and which opened up with great expectations is that the Conference concluded even without a communiqué. This was unlike previous meetings held between Foncha and Ahidjo on federalism which were always concluded with official press releases and communiqués. As can easily be deduced the conference was notable for the frequent interjections of open disagreements and quarrels among the delegates, which led to the substantial charges of open partiality against the Chairman and of deliberate collusion between the British and Republic of Cameroon delegations. Equally peculiar was the self-centeredness, arrogance and megalomaniac attitude of President Ahidjo and even worse, his utter disregard for previous accords to which he had been signatory. That he absconded after the first day leaving the discussions halfway simply because he could not brood any contrary views to his own rendered the entire conference sham. Consequently, there was little of substance that could be quoted as achievements at the conference.

Mr. J.O Field and the British team brazenly and openly took sides with Ahidjo and the Republic of Cameroon leaving Foncha to accuse them of colluding with the Republic of Cameroon delegation. Even worse, Ahidjo reneged on earlier agreements reached based on a federal constitution. He introduced a monarchical and dictatorial type constitution with all power radiating from his person which Foncha and Muna objected. Ahidjo stressed:

> It is the view of the Republic of Cameroon that after 1st October and pending the establishment of the federal government, those powers which will become federal would be transmitted to the President of the Republic who would exercise them in association with the Prime Minister of the Southern Cameroons.[296]

These views were not shared by the Government of Southern Cameroons. Nor was this in accordance with the UN resolution. The legal implications were rather too refined and complicated. It meant that:

> If at midnight the sovereignty of the Southern Cameroons is transmitted to the Republic of Cameroon the people of the southern Cameroons do not at the moment achieve independence. They lose their identity and become subjects of the Republic of Cameroon. It may be that within a matter of minutes, hours or days the Republic will be by an act of state transform itself into a federation of the two states composed of the former Republic of Cameroon and the former trust territory of Southern Cameroons. The Southern Cameroons would then have achieved independence

---

[296] PRO CO 554/2260 XC of 11 August 1961; see also, Mr. Fraser at the hands of GM Thomson MP.

not by joining the Republic of Cameroon but after joining the republic of Cameroon.[297]

This view taken by the Republic of Cameroon was at variance with the undertaking made before the plebiscite in the joint communiqué of 10 December 1960 in accordance with Resolution 2013of the UN Trusteeship Council which the UK Government extracted from the two governments. In it, it was agreed that:

> By an early date to be decided by the United Nations... the Southern Cameroons and the Cameroon Republic would unite in a Federal United Cameroon republic. Head 3, paragraph(b)of the communiqué postulated..." the transfer of sovereign powers to an organization representing the future federation.[298]

Reporting about the failure of the Tripartite meeting at Buea from 15-17 May 1961 in his autobiography, Malcolm Milne reiterates the hard stance taken by Ahidjo; analyses the representation and notes brusquely the Tower of Babel in which it resulted:

> The report of the conference, with appendices, runs to fifty pages; it reads more like a dossier of differences than an agreed solution of outstanding difficulties... Ahidjo had produced a very clear statement of the relationship between the two territories a she hoped it would develop, Foncha, as I deduced from the minutes of the meeting, had a number of reservations the most cogent of which concerned the arrangements for security in the federal republic....the conference broke up after four sessions without being able to agree on a statement to the press.[299]

---

[297] Ibid
[298] Ibid
[299] Milne., *No telephone* P. 436. .

Conclusion

The issues raised at the failed Buea Tripartite Conference especially over defence were further discussed at an Anglo-French meeting in Paris from 24-25 May 1961withoutanyheadway. However, it was clear that the stance taken by Ahidjo at the Buea Tripartite Conference had been tele-guided by France.[32]Critically examined it will be seen that; the open indictment that Foncha decided to "hide" the highly centralized draft federal constitution he received from President Ahidjo is not based on any palpable evidence. Nor is there any logical reason why he should have hidden a document which he shared with his cabinet and which was certain to popup at Foumban since it was proposed by President Ahidjo as a working document. Finally, the Bamenda All Party Conference and the Foumban Constitutional Conferences are now history thus obviating any notion or relevance of the supposed hidden highly centralized draft federal constitution which Ahidjo finally presented for discussion at Foumban.

That a part, Foncha's way of life and the KNDP motto were perched on "Truth", which it was maintained would always prevail. Furthermore, even before the plebiscite, the UC and the KNDP had set up a "Joint Committee" which met routinely from July till October 1960 and produced two broadly federal constitutions on which basis Southern Cameroons and Republic of Cameroon would unite in the event that "Reunification" won in the impending plebiscite of 11 February 1961. After success in the plebiscite the two ruling parties established the "UC-KNDP waking Group", which was a sort of loose coalition because by it, they agreed to contribute towards joint leadership at the centre. Logically therefore, there was no need for secret deals–this was simply illogical.

However, since the colonial Administration had decided to teach Foncha a lesson because he rejected integration with Nigeria, JO Field, Malcolm Milne (Commissioner and Deputy respectively) and CE King, the British Ambassador to Cameroon in Yaoundé raised in surmountable obstacle against Foncha, his cabinet and party. The Climax was reached at the Buea Tripartite Conference which met from 15-17 May 1961 just before the Bamenda All Party Conference, at which the British and Republic of Cameroon delegates openly colluded "against Foncha and his cabinet". The idea was to totally discredit and humiliate him before Ahidjo and his delegation. Worse than this, by openly declaring the withdrawal of British defence forces just as the various delegates were gathering for the Bamenda All Party Conference, as Malcolm Milne boldly pointed out; the idea was to cause division within Foncha's own party followed by rebellion of all the other delegates against the ruling KNDP. In fact, JO Field and Malcolm Milne expected a civil war to erupt but the delegates at the Bamenda All Party Conference declared their unanimous support for Foncha. Instead they sent a strong letter of protest, disappointment to JO Field for the British withdrawal of their defence forces at such a critical moment without any replacement. This precisely is the context in which the concoction of the so called "secret deals" was cooked. In fact, this was the pattern in which they wrote every single report about Foncha to the colonial office.

In other words, the "Secret Deals" theory was at the heart of the plot of the "inescapable traps" carefully set a foot by the British colonial Administration and directly targeted at Foncha as a person and his party as a whole. Tragically, this has found fertile ground in certain influential circles under the guise of Conspiracy Theories-precisely fifty-two years since Malcolm Milne the originator confessed and denounced all that had taken place at a round one O'clock in the morning of 1 October 1961. In historical terms, the whole process therefore is anachronistic and in local parlance, it is like a group of people continuing to dance long after the drums had stopped beating.

Chapter 8

Indictments: Foncha Opposed Southern Cameroons Independence

Brash Unsubstantiated Accusations

Of the litany of accusations piled up against Foncha, two stick out poignantly. One is with regard to his policy towards autonomy or independence for Southern Cameroons and the other about secret deals he is supposed to have struck with President Ahmadou Ahidjo in 1961 over positions for himself and Muna in Ahidjo's Government. In fact, there are repeated instances in the Summit Magazine interview where Professor Ngoh is absolute on the fact that: "Foncha was not really in favour of Southern Cameroons attaining independence as a separate state".[300] As if this is not sufficiently absurd considering the overwhelming revelations now available in the declassified British secret papers which bear overwhelming testimony to the invidious role the officials of the Colonial and Foreign Offices played to obstruct any attempts towards securing independence for Southern Cameroons by Foncha. Further reference is made in the interview to an obscure, possibly inconsequential discussion Foncha is supposed to have had with Mr. Eastwood of the Colonial Office in March 1956, to substantiate the accusation. However, when placed in context, this was when the KNDP was barely one year old and five tedious political years away from the actual battle for reunification and independence which only gathered pace during the period 1958-1961.

Although Professor Ngoh's word alone is taken on its own authority, it would have been more credible to situate the "circumstance" in which such a conversation took place to accord it such prominence. It is an acknowledged fact that a week in politics is a long time as any of a number of events could have happened to necessitate a change of attitude, if indeed this were to have been the case. That is why such an important indictment ought to have been

---

[300] See Epilogue

concretely contextualized. Furthermore, on the balance, if such meticulous attention could be given to Foncha, who at the time was only the leader of the KNDP which was the opposition party, this assertion could also have been considered in comparative terms for example, how often Dr. Endeley, Leader of Government Business and Foncha's direct political opponent changed his mind on the same crucial political issue during that same period. In fact, it deserves in this instance, to emphasize that it was precisely Endeley's complete volte face from reunification with French Cameroon to integration with Nigeria that forced Foncha and Jua out of the KNC to form the KNDP.

It was certainly "hitting below the belt" to single out Foncha for attack on such a subject and even worse, quoting the same British Colonial Office source; comprising people who, as has been demonstrated, placed every conceivable hurdle on Foncha's path against achieving the goal of independence for Southern Cameroons through the "Third Question", which they blocked.[301] These revelations in point of fact constitute the totality of the subject matter of the correspondence: to "Stop Foncha" from pursuing the famous "Third Question" of independence for Southern Cameroons in the anticipated plebiscite.[302] However, what is available on record about Mr. Christopher Eastwood's attitude to Foncha's bid for independence is exactly the opposite of that referred to above. With reference to a pertinent minute from Mr. Eastwood, the following action was taken on the specific issue of independence for Southern Cameroons. This rejoinder was made apparently after the botched Tripartite Conference held at Buea in mid-May 1961 at which Foncha and Ahidjo were locked up in a bitter deadlock. Both men openly disagreed on the floor of the conference over the issue of defence, the deployment of Republican Forces in Southern Cameroons and Ahidjo's demand for greater powers to be conferred on him during the intervening period between independence and the application of the Federal Constitution. Note was taken in response to Eastwood that:

---

[301] The declassified British secret papers Appendix 2.
[302] Ibid., Appendix..

Foncha might go to the UN asking not for extension of Trusteeship at all but for Independence, possibly within the commonwealth. He would argue that it was not possible to agree terms for gaining independence by joining the Republic in accordance with the Assembly's resolution.... Independence for Southern Cameroons would face us with considerable problems.... In short, this is not a course which we should at all encourage Foncha to adopt. ... The departments are strongly of the opinion that we should not encourage Foncha to go to the UN at all.[303]

The above quotation clearly and emphatically refers to action taken in accordance with a directive from Mr. Christopher Eastwood paradoxically preventing the same Foncha from going to the UN to demand for independence for Southern Cameroons. This is wholly irreconcilable with reference to the same Foncha and the same Christopher Eastwood of the Colonial Office over the issue of independence in the discussion they are alleged to have had in March 1956 unless it can be proved that there was more than one [Christopher] Eastwood in the Colonial Office.[304] Or if it was the same Eastwood, he had definitely changed his mind whereas Foncha was not expected to budge on such an issue. However, in this instant Foncha was consistent.

"Independence" Foncha's Passion

The accusations that Foncha was opposed to Southern Cameroons attaining independence fly openly in the face of massive historical evidence which abounds to indicate the extent to which independence was his passion and preoccupation for Southern Cameroons. Indeed, it was a creed entrenched in the KNDP's philosophy of reunification. Because of the persistent slander and conspiracy theories heaped on his person and the KNDP Government, liberty has been taken to quote Foncha extensively on his stand with regard to the cardinal

---

[303] PRO CO554/2188 XC 3406 CPC 61(19) paras. 11-14 of 28 June 1961.
[304] Ibid.

policy of 'independence before reunification' for Southern Cameroons. Njeuma, who lived the era clearly thought that it was:

> Nevertheless, the British employed much arm-twisting at the UN to line up western and anti-communist representatives to block Foncha's bid to make secession the second question in the British-inspired plebiscite[305].

At a last ditch stand, after all attempts to reach a consensus at the Mamfe Plebiscite Conference had failed followed by those at the Southern Cameroons House of Assembly and then in New York for the second time on this issue; a delegation comprising: Foncha for the KNDP, Endeley for the KNC and Mbile for the KPP, found themselves before the UN General Assembly in New York to defend the options they had chosen to be presented to the people of Southern Cameroons during the impending plebiscite. It was crucial and to Foncha what follows is unquestionably a statement of capital political significance that cannot be improved upon given the weight, venue and circumstances under which it was pronounced.

With France about to grant independence to French Cameroon in January 1960 and Nigeria assuring Southern Cameroons the status of a full autonomous Region within the Federation if it opted for integration with Nigeria at the plebiscite, Endeley was accorded high political standing with this attractive political proposition. In contrast, alone and disproportionately outweighed at the UN, Foncha fought back fiercely. He declared before that august body:

> I wish to say that I am mandated by the house of assembly and the majority of the people of Southern Cameroons to place the following before the UN General Assembly as what they want:

> a) That we want the separation of southern Cameroons from the federation of Nigeria before the latter attains independence in 1960 (Sic)

---

[305] Ibid.

b) That Southern Cameroons be constituted into a separate entity and continue for a short time under the United Kingdom Trusteeship. The Trusteeship Agreement should be modified to allow the Southern Cameroons to be administered separately from Nigeria. During this interim period, the Southern Cameroons will work towards complete independence.

c) That during the period of continued trusteeship the Southern Cameroons government will explore the possibility and suitable terms of unification with an independent French Cameroon and that the form of such a union should be federation.

He also added that:

The Southern Cameroons will watch political progress in Northern Cameroons, and if in the meantime they have worked out their separation from the federation of Nigeria, then a reunion will be welcomed.[306]

This declaration rendered here in extensor is far removed from the accusations levied against Foncha in the interview as not being in favour of independence for Southern Cameroons. Nothing could have been closest to Foncha's heart. Way back in 1958, while in London for constitutional talks, then merely as leaders of the KNDP Opposition, Foncha and Jua were recorded to have lobbied seriously for an independent Southern Cameroons expecting financial assistance from the British Government. They discussed this option openly with the Cameroon students studying in Britain at the time as reported by Omer B Sendze who was present.[307]

Nevertheless, the British stuck steadfastly to the Phillipson Report, which stated that the Southern Cameroons economy was wholly dependent on bananas, the only main source of revenue for the Buea Government and that "it took only one serious storm to wipe out the

---

[306] *Press Release* No. 485: "PlebisciteQuestions, Premier and Opposition Leader Disagree at UN", 29/09/59.

[307] Ibid.,Sendze; also, Foreword by Dr. Endeley, *Victoria Southern Cameroons – 1858 – 1968*.

whole crop and there would be nothing to fall back on". This was even though timber export had become a significant source of income. Consequently, on this ground their pleas fell on deaf ears.[308] Foncha's stand on independence for Southern Cameroons was indubitable. As finally divulged by no other person than Malcolm Milne himself, Sir Sydney Phillipson had stealthily been slotted in by the Governor General of Nigeria Sir James Robertson to produce an adverse economic report that would block any attempt by Foncha to secede from Nigeria.[309]

From the annals it is clear in the Southern Cameroons House of Assembly debate of 23 March 1959 that Mr. Peter M Kemcha, Secretary of State for Finance in the KNDP Government, described as "an intellectual of sorts" made a strong case for the economic strength of Southern Cameroons. He argued that it could stand alone, in other words, it was ready for "independence". This was in response to NN Mbile of the KNC/KPP alliance's stand for integration with Nigeria maintaining that, 'Only the British Government will discuss with us over where we should be. We shall not compromise on this issue'. On the other hand, Kemcha made apt comparisons with: Zanzibar, Gambia, Somaliland and even within the Nigerian Federation, to Northern Nigeria and Eastern Nigeria, using appropriate statistics.

In fact, he was able to demonstrate that Southern Cameroons was losing more by being administered as an integral part of Nigeria with the low dividends it derived from the Commonwealth Development and Social Welfare Fund. Even before secession in 1954, no one had said how Southern Cameroons was going to survive financially. He ran through the budget for 1st April 1957 to 31 March 1958 and then argued prophetically: "We have our natural resources. No geologist has been able to prove that Cameroons has not got minerals, natural resources here. ... you will see what is the current revenue we get from our natural resources".[310] Finally, on the issue of reunification, Kemncha was irritated and emphasized:

---

[308] Ibid., Sendze, among many Cameroonian students studying in London was addressed by them.

[309] Malcolm Milne in his own words.

[310] Ibid.,*Cameroon Life* pp. 32-33.

> People have been trying to distort the facts. They talk of immediate unification. If we wanted immediate unification there would have been no reason why we would not have been together with the UPC or OK. Our policy has always been secession from the Federation of Nigeria and to continue under Trusteeship Agreement for a short time after which we will explore the possibility of unification.[311]

The KNDP policy had been consistent all along and he challenged anybody to bring out information to the contrary.[312] Placed in proper perspective, tracing the stages that the KNDP had undertaken in the struggle for reunification in search of an appropriate French Cameroon political party which shared its ideology with which it could coalesce prior to forming the concord with Ahidjo's UC in 1959, Foncha stated clearly in his letter of resignation:

> Earlier, we had received, the UPC and hosted them as partners to the KNDP in the struggle for reunification. It was unfortunate that we disagreed on the procedure of achieving it. We were pleased to cooperate with the Action Nationale before it was dissolved. The tribal organizations of Dschang for the Bamileke and the Ngondo Society of Douala played the role of animators in reunification.[313]

This was part of the KNDP platform in seeking for an agreeable partner on the French Cameroon side with which it could tango towards negotiated independence. Thus in the circumstances the:

> UC then remained the only political party in French Cameroon with which the KNDP met to cooperate to achieve independence

---

[311] Ibid, see also, *Federated State of West Cameroon, Budget Speech by the Hon. PM Kemcha*, printed by the Government Printer, Buea, 1966. This was another powerful presentation by him.

[312] Ibid.

[313] An Open Letter Addressed to the Government of the Republic of Cameroon on The Operation of Reunification: Federal Republic of Cameroon 1961-1971, by Dr. JN Foncha p.6.

on 1stOctober, 1961. It was our tenacious stand for Truth to the People that the KNDP defeated the Government of the KNC in the General Election of 24thJanuary 1959. Then the Southern Cameroons became an autonomous region of Nigeria while preparing to severe links with Nigeria at independence.[314]

KNDP Ideology: "Independence before Reunification"

This was a major reason why the KNDP disagreed with the UPC and the OK party who, while sharing the common platform of independence for Southern Cameroons and reunification with French Cameroon, chose the fast track. They opted for "immediate reunification and independence", while the KNDP emphasized extended trusteeship and "independence before reunification" so that differences in economic development between the two Trust Territories could be bridged. This was precisely because Southern Cameroons had a "leeway to make" before reunification.[315]

Presented with this scenario, East and West Cameroons should have reunified as equals, as two independent countries. The failure to achieve this objective resulted from a combination of factors the most important of which was projected by Dr. EML Endeley. This is best expressed by the Commissioner of Southern Cameroons, Mr. JO Field. As the plebiscite approached, he reported:

> It is relevant to recall that Mr. Foncha and his colleagues have never favoured immediate reunification and have always wanted a period of separate existence. It was Dr. Endeley who insisted that the second choice in the plebiscite should be for joining the republic and Mr. Foncha only accepted it with reluctance when he was out-manoeuvred and subjected to heavy pressure by the afro-Asian bloc at the United Nations.[316]

---

[314] Ibid., Foncha, open letter.
[315] David Killingray and Richard Ratbone, eds., *Africa and the Second World War*, (Macmillan Press Ltd. , London).
[316] PRO COS54/2412 XC 3343 Dispatch of 12 October 1960

This justifies the title of this work with regard to international conspiracies against Southern Cameroons attaining independence. Referring to this painful issue of "independence for Southern Cameroons" before reunification and that he had been cheated out of this option by a combination of impenetrable forces: the British Government in collaboration with Endeley's KNC/KPP alliance and the UN, Foncha succinctly revisited this issue during his last message as Prime Minister of West Cameroon, to the people of that state. In a manner consonant with what weight this had placed on his mind, in that ultimate address, Foncha unburdened his heart, noting in retrospect:

> Although our first step was independence before unification, nevertheless independence was denied us. This was a clever move against unification itself. At the UN the British put up a strong fight against independence for Southern Cameroons and manoeuvred the UN to accept their proposal.[317]

So, on both counts, the charges against Foncha in that interview as in other historical works by Professor Ngoh[318] are hugely misplaced. Foncha at all times stood for independence for Southern Cameroons and even so, independence before reunification because he, like most of his compatriots was cognizant of the wide economic disparities existing between the two Trust Territories for the reason that Britain had failed woefully in its obligations as prescribed by Article 76(b) of the Charter of the UN, towards the Trusteeship. By that charter Britain as the administering authority was expected:

> To promote the political, economic, social and educational advancement of the inhabitants of the Trust Territories, and their progressive development towards self-government or independence as may be appropriate to the particular circumstances of each territory and its peoples and the freely expressed wishes of the people concerned, and as may be provided

---

[317] Message to PM and people of West Cameroon by Dr. JN Foncha June 1965.
[318] Epilogue Prof. VJ Ngoh, also, his recent book, the *Untold Story*.

by the terms of each trusteeship agreement.... It applied to Southern Cameroons as well: Industry ... was non-existent and agriculture still very backward. There were no railways and the inadequacy of road network made certain areas inaccessible during the rainy season. The situation in the educational and medical fields particularly in the Northern Cameroons was far from being satisfactory.[319]

It did not therefore necessitate a five day safari study trip for an official from the Colonial Office in Britain (Mr. Eastwood) to come and assess a reality that Cameroonians on the spot were living and complaining about. In fact, in the circumstance it was ample evidence of British failure in executing their Trusteeship commitment to the United Nations Trusteeship Council (UNTC) in Southern Cameroons.

Double British Standards

Even at the UN Trusteeship Council meeting during an examination of the official documents submitted by Britain itself, the Soviet Union delegate graphically painted the derelict state of the economy and the extremely low level of development in the territory after forty years of British rule. The performance of the British in Southern Cameroons was so dismal that the Russian representative on UNVM Team noted with enormous disappointment:

> Industry in Cameroons was non-existent and agriculture still very backward. There were no railways and the inadequacy of the road network made certain areas inaccessible during the rainy season. The situation in the educational and medical fields...was far from being satisfactory. The indigenous inhabitants had obviously come to the conclusion that they must take matters into their own hands recognizing that independence provided the constitutions in

---

[319] UN, Doc T/8, March 25, 1957.

which former ...trust territories would develop their full potentialities.[320]

The above is an extract from the "British Report" in 1958 at the UNTC, a situation which makes it extremely ridiculous that the same British Colonial Government should have dispatched an official on a "five day study trip" to find out what they had already reported on, and even more ridiculously, "prophesying" on their own failure as Malcolm Milne was later to confess.[321] It must have been some idle official from the Colonial Office coming to rediscover the wheel.

To the British Government, Southern Cameroons remained a great liability and every venue was sought to dump it as was the case at the Buea Tripartite Conference. They were hastily in search of someone to "foster" it and the only available person to do the unpleasant job was an unwilling and reluctant President Ahidjo, who as well did not see any gain in the bargain. This came out clearly in a dispatch from Mr. CB Boothby, Head of the African Department at the Foreign Office to Mr. PM Johnston, the British Ambassador to Cameroon Republic in June 1960. In opposition to a suggestion for independence for Southern Cameroons by the former, speaking for the government, he firmly declared:

> We are not attracted to the idea of an independent Southern Cameroons because it would certainly not be able to pay its way as you suggest, we are not anxious to do so on its behalf. We cannot expect to have any advantage from being foster mother to an independent Southern Cameroons and it is clear that it would have to be fostered by somebody. ... In fact, the sooner we provide decently for Southern Cameroons and wash our hands off it, the more pleased we shall be[322]

---

[320] *The Cameroons under United Kingdom Administration: Report by Her Majesty's Government in UK to the General Assembly of the UN for 1959*, London, 1960,p.104; seeNdi in, *Africa and World War II*, also, *Golden Age* p.57.

[321] Ibid., Malcolm Milne p.447.

[322] PRO, Declassified doc. 13 June 1960, quoted in Carlson Anyangwe, p. 54.

This is a terrible sordid picture of the Cameroons we know. Obviously this was also, largely because the British officials on the spot in Southern Cameroons were in the habit of feeding the Colonial Office with conspiracy theories and false information intended to paint Foncha and the KNDP secessionists as negatively as possible. To make the point emphatically clear, the note below from Sir, Andrew Cohen to the Secretary of State at the Foreign Office of 11 October 1960 on the British stand as regards the independence of Southern Cameroons is instructive: He was categorical:

> Our policy remains strongly against a separate Southern Cameroons state.... If Cameroons political parties combine to take action to establish an independent state, this would place us in a very embarrassing position. With support of moderate Afro-Asians and others, we have always argued that separate independence would produce an entirely unviable state.[323]

This is perfect explanation for the failure of the London visit of all political parties in 1960 the failure of which Mbile heaped on Foncha asking for a 14 million pound handshake. This double dealing by the British officials was patent. Taking the cue a month later, Lord Perth, British Minister of State at the Colonial Office in a minute to Sir John Marten of the same office did not hide his spite not just for Foncha as an individual but for the entire Southern Cameroons population, especially when it came to comparing it with Northern Cameroons. Without any qualms of conscience, he bluntly declared:

> What would worry me is if a sequel to the Southern Cameroons try (sic) for independence was that the northern Cameroons went the same way. That would, really, I think, upset our relationship with Nigeria as a whole for which, we must, at all costs, avoid.[324]

---

[323] Ibid., Secret brief of 11 Oct. 1960,
[324] Lord Perth to Sir John Marten of the Colonial Office, dated 12 October 1960, See also Cohen from New York of 11 October 1960 to JO Field. "The Southern Cameroons and its inhabitants are undoubtedly expendable in relation to this". .

Dislike for individuals such as was expressed for Foncha might be understandable and even excusable, but venting this on a whole people for whom they were officially responsible becomes difficult to understand and justify.

This attitude seems to have been patent, deep-rooted and entrenched in the psyche of those at the British Colonial and Foreign Offices. It will be recalled that Foncha's appeal for an extended period of Trusteeship to enable Southern Cameroons to prepare for independence and to negotiate for reunification was turned down with impunity. He was further told that he could not hope to have access to "the golden key to the Bank of England." With reference to Northern Cameroons the British took a completely different approach.

At the United Nations Trusteeship Council in November1959 the British representative at the UN General Assembly envisaging Nigerian independence on 1 October 1960, volunteered rapid reforms for Northern Cameroons by Britain. He proceeded gratuitously to inform the Assembly that:

> As it would no longer be possible to administer the Northern Cameroons as an integral part of Nigeria after the date of Nigerian independence, the administering authority intended to administer the territory separately through an administrator responsible to Her Majesty's Government in the United Kingdom.[325]

This was at about the same time that Foncha was labouring for the extension of the British Trusteeship Mandate for Southern Cameroons, which in the circumstance was rejected instantly and spitefully. The version quoted above conveyed much more than just spitefulness and the surprise therefore is why there should have been such inordinate abhorrence for Southern Cameroons as a state and for its leadership. This eventually translated into Britain simply dumping Southern Cameroons and its inhabitants into the hands of the Republic of Cameroon to please France. This was carefully done and the blames made over to Foncha as in the example cited earlier.

---

[325] "Resolution 1350 (XIII,} para 6 of the General Assembly on the Future of Northern Cameroons".

The same approach was pursued in the case of selecting questions to be put to the electorate in Northern Cameroons during their own plebiscite. This process had taken Foncha, Endeley and Mbile working full steam, at great cost, sowing seeds of distrust, and hatred and tearing the entire country into shreds starting from the Mamfe Plebiscite Conference in August 1959 till February1961. Yet, at the nick of time in the case of Northern Cameroons, the people were not required to campaign for the choice of questions, the British administration simply turned round, uplifted in whole, the questions that had been composed at such great cost in the case of Southern Cameroons and endorsed for use in Northern Cameroons; a clear case of political plagiarism and blatant favouritism by Britain.[326]

Towards Provoking Civil Strife

The picture of benign neglect became all the more glaring during the closing months of 1960 when the French were sponsoring numerous gigantic economic projects involving colossal sums of money, technical assistance and personnel, as well as strengthening the military defences in French Cameroun. It was at this same time that British civil servants and expatriates in the private sector in Southern Cameroons were resigning in droves. Still worse, at its most vulnerable point, British troops were loudly and dramatically being prepared for withdrawal in a bid to teach Foncha a lesson while leaving the country absolutely defenceless.[327] This momentous irrevocable declaration by JO Field the Commissioner was strategically timed to come just before the All Party, Pre-Foumban Conference in Bamenda so as to have maximum effect. It was equally intended to strike fright, terror, confusion and cut as much ground from under Foncha's feet as possible. The situation was so alarming that the delegates at the Conference unanimously protested to the British Government but to no avail.[328]

---

[326] Ibid., Directly linked to Foncha's policy on independence for Southern Cameroons was the subject of the so called 'Third Question' in the options for the plebiscite questions.
[327] Ibid., Malcolm Milne, traps set for Foncha.
[328] Ibid., OBB Sendze.

The memorandum to this effect surprisingly was jointly issued by the KNDP, CPNC, OK Party, Funs and all the participants at the Conference at Bamenda on security matters. This was a shock to JO Field and Malcolm Milne, who had expected that this would get a combination of the CPNC, the OK party and even KNDP back benchers to rise up against Foncha and his Government, but instead it welded them firmly together against Britain. Thus, with one voice the delegates at the Bamenda All Party Conference energetically decried:

> The Press Release by the Commissioner of Southern Cameroons on the United Kingdom forces that on October 1, the United Kingdom will leave the Southern Cameroons undefended….It is therefore with deep regret that we protest against this action by Her Majesty's Government to withdraw its forces from Southern Cameroons without any arrangements for other security measures.[329]

It is in this sequence that the rather strange and bizarre behaviour of His Excellency JO Field, Commissioner of Southern Cameroons can fittingly be situated. He did not wait to execute his ultimate most celebrated, diplomatic and historic function of handing over the United Nations Trust Territory of Southern Cameroons Under the Administration of Great Britain for over forty years to President Ahmadou Ahidjo. Rather, he delegated this all too momentous function to his Assistant, Malcolm Milne to perform. Meanwhile, he, JO Field boarded a British warship at Victoria Wharf on the morning of September 30, 1961and stayed there on board in Cameroons territorial waters until 1st October 1961 before sailing off to Lagos. At about the same time in the British House of Commons, Hon Fraser, the Minister for Colonies was being grilled for abandoning Southern Cameroons without adequate arrangements for its defence.[330]

Reasons for the weird behaviour of JO Field remain a matter of conjecture but given the trend of events building up to this episode, it was largely an expression of the ambiguous role he and his colleagues

---

[329] David Kingah and Tazifor John, *Introducing Cameroon History* p, 86, quoted in Pius Soh, *Dr. John Ngu Foncha: the Cameroonian Statesman* p.140.

[330] Of course, he had no convincing excuses to offer. See, OBB Sendze.

at the Colonial and Foreign Office had played in the affairs of the Trust Territory of Southern Cameroons thus fulfilling the adage that: "By their fruits we shall know them." There is also a strong current of opinion which maintains that Field actually expected a civil war to break out. This was expressly his intention in loudly announcing the withdrawal of British defence forces at that vulnerable moment to incite the public into insurrection against the Foncha Government. Both he and his assistant Malcolm Milne had been preparing the minds of attendants at the Bamenda All Party Conference for a rebellion within the KNDP in particular and, generally among the participants. When things passed off peacefully, Malcolm Milne openly expressed his disappointment pugnaciously noting:

> At one time we thought there might have been a showdown at the Bamenda All Party Conference with everyone's cards on the table… it seems that Foncha will now trot off to Bamum armed with the views of all parties in Southern Cameroons.[331]

---

[331] PRO CO554/2247 XC 3343 of 1 July 1961.

Foncha and Team at site of the Ebubu Massacre in Tombel

Note the expression of disgust on their faces

It is inconceivable that up to the last moment, these top British officials were still intent on inflicting maximum punishment on the Foncha Administration and dismembering the fragile territory they had administered half-heartedly for over forty years. The pattern of seditious correspondence above facilitates admission of the argument that the British were indeed directly or indirectly responsible for the Ebubu Massacre; either in an attempt to scare the "natives" against the Republic of Cameroun; punish them for having chosen reunification instead of integration or still worse, stir up the intended rebellion against the Foncha Government.[332] There can hardly be any other logic in their insistence to ensure both the failure of the Bamenda All Party Conference and the Foumban Constitutional Conference or, much less, why finally power was passed on directly to Ahidjo and not to Foncha on the eve of 30 September 1961 as previewed in all other correspondence before that event.[333]

---

[332] In fact, there is the story told of a young labourer at the Ebubu Plantation from Nkor, Bui Division, who witnessedthe horror and after trekking for ten days in the forest along the River Nkam eventually got home. He recounted that those who carried out the massacre were whites dressed in military uniform. Discussion with Hon. Joseph K Kwi, (aged 74), January 2013.

[333] PRO COS54/2412 XC 3343 cc. 74'69 of 18/1160.

Picture Omar BB Sendze President Emeritus: National Order of Civil Engineers, Cameroon

A main Actor: he lived through the early political experiences as a student in London, the FRC and Unitary State of Cameroon. He was one of two Cameroon Civil Engineers left after massive resignation of British expatriates.

Consequently, all British citizens were put on the alert. Foncha as PM struggled tirelessly to reassure the population; especially the expatriates that even with the unfortunate withdrawal of the Grenadier Guards, peace would continue to prevail. All British civil servants were barricaded behind barbwire fences, while those working with the CDC at Bota, were packed like cattle in a fence and guarded by the police.[334] Nonetheless, there were sceptics among whom were some missionary organizations and individuals, who took the scare seriously and withdrew from the territory.[335] On the night of the handing-over, the British civil servants in Buea were evacuated to a warship anchored

---

[334] Mr. OBB Sendze, who visited the Bota Senior Service Club that evening, lived the experience. He encountered unusual police checks, while an eerie atmosphere pervaded the club.

[335] Franciscan Sisters at Fiango Kumba; There was also, Rev. Fr. Frank McCarthy, former principal of St. Joseph's College, Sasse, see, Frank M'carthy, *The Wanderings- An APF Organiser's Wanderings*, pp. 157-158.

at Victoria Bay, while those working in the CDC were herded behind high barbed wire fences.[336]

Put together, the British Colonial Government's attitude; the elaborate and relentless attacks by the CPNC opposition engaging the press and much more, produced invidious accounts of "John Ngu Foncha", which constituted conspiracy theories ultimately making a myth of a simple man. Since he is central in this study and given that space has been allotted to President Ahidjo and Malcolm Milne, who were major political actors in this story, it is equally important to see in profile the face behind the mask of who really John Ngu Foncha was.

John Ngu Foncha: Sketch Biography

Born on 21 June 1921, John Ngu Foncha was the son of a Prince of the Nkwen Royal Family, a Fondom in Bamenda, North- West Region, Cameroon. He attended Bamenda Government Primary School, the only one in the Division (the entire North- West Region today!), 1926-30 and proceeded to Calabar, Nigeria, where he completed Standard Six, earning the highly coveted First School Leaving Certificate at St. Michael's Roman Catholic School, Boguma, Calabar, Nigeria in 1934.

He then served as a Pupil Teacher (PT) for the year 1934-35 in Sacred Heart School, Shisong-Nso, and immediately thereafter, went back to do post-primary education in Nigeria gaining admission into St. Charles' College, Onitsha for the Teacher's Grade II certificate. On completion, he taught in St. Anthony's Roman Catholic School, Njinikom for the year, 1939-40. With passion for further education, barely after another interval of one year, Foncha was back to Nigeria, where he sought admission in the Moore Plantation School, Ibadan. There, he pursued a course which earned him the Agricultural Teacher's Grade I Certificate in 1941. In the context of the time and even presently, this was obviously a brilliant fast-track academic record. It should be noted that the teaching profession up to the early 1970s throughout Southern Cameroons was one of the most prestigious, respected and dignified professions. A teacher was the epitome of all that was desirable since he symbolized progress,

---

[336] See Sendze, reminiscences.

integrity, wisdom and was the exemplar in his society. He was the letter writer, sanitary inspector and an emblem of knowledge, decorum and orderliness. The Headmaster additionally was highly respected and played the role of adviser to the Fon, Chief or the Village Head and the Village Council. "The HM represented the acme of academic achievement".[337] His wisdom was most sought after. With the introduction of political life, they were the most eligible for elective office.

The Professional Teacher

Despite brighter professional and financial prospects offered by service with the government as an Executive Officer (EO), Foncha preferred to return to the Roman Catholic Mission as a humble classroom teacher in St. Anthony's Primary School, Njinikom, where for a while; he was also a tutor on the staff of the newly opened Teacher's Training College (1943-1947). It was at this point that he wedded Miss Anna Atang, daughter of Mr. Martin Atang, pioneer Catechist and founder of St. Joseph's Mission, Mankon, Bamenda, present day, Cathedral Parish, and Seat of the Archdiocese of Bamenda.[338] The bride was a fresh graduate from Ifuoma Teachers' Training Centre, Calabar, Nigeria.

Launching into Political Life

Foncha was next posted to head; St. Joseph's Roman Catholic School, Mankon, 1948-51, the largest Roman Catholic School in the Province. Here, he quickly rose in rank and successively became: Supervisor, Headmaster and then, Visiting Teacher. These were the highest positions available to any individual teacher at the time. His political ambitions found fertile ground and rapidly sprouted. A typical product of his time: an epoch characterized by the ferment of political consciousness and proto-nationalism, Foncha began by organizing common break-time meals among his staff, a practice which quickly

---

[337] Cameroon life, March 1991, p7; "The Plebiscite Thirty Years After", by Francis K Wache.
[338] Manuscript by Mgr. Luke Atang.

spread throughout Bamenda Division (the entire North-West Region) among teachers of all denominations. Soon these were transformed into njangis or thrift and loan societies. Still, out of these, mushroomed socio-economic, cultural, development and budding political associations, trade unions and other pressure groups, which were later to become the pools from which the grass root supporters of his KNDP were enrolled.

While studying in Nigeria, Foncha had come into contact with leading compatriots including: Messrs Paul M Kale, Nerius N Mbile, NN Namme and especially Dr. Emmanuel M L Endeley and a host of other Southern Cameroonians. Together, under the leadership of Paul M Kale and, in imitation of the Nigerian Youth League (NYL) they formed the Cameroon Youth League (CYL) which in later years became a branch of Dr. Nnamdi Azikiwe's National Congress of Nigeria and Cameroons (NCNC), the first ever Nigerian national political party inaugurated in 1944.

Already widely popular, it was as Branch Secretary of the NCNC and the Cameroon National Federation (CNF) that Foncha hosted Dr. Nnamdi Azikiwe during his national tour in which he addressed a political rally at the RCM Field, Mankon, Bamenda in 1946. Mbile's memories of Foncha in those early years remained pretty fresh such that when writing his biography forty years later, he could still vividly recall how: "My early contact with Foncha created a special place in my heart for a man who despite his simple ways had shown himself as one of conviction in the African cause for freedom from foreign rule."[339] And in later years, after all the hustle and bustle in political life, he could still concede: "All said and done, we cannot fail to hail John Ngu Foncha as a hero in Cameroon political history. Despite faltering steps he is an acknowledged champion of Cameroonian unification."[340]

Member of Parliament and Party Leader

Henceforth, Foncha was launched into national politics. With a little more effort, he was elected for Bamenda Central with 12 other

---

[339] NN Mbile, *Cameroon Political Story; Memories of an Eye-Witness*, (Limbe, Presbyterian Printing Press, 1999), p. 322.
[340] Ibid., p. 199.

Southern Cameroonians as Members of Parliament (MPs) to the Eastern House of Assembly in 1951.These were known as the "Original Thirteen". With the formation of the "Neutrality Bloc" in Nigerian politics by Endeley, Foncha became one of his most fervent followers devoted to Southern Cameroons seceding from Nigeria and subsequently a staunch member of the KNC, which espoused that ideology. However, when, Endeley turned tail in1955, Foncha, supported by Hon. Augustine Ngom Jua, tore off to form the Kamerun National Democratic Party (KNDP). Barely two years later in the 1957 elections, while the (KNC) won 06/13, the KNDP won 05/13 and the Kamerun Peoples Party (KPP)02/13 seats thus forcing the KNC into a coalition with the KPP to hold to power, 1957-59.

After winning the 1959 elections by a narrow margin of 14:12, and later stalemating at 13:13 following the carpet crossing from the ruling KNDP to the Opposition KNC/KPP alliance by Hon JM Boja, Foncha's KNDP soon picked up and rapidly grew from strength to strength. Thus, it overwhelmingly swept through the famous 11 February Plebiscite in 1961, the parliamentary elections to an enlarged House of Assembly of that year and subsequently again swept the slates clean in the Municipal and Federal elections of 1963 and 1964 respectively in which the Cameroons Peoples National Congress (CPNC) lost its deposit. Thus, Foncha became Prime Minister of Southern Cameroons, (1959-61); joint PM of West Cameroon and Vice President (VP) of the Federal Republic of Cameroon, (FRC) from 1961-65 and then VP of the Federal Republic of Cameroon (1965-70). Sacked in 1970, he held obscure political positions until his resignation from political life in 1990.

Socio-Cultural and Spiritual Life: House Arrest, Trapped!

John Ngu Foncha lived an intensely spiritual life, firmly convinced that religious and political life were mutually compatible and supportive of each other. As a matter of course, his day began with Morning Prayers and Holy Mass and concluded with family prayers before bed time. Even as Prime Minister, he would carry out the same routine and if it was too early when he had to travel, a special Mass was arranged and quite often he himself would serve if there was no Mass

Servant. On retirement, he led Prayers in the St. John the Baptist Mission Station Church, Bayelle Nkwen a practice he carried out till he fell gravely ill.[341]

His spiritual and charitable activities at the level of the "All Saints Parish, Bayelle" intensified. This was the case after he was sacked as Vice President, quarantined and literally placed under house arrest in Nkwen. This harrowing experience, characterized by searches and harassment by the forces of law and order of all visitors and passers-by who came close to, or much worse attempted to visit the house lasted for about a year.[342] Mrs. Foncha's cousin, who had constructed the house in which they were living, was not allowed to visit them. These police and gendarmes slept under cover in the shrubs surrounding the compound both day and night making life most uncomfortable.[343]

In addition to membership in parochial Prayer and Christian Action Groups, Foncha was actively involved in humanitarian organizations such as the Father Samson Foundation for Underprivileged Children (FASAF), the fortnightly meetings of which he attended with religious tenacity.[344] It was only one of several philanthropic groups to which he belonged. These apart, the Foncha compound then and since then, has remained a haven for the poor, mentally deranged and physically handicapped as well as stranded wayfarers. This was a venture in which he and his wife, Mrs. Anna Atang Foncha as founder of the Catholic Women's Association (CWA) were further blended.[345]

Interestingly, for his long life and responsible positions held, Foncha never built a family house and the present four-bed room

---

[341] There are even those who feel that he took ill because of the exposure to the cold April morning droughts that invaded the church which was still under construction and had no window shutters as he participated in the Lenten Stations of the Cross.

[342] Even Mr. DA Nangah, Mrs. Foncha's cousin.

[343] Memories recollected by Mrs. Anna Atang Foncha and family.

[344] This initially undertook the education of deprived and poor children exclusively in Akwaya Subdivision, especially the "girl children who were betrothed in childhood sometimes even before they were born" by tradition. Since then the policy has been adjusted so that it caters for underprivileged children elsewhere in Cameroon.

[345] A good number of these come from distant places and could be found around the compound! I talked to one from Bafia!.

bungalow and premises, after which "Foncha Street" is named was the initiative of Mrs. Foncha, who realizing that they were likely to go on retirement without a family home requested her cousin, Mr. Daniel A Nangah, a contractor to put up the structure which she meant to use as her farm house. Ultimately, it became and has remained the Foncha family house. It is the most ordinary of houses in "Foncha Street," distinguished by the fact that unlike typical Foncha Street houses, it has no fence or enclosure of any kind demarcating it.[346]

After the abrupt and causeless dismissal of Foncha in 1970, the entire Cameroon nation was gripped with fear. All of Yaoundé was pervaded by *DIRDOC* Security (secret security) agents in the university campus; lecture halls, restaurants and bars to pick up dissidents who were taken to the brutal gendarme detention centres as his family flew back home. Civil administrators especially in Bamenda were instructed to prevent crowds turning out to receive him. However, despite massive police presence, the Fon of Bali organized a rousing welcome for him at Bali Airport and, on entry into Bamenda Town, huge crowds lined the streets right to his residence in Nkwen.

Thereafter, he was practically placed under house arrest, thoroughly quarantined with squads of fierce looking Francophone security officers who blocked entry to the area even to passers-by taking down their names and car numbers. They infiltrated and dug around the premises and bushes in search of hidden arms. Even priests of the local Bayelle Parish Church, which the Foncha family attended, were held to explain why so many masses were being offered for the "protection of the Foncha family", suspicious that he was setting up an army for the secession of Southern Cameroons.

Among notable individuals who defied the banning orders to visit Foncha was Professor Bernard Nsokika Fonlon, who requested to be relieved of his ministerial position because of the disrespectful manner in which Foncha had been dismissed.[347] This was the practical application of Malcolm Milne's "Nkambe-type inescapable trap" promised Foncha. It was actually reported that: "Foncha was like a

---

[346] His son and successor, Martin Foncha a businessman is presently putting up a more befitting family house in the Foncha compound.

[347] Fonlon was actually deposed from his ministerial portfolio and went back to the University of Yaoundé as a lecturer that year, in 1970.

caged 'rat'".³⁴⁸ The only addition was that this time it was being administered by the Ahidjo Regime to whom the British had "safely" handed him over on 1 October 1961. Ahidjo's fear was increased by the fact that Foncha did not utter a word or show any sign of resistance given that he still enjoyed massive popularity.³⁴⁹

Foncha as observed in his Nkwen Home Town

Opinion about Foncha and the Foncha family in Nkwen, the village of his birth, is fairly mixed. There is a significant vocal minority, who hold that he did "nothing" practically nothing to "train" or bring up Nkwen sons and daughters to become prominent national figures, while others maintain that he "surrendered" everything to his wife, whose family members are relatively better placed. All of these allegations sound credible until the facts are brought to light. Indeed, none of the three Foncha siblings³⁵⁰ improved their statures in life

---

³⁴⁸ Pius Soh, Dr. John Ngu Foncha the Cameroonian Statesman, (Bamenda, 1999), pp.210-12. This was precisely in the manner of the Nkambe type trap described by Malcolm Milne.

³⁴⁹ The other, was Mr. DA Nangah, Mrs. Foncha's cousin. Pius B Soh, Dr. John Ngu Foncha the Cameroonian Statesman, Bamenda, 1999, pp.210-212, also in-depth discussion with Ba Tita Fokum, who had taught with Foncha. He recounted the awful harassment and torture of the Nkwen population following the inexplicable death of one of the policemen keeping watch at the Foncha compound. He tells how: women just discharged from the maternity hospital, all young men and girls and even octogenarians were arrested and locked up. As a senior policeman, he was sent to resolve the problems; Interviewed on 25 October 2012. Yet, Foncha had acquired a relatively vast stretch of land in Nkwen, while still Headmaster of St. Joseph's Roman Catholic School, Mankon. As a specialist in Agriculture, he intended to use this land for mixed-farming; cattle/animal rearing, fishery, poultry, piggery, coffee, palm oil and eucalyptus fuel plantations. At the time far removed from 'Abakwa' Town; today it has been engulfed by the fast growing population and is demographically at the heart of Nkwen. As a consequence there are murmurs and veiled criticisms that the Foncha family is hoarding land, and obstructing development. In reality, this is insignificant when compared to the holdings of his colleagues, who acquired vast estates directly for commercial purposes. However, what is noteworthy is that Foncha has given out substantial portions of the land to the Bayelle Parish and various groups in the Catholic Church and he was ready to add to these just before his death.

³⁵⁰ These were: Godfrey Awantoh, traditional musician; Paul Ndasi, a soldier and Martin Ngangni, a tailor in the South West Region

above being: the night-watch, village tailor and ordinary soldier (l'homme de troupe'), as a consequence of their brother having become Prime Minister or "whatever."[351] In other words, they were simple villagers like everybody else if not "wretched" to say the least. As for the Foncha children, they were each given a sound Catholic primary, secondary and high school formation even up to university level but there are no renowned professors, doctors, lawyers and architects among them. Most of all, there is none of them who has taken up politics or who holds a prominent position in national life as a consequence of who and what their father was in public life.

Some Atang family members definitely acquired career positions, but they did this because of their father's position, influence as the first catechist in Mankon and by dint of their individual hard work, intelligence and resourcefulness without undue assistance from their sister or brother–in–law. The big accusation Foncha faced was that he was "tribalistic", a trait which he incidentally loathed and repeatedly condemned. This becomes difficult to locate in these circumstances or it acquires another definition.[352] Proof is that some of Mrs. Foncha's sisters at best have not risen above being considered as dutiful house wives and good Christians with no distinguished source of livelihood. Actually, throughout their education especially from primary to high school, the Foncha children received no privileged treatment. One of them recalls the public snake beating he received at the hands of his father for daring to commit a misdemeanour among other school children. They were expected to be of exemplary conduct. The author recalls an occasion when he accompanied a friend in 1976 to Sacred Heart College, Mankon, Bamenda to check out how it was that his son had ruined two pairs of shoes in one term and was asking for yet another. He knew this because he wore the same size of shoe with his father.

We discovered that the boy actually had been playing football in such durable and expensive, imported shoes. The point, however, is

---

[351] Discussions with Mr. Clement Awasum, octogenarian, July 2010 (late)

[352] My struggle in the Catholic Priesthood by (Mgr. Luke Atang , nd, 2003); while, Dr. Protus Atang literally fought every inch of his way from St. Anthony's Catholic Primary School, Njinikom to Government College Umahia, Jakiri, Vom and Glasgow etc. He retired as a diplomat having served with the Food and Agricultural Organisation (FAO) with distinction and earned several international decorations.

that we chanced on Dr. Foncha, then retired Vice President, who also had come to find out why his own son, who was in the same school was asking for another pair of "sandals". In our presence, the principal brought out the sandals, which were still intact explaining that the Foncha son had simply outgrown his size and needed a bigger size. We were stunned that, he could be so meticulous.

However, this experience was not limited to Foncha alone but common to the bulk of his colleagues across the entire political spectrum. At Sacred Heart College, Mankon, Bamenda and Bilingual Grammar School, Molyko, Buea, the author as a secondary school teacher taught the sons of: AN Jua, Christian Bongwa and ST Muna between 1968 and 1974. He noted the same austere and highly disciplined attitude towards their sons. It was normal for a Muna son to walk the distance between Buea Town and Bilingual Grammar School (BGS), Molyko, Buea just like all the other students. There were absolutely no extrinsic privileges and distinctions enjoyed by their offspring in any confessional or public establishments. The same formation was accorded to the future Fon Abumbi III of Bafut, while a student at BGS Molyko. Of course, outside school and upon graduation, he became an "untouchable" and revered almost as a deity in the traditional Tikar Bamenda Grassland setting. Simplicity, austerity, probity and discipline were the order of the day among the political leadership.

Conclusion

If anything, it can be observed that till the end, Foncha was as fallible as all human beings are but distinguished himself by being consistent both in his private and public life. He tried to live the life he had envisaged for himself, his family from the onset and his people based on: simplicity, humility, diligence, assiduity, generosity, honesty, fear of God and respect for the law. These are not issues over which any unanimity especially of a political figure can be expected. While there are those who crave that Foncha ought to have been sent to the 'gallows' like in the Summit Magazine, his surviving products, schoolmates and the masses who knew him closely, think he should be beatified.

The truth definitely lies somewhere in between and as he maintained in the KNDP motto, which he coined: "The truth shall prevail."[353] The other incontestable fact about Foncha is that he was extensively charismatic, popular and a crowd puller even when appearing in public with President Ahidjo. This was amply demonstrated during his decorations at Foumban and, paradoxically this fact was acknowledged by none other than Malcolm Milne, who openly voiced his dislike for the fact that Foncha was too popular for his liking, and was honest enough to say so.[354] Other frequently heard criticisms of Foncha turn to the fact that he allowed his Christian inclinations to overshadow his political life and that his extreme dedication to peace, modesty and fear of bloodshed gave Ahidjo the leeway to subjugate Southern Cameroons. In fact, radical critics of him like Nde Ntumazah thought he was timid and a coward, qualities which Ahidjo was quick to take advantage of to suppress Anglophone Southern Cameroonians. However, there are political analysts who forcefully argue that when it came to the quest for amassing power, Ahidjo was unstoppable, reason why he is considered a megalomaniac, while in contrast, there was practically nothing which Foncha would not sacrifice for peace. In other words, between the two men, there was a whole world of difference.[355]

---

[353] Kamerun National Democratic Party (KNDP) *Tenth Annual Convention Working Papers, Kumba*, Nov, 1964.

[354] *No telephone*, p. 446.

[355] Bayart and Richard Joseph in *Gaullist Africa* and *Radical Nationalism in Cameroon* respectively. See also, Malcolm Milne, No telephone, p. 446.

Chapter 9

Malcolm Milne: "*Dr. Jerkyll and Mr. Hyde*"

The "Nadir": Malcolm Milne Awful Disclosures

In essence, the "Nadir comprises historically contextualised excerpts from Malcolm Milne's rich autobiography entitled: *No Telephone to Heaven – From Apex to Nadir- Colonial Service in Nigeria, Eden, the Cameroons and the Gold Coast.*"[356] The entire volume recounts his experiences in the British colonial service but the focus here is on his time in Southern Cameroons, which saw the end of his life in the colonial service. It is therefore, also, a sort of comparative account of his life in Southern Cameroons relative to the other colonial experiences. Southern Cameroons was his last posting and it was his lot to preside over the closing of a glorious epoch in the history of the British Empire and, it is these bitter – sweet memories that constitute the contents of this epic account.

In all, he is left to speak in a historical perspective encompassing his exploits together with those of his colleagues in the colonial service as well as the Southern Cameroonian politicians and people with whom he interacted in all capacities. As it turns out it is an exposition of Malcolm Milne's: regrets, disclosures, fears, apologies, contradictions, explanations, admissions, confessions, lessons learnt and to learn, and reaffirmations of the revelations of the macabre goings on in the British colonial service in the Southern Cameroons, later confirmed almost in toto in the declassified British secret papers. For these latter, he says he has no regrets and no apologies to make and so in one word affirms the ugly utterances contained therein.[357]

---

[356] For details see Johnson, Part II; Edwin Ardener, "The Kamerun Idea" West Africa, June 7and 14, 1958; Ardener, EO *Coastal Bantu of the Cameroons*, Part XI, Daryll Forde, ed.(London, International African institute),p.434.
[357] Ibid.

Writing his report was Malcolm Milne's last act on his last day; in the small hours of 1 October 1961, as he grappled with drafting, "a telegram for Eastwood on Field's departure and Ahidjo's take-over."[358]

This was a historic function he had solemnly executed that evening; watching the Union Jack lowered for the last time and the Green, Red and Yellow striped flag with two gold stars that ushered in the brand new "Federal Republic of Cameroon", raised for the first time that evening at Tiko International Airport. Something "miraculous" happened, on his being conferred the reins of power as Acting Commissioner of Southern Cameroons. All of a sudden, the scales of deceit fell from his eyes and Malcolm Milne in that brief moment of truth, heartily regretted and fervently rather poetically and emotionally confessed:

> That afternoon of 30th September had been exceptionally brilliant. There weren't many days in the year Ambas Bay could be like that. But l for one – and l think others of my colleagues as well - felt that the beauty of the scene was an ironic comment on what we'd been up to rather than a sign of approbation for what we'd done. May be we'd let "these nice little people down "to use Foley Newn's words and one day would rue it.[359]

The last sentence of this heavily loaded quotation is all that is required in the close to the 500 page volume to drive home the topical message of Malcolm Milne's regret, apology and confession not only for himself but for the entire British colonial establishment of the mess they had made of their watch over Southern Cameroons after forty years of administration. Yet, this is not all, in a vain search for an explanation, Malcolm Milne continues:

> We'd come to the end of a pretty sorry saga. We had - obedient to orders – given away what once we'd been charged with constructing. On the other hand none of us felt competent to question the orders emanating from cabinet level; our experience

---

[358] Ibid., p. 447.
[359] Ibid.

had always been that such orders, based upon all the facts were correct, infallible.[360]

Apparently these are not crocodile's tears, but genuine as they were, they were being shed over spilt milk; closing the stable door after the horse had escaped. In other words, as indicated in the preface to Malcolm Milne's book by Kirk Green, the Holy Spirit had all of a sudden happened on Malcolm Milne and providentially he saw the light; far, far too late for any amends to be made. And what is worse, he and Field had been the very instruments of that destruction. Whatever, political wrongs he might have committed, turned on him with incalculable vengeance and Malcolm further confesses:

> My head full of such conflicts I found drafting what might have been a simple relatively straightforward telegram that night desperately difficult. I felt that some of the 'Whitehall Warriors', as we referred facetiously to our London colleagues, were treating the whole matter too casually by half. Most of them seemed incapable of understanding that our role had been a painful one.[361]

This is a chilling revelation hard to believe, alleging that Johnson Field and Malcolm Milne had during those crucial years been merely helpless, docile instruments of a mindless political machine in London that drove them to conduct the irreparable destruction of the future of the trusting 'nice little people' of British Southern Cameroons. This, to say the least marks one of the lowest points in British colonial history. Much less is it possible to understand how this was translated by these two high officials in the territory into the rancour that they built against Foncha as a person, for his cabinet and the people.

---

[360] Ibid.
[361] Ibid.

Dread of Destitution

However, Malcolm Milne's one great worry is that his tenure in the colonial service in Southern Cameroons from 1959-1961 coincided with when the colonial empire was folding up and with it, his career ambitions. His life's dream, a career in the colonial service was being to preside over that painful fateful exercise of the lowering of the Union Jack for the last time as the two star Federal Republic of Cameroon flag was hoisted for the first time ever in the territory at Tiko. The other great worry was the looming reality of destitution; what did the future outside the colonial office hold for him – simply a void? This was scary to say the least. In writing the introduction to the work, Anthony Kirk Green, Malcolm Milne's erudite colleague in the colonial service and author of the classic work, "Adamawa Past and Present", fired the first friendly salvo when he took an exception to Malcolm's position maintaining:

> I find that for all my admiration of Malcolm Milne's memoir, I have to express my disagreement with one of his interpretations. Such an option to differ was one we in the colonial service were always open to exercise as he himself neatly encapsulates the ethos. 'The service was not only eminently fair to us, it took care of us. We in turn, obeyed the accepted usages of the service: we were encouraged at whatever level we served, to say what we thought but we did what we were told. [362]

Then, Green continues:

> In particular, l am far happier over the executive role of the colonial administrative service in the dismantling of the colonial empire than he is with his belief that whereas the pre-war administration represented its apex, its post- war involvement in the mechanics of the transfer of power constituted its nadir.[363]

---

[362]Ibid., *No Telephone* p. xiv. .
[363]Ibid.

To Green, such an argument was too negative. However, it turned out that Malcolm Milne had moulded his career in the colonial service entirely set on the premise that the British Empire would continue to be one over which the "sun never sets".[364]

Harold MacMillan: "Winds of Change Address"

As indicated by his colleague, Kirk Green, it is apparent that Malcolm Milne actually was out of step with the current thought in British colonial policy. He belonged to the "old school" constructed on past glories. Harold Macmillan set the ball rolling during his visit to southern Africa and specifically in the historic address he made to the joint Houses of Parliament. He was succinct and drove home the message forcefully in that bastion of apartheid leaving no one in doubt. After that, nothing in colonial Africa was ever to remain the same. In this context:

> The British Prime Minister, Mr. Harold Macmillan, arrived in the Union after visiting other African countries and on February 3 addressed the members of both houses of Parliament in Cape Town. His speech covered many topics. He spoke of the traditional ties of friendship between Britain and the Union, deplored the boycott of South African goods being promoted in some countries, and referred to the 'winds of change' blowing over Africa.[365]

---

[364]Children were taught to sing this in Primary School especially on Empire Day and the Queen's Birthday

[365]Microsoft ® Encarta ® 2009. © 1993-2008 Microsoft Corporation. All rights reserved.

Harold Macmillan

British P.M: 1957 - 1963

However, the core of the speech was his avowal of the principles on which British policy in Africa was based: Everything apart, he emphasised equality and the rise of Nelson Mandela could logically be traced to that speech. He continued: "We reject the idea of any inherent superiority of one race over another." The British ideal was a society 'in which individual merit and individual merit alone"[366]was the epitome. The echoes of this famous address seem to have caught the attention of members at the UN and UNTC as well. The 1960s were to witness attacks by the US and the Afro-Asian bloc of nations at the UN against all forms of imperialism and colonialism. There is therefore no wonder that even France which had not given any thought to granting its African colonies any form of independence outside the French Union that year alone, of a sudden discharged most of them from its political stranglehold. This included "French Cameroon", which became "Republic of Cameroon" on First January 1960, even before British Southern Cameroons, which had begun enjoying self-government since1954.

Given the importance Malcolm Milne attached to professional motivation, it is interesting to know that he had joined the colonial service intending to become a Divisional Officer with a permanent and

---

[366]Ibid., Milne, *No Telephone*.

pensionable career.³⁶⁷ These expectations were initially surpassed but, finally prematurely, shattered and terminated as Southern Cameroons prepared for reunification and independence in 1961. He himself put it desolately but intelligibly:

> By 1959, after twenty years of service, I found myself working with confidence in the higher ranks of a unified and closely knit service. At the same time, in keeping with my friends, I saw that the service itself was coming to an end. I had taken a job for my working life. Half way through, the ground below had been cut away; it was no longer a job for life. A continually reducing service would be required for a few years but even that would bear little resemblance to the service I'd joined. Great Britain had decided, rightly or wrongly to abandon the colonial role.³⁶⁸

These were irrecoverable experiences with which Malcolm Milne was reluctant to reconcile. To Green, Malcolm belonged to the "old school" and was out of step with the evolving times. But since this concept remained the recurrent theme in his book it most likely affected his attitude to politicians and political decisions in Southern Cameroons.

Malcolm and Field Innately Idiosyncratic

This was the regrettable reality that dogged Malcolm Milne's thoughts throughout his years in the service in Southern Cameroons and affected a lot of the decisions he took, in fact, his pattern of life, thought and action. Relatively early in this commentary, it deserves to be added that one of the greatest errors was that Malcolm Milne and his boss, JO Field saw reunification for Southern Cameroons with the terrorist- ridden French Cameroun as nothing more than a pipe dream and consequently paid scant if not scornful attention to the KNDP and its leadership which championed that "hollow" option. This

---

³⁶⁷Ibid. , p,xv.
³⁶⁸Ibid., p. 403.

turned out to be one of Malcolm Milne's greatest shocks when ultimately reunification won.

Directly or indirectly, the effects were devastating on him.[369] It was something of a tragedy that both Malcolm Milne and his boss Johnson Field were so innately idiosyncratic and blinded that they passionately believed that Endeley's KNC-KPP alliance with Mbile, which stood for integration with Nigeria would win convincingly. Possibly it was in respect of "laid down colonial policy" as indicated by Kirk Green: that, Malcolm Milne saw everything wrong with the Foncha and KNDP option. Consequently, he veered round to castigate:

> Foncha, as the past thirty-seven years has demonstrated, was battling on a much more difficult wicket. He himself was prejudiced against the Ibos ... alleging the majority in his small country felt the same. The Ibos were quite simply better traders, better politicians and more tightly organized than his own disparate peoples, charming as the latter could be.[370]

Malcolm Milne had a contemptuous and low opinion of Foncha and the KNDP, casually dismissing 'Ibo-phobia' as of no consequence in the forthcoming contest. He was overly confident that reunification was by far a lost cause, reason why he pitied Foncha's futile travails. As a result he boldly declared contemptuously that:

> Foncha's most fervent supporters did not relish the possibility of Southern Cameroons becoming absorbed into a Cameroun state… Reunification was a romantic, almost poetic concept. It was a useful flag to wave but not a plebiscite winning conception.[371]

The statistical degree of error resulting from this great diplomat's miscalculations was enormous and was soon demonstrated in the

---

[369] He took his family for a holiday in Europe at the end of February 1961 and within one week, he was very sick. In fact, he was hospitalized in the London Tropical Diseases Hospital for three long weeks. This could well have been a shock resulting from the Plebiscite results, See, Telephone, p.427.

[370] Ibid. p. 424.

[371] Ibid.

daunting vote of: 233.371 to 97.741 in favour of reunification. This was equally illustrative of how much those of the diplomats on the spot were incorrigibly myopic. As a result they misled officials at the colonial office in London on the correct picture of the political situation on the ground in Cameroons by reading everything through tainted glasses, upside down.[372]

Foncha KNDP Government 1959

Sitting Left to Right: JO Field, James Robertson, Foncha and Malcolm Milne

Milne Pays Generous Tributes to Civil Servants

Nevertheless, for all that can be said and his idiosyncrasy apart, Malcolm Milne is a great writer and No Telephone to Heaven, on the whole is a lucid, classic account of his autobiography, a masterpiece. He genuinely believed in what he wrote. Malcolm Milne's assessment of the typical Cameroonian was somewhat mercurial and temperamental but generous, although he was loath to think so, as was the case in the choice of friends, like Muna and Foncha. Thus after an inspection tour of councils in Bamenda Province, Malcolm Milne was full of praise and admiration for what he saw, the intelligence and tact of the people, who would ,while knowing the solution to a problem,

---

[372]See declassified docs.

carefully design the final decision and leave it for the DO to make the pronouncement himself. of the quality of people he noted:

> The situation has changed again during the last four or five years of my service when l was operating at permanent secretary level or above. Then l was dealing with individual ministers, with cabinet committees or in the case of southern Cameroons with a small government. Almost without exception they were people of high intelligence who knew exactly what they wanted.[373]

Most interestingly, here, Malcolm Milne was precisely referring to the Foncha Cabinet. His thoughts again went to the Bamenda corps of messengers with whom he had worked ten years earlier. With current reports from Mr. ED Quan, Assistant Secretary for Establishment; from this corps only one person had retired, Mr. A Dinga. Of this valiant unit in 1961, Malcolm Milne was passionate: "I felt vaguely then, and know for certain now, that working with these men had greatly enriched my time in the colonial service. There was something very special about that corps; their service was their watch word".[374] This was generous, glowing tribute typical of Malcolm, when he felt pleased to do so. However, if it could be said this was largely the case then, the exceptions came in when he had to talk about Foncha, the KNDP and reunification. At that point he was reminded of the creed that bound them in the colonial service, namely: "We were encouraged at whatever level we served, to say whatever we thought but we did whatever we were told".[375] Only it is not obvious as to who exactly was calling the shots.

---

[373] Ibid., *No Telephone*, p.254. .
[374] Ibid., p.409.
[375] Ibid., p. xiv.

Bamenda Corps, Valiant Unit

"Service was their watch word"

Mr. A Dinga Messenger   **Muna and Milne**

Trustworthy, Diligent and Reliable   Live long friends

Remorse and Regret

The next cardinal pronouncement was about Malcolm Milne himself. This view came to influence his attitude to his work as the morbid fear of a leap into the dark increasingly dominated his thoughts as can easily be discerned in his work, which is marked by a recurrent regret of the unwinding of the vast British colonial empire. Apparently, the officials were being used by the Colonial Office for supreme British national interest. In other words, this was a service in decline, without any real motivation and far from being inspirational as had been the case at the zenith in the 1930s-1950s replete with great hope and glory, a "Golden age" to which he belonged. Then referring to his own evolution over the years in the service, Malcolm Milne noted with much nostalgia for the glorious past and regret of the uncertain future. He openly confessed:

> Throughout this work I have done my best to portray as faithfully as possible what my own attitudes were at each particular moment in my service. They changed because I was getting older, they changed because the whole objective of my work changed: I joined a service with what I believed was a job for life eventually to find that that same service was being used to disband the empire, no longer to continue to maintain it.[376]

He made some unnerving revelations especially given his stance and that of his colleagues in the declassified documents. On being appointed substantive Deputy Commissioner to Johnson O Field, for Southern Cameroons in 1959, he again most repentantly confessed:

> [What] I had not come to terms with the conviction myself – was that we were doing the Cameroons a wrong. We should have struggled harder to continue our trusteeship for several years longer. But the forces against us were too strong and I judge now that had I, as Commissioner of the Cameroons taken this line in 1959 –61, I should merely have made a great nuisance of myself and achieved nothing.[377]

This is easily as far as any culpable mortal could go and makes a very sad commentary when examined in the context that while this concession was repeatedly and emphatically refused to Foncha and Southern Cameroons, it was gratuitously made over to Northern Cameroons without any request on their part. Blended with overall British colonial policy, this perfectly dovetails into Sir Perth's untoward comment that compared to Northern Cameroons, Southern

---

[376]Milne, *No Telephone*, pp. 254-255.
[377]Ibid., p. 395.

Cameroons was expendable. This was with regard to the emphatic rejection of the third question for Southern Cameroons standing alone or for independence during the plebiscite of 11 February 1961.[378] Here, not even reason, logic or ethics came into play; it was largely a matter of sheer bad faith on the part of the British Colonial Administration towards Southern Cameroons. On visiting Buea in 1960 Malcolm reports:

> Regarding views then current in the colonial and foreign offices and the treasury, Perth said that they could best be summarised as a balance against further trusteeship, the cost and defence considerations weighed heavily against as did the relatively small size of the territory – about one million people in all. However, Perth emphasised that the matter was still open.[379]

Yet, this was not the last confession and apology that was being made by Malcolm Milne about British disservice to Southern Cameroons. As the man who presided over the lowering of the Union Jack at Tiko International Airport for the last time on 30 September1961, Malcolm Milne profoundly regretted that the British had let these "nice little people down and one day would rue it".[380] By any means, these indeed were solemn prophetic words and given their context and the current trends in the history of Cameroon, certainly we are in early days and no one dares sing the swan song yet. For what reason would the British have dumped Southern Cameroonians the way they did? This is a capital rhetoric question that pleads for veritable equity at the gate of justice.

Phillipson's Appointment: Seals Fate of Southern Cameroons

Divulging the fact that he was largely responsible for the appointment of Sir Sydney Phillipson as consultant to the Southern Cameroons Government is one of those characteristics for which historians would no doubt credit Malcolm Milne as one who made a

---

[378] See declassified documents.
[379] Malcolm, p. 397.
[380] Ibid., p. 447.

clean breast of himself in his autobiography. Interestingly, this was not a planned act except that he used his diplomatic instinct in this situation to the immeasurable advantage of the British Government and total damage to the future of Southern Cameroons.

Nkrumah Delegation to Southern Cameroons February 1961

Endeley, Padmore, Nkrumah, and Foncha

As a consequence of the cordial relations that had developed between ST Muna and Malcolm Milne, there arose an episode that was to cost Southern Cameroons dearly. In Foncha's absence, Muna approached Malcolm Milne precisely, on 23 February 1959 and inadvertently disclosed to him the policy the KNDP Government intended to pursue with regard to the staffing problems which the cabinet anticipated would arise in the event of Nigerian independence in 1960. He plainly told Malcolm, who recounted:

> It was the policy of Foncha's government to rely on Ghanaians or expatriates rather than on the continued services of Nigerians. He also said that he and his colleagues had agreed with Foncha before the latter's departure that they really needed an expert to advice on the implications of secession. He asked me if l could

help by suggesting the sort of background the advisor should ideally have and by suggesting names.[381]

This was a gaffe that Malcolm Milne quickly grasped and was to play a decisive role in determining the future of Southern Cameroons. By this inadvertence, Muna had played directly into the hands of the beguiled enemy. The Cold War politics of the time and the game of the Afro-Asian bloc of nations at the UN apart, the British Government was in full partnership with Nigeria on the crucial issue of secession and so Muna had admitted the fox into the poultry. It was a chance Malcolm seized with zeal and acted on with alacrity and, as he put it: "It seemed clear to me that the Cameroonians were wide open to the wrong sort of influence and advice unless a suitable secessionist expert was found as soon as possible."[382] The consequences spelt doom for the future of Southern Cameroons.

Intuitively, by his diplomatic upbringing, Malcolm quickly reasoned that following the recent visit by President Kwame Nkrumah to Southern Cameroons, George Padmore might likely be appointed to that delicate position with obvious dire consequences; the loss of Southern Cameroons to Nigeria and the British and in the Cold War climate, into communist hands. Malcolm made urgent contacts through Gardner-Brown to Sir James Robertson, the Governor General of Nigeria, which finally and appropriately led to the appointment of Sir Sydney Phillipson KBE, CMG to that crucial position. He had served in Ceylon, and was Financial Secretary in Uganda and Nigeria.[383]

Thus installed, Sir Sydney Phillipson was charged with having to report on financial, economic and administrative consequences to Southern Cameroons of separation from the Federation of Nigeria. Of course, he performed an excellent job the results of which were to be far reaching and predictable. As expected, the report concluded that: "The available revenues would just suffice to enable it to maintain... a precarious hand-to-mouth existence". In short it meant that Southern Cameroons could not hope to survive as a completely viable,

---

[381] Ibid., p.447.
[382] Ibid., Milne, No Telephone, p. 168.
[383] Ibid

independent and sovereign state without continued assistance from Nigeria as had been the case so far.[384] This was a deliberate act that sealed the fate of Southern Cameroons. It is doubtful, whether till his demise Muna ever realized what harm he had inadvertently done by turning to the 'British', the "fox among the chickens" in Malcolm Milne's words, for assistance "to secede from Nigeria."

"Independence" Excluded as Plebiscite Option

In the circumstance, Sir Sydney Phillipson arrived in Southern Cameroons in mid-July 1959 and already by third September after only a two day visit to the CDC plantations at Victoria and Tiko, coupled with interviews with some civil servants and economic operators, submitted a rushed 'interim' report in which he expressed the opinion that the "Southern Cameroons would not be viable as a separate independent state". The whole idea was that the British Government urgently wanted a report confirming evidence of the "economic non-viability" of Southern Cameroons for submission at the 14thsession of the UN General Assembly. Sir Sydney Phillipson also calculatedly made his interim report to politicians from Southern Cameroons attending that Commission. It will be recalled that this report played well in the hands of the integrationists and was quoted by the whole range of CPNC leadership: Endeley, Mbile, Motomby Woleta, Kangsen and Ajebe Sone ad nauseam during the campaigns for the plebiscite.

It was only one week later after he had submitted the report that Sir Sydney Philippson undertook his three day whirlwind field trip inland to Bamenda, Wum and Nkambe. This means that his visits to Ndu Tea Estate and Santa Coffee Estate were only perfunctory, merely seeking data to validate the report he had already dispatched. His later fine-tuned report stated that the interim one of five weeks earlier had been of restricted circulation and was of no effect. The immediate political consequence of that report however, was the decision to out rightly exclude "independence as an option" for Southern Cameroons during the plebiscite. Thus Miss Angela Brooks the Liberian Chairlady

---

[384]Ngoh, pp.167-8 also Sendze, Reflections.

for that Session of the Fourth Committee fed by Colonial Office with the Phillipson report, concluded the debates advising that:

> The plebiscite questions in the draft resolution of the committee were to be framed in such a way that it would serve to allay any apprehension that the Southern Cameroons might become independent as a separate entity; an eventuality which all were agreed should be ruled out in view of the territory's limited economic potential.[385]

This abundantly explains the futility of Foncha's Labours at the UN faced with a Phalanx of : the British , Afro-Asian Bloc, UPC and the threat by Jua and the rest of the KNDP leadership back in Cameroon to have him resign or be replaced as leader. These are painful revelations coming out after the demise of that whole generation.

Phillipson: Constitutional and Economic Adviser

Sir Sydney Phillipson's fame in the territory as an "honest broker" soared to inconceivable heights. He was next appointed "Constitutional and Economic Adviser" to "assist" the Southern Cameroons Government in the examination of constitutional, fiscal and economic problems likely to arise out of joining the Cameroon Republic. Clearly, the extent to which this commission was "perfectly executed" could be seen in the manner in which the British Delegation openly colluded with the Cameroon Republic at the Buea Tripartite Conference and carefully delivered Foncha and his cabinet, together with the entire territory so to speak, into the "safe keeping" of President Ahidjo.

Nor was this all, Sir Sydney Phillipson, who openly had become the British hatchet man had earlier been appointed the 'neutral chairman' of the Mamfe Plebiscite Conference, 10-11 August 1959. As expected, "he demonstrated his "neutrality" by hurriedly closing the

---

[385]See 898th Meeting of the Fourth Committee in October 1959, quoted in Anyangwe p. 51.

conference, declaring in spite of clear evidence to the contrary, that the delegates had failed to reach agreement on the alternatives that should be presented at the plebiscite."[386] He had barely finished his consultancy report on this than the British Government appointed him yet again as double expert on "constitutional law and economics" to assist the Southern Cameroons in its negotiations with Cameroon Republic. In effect, he ensured that the noose was firmly tied round the neck of the territory and tethered to Cameroon Republic under the Ahidjo's leadership: A typical Nkambe type trap!

During the Anglo-Southern Cameroons talks in London in October 1960, the British Government told the Southern Cameroons delegation, that by framing the plebiscite questions the way it did, the UN had ruled out any period of continuing trusteeship as well as of independence. Consequently, they returned home cursed to choose between two options neither of which was their intrinsic choice. Still based on this information, the Secretary of State for Colonies, Mr. Iain Macleod clearly enunciated that if the plebiscite went in favour of joining Cameroon Republic, arrangements would be made for the early termination of Trusteeship and the transfer of sovereignty to the Republic of Cameroon even though this was not enshrined in any UN resolution.[387] These and other decisions of the British Government all derived their potency from the reports framed by Sir Sydney Phillipson, their hatchet man, whose appointment originated from the fertile mind of Malcolm Milne and inadvertence of ST Muna. Placed in sequence this saga is more theatrical than historical.

Open Support for KNC/KPP Alliance

The open assistance rendered to the opposition KNC/KPP Alliance (and later the CPNC party) by Malcolm Milne and his colleagues of the Colonial Office was probably because they were cocksure that with integration as its flagstaff, it would succeed. This was done in various ways. Returning to the situation in 1960, when the CPNC and the KNDP were seriously logged up in contest, Malcolm notes:

---

[386] Ibid., Anyangwe, p. 52.
[387] Report of the Plebiscite Commissioner, para. 68.

I tried to explain that Endeley and the members of the KNC/KPP alliance wasted no time in procuring the agreements of the United Kingdom and Nigerian governments to the steps that would be taken should the plebiscite of 11thFebruary1961 go in favour of Nigeria. The southern Cameroons would become a separate Region of independent Nigeria with all that entailed.[388]

Foncha and his KNDP on the other hand were blocked in every single direction as far as it went. For example, JO Field having buttressed the chances of Endeley and the KNC/KPP alliance in the forthcoming plebiscite, at the same time was mounting relentless pressure on Foncha and the KNDP to produce their own agreed stand with Ahidjo on reunification. Yet given his exalted position as the Commissioner of Southern Cameroons, he was looked up to as the Queen's Representative. As the ultimate person in charge, JO Field ought to have been a disinterested arbiter, but unfortunately:

> Foncha and his ministers hadn't reached agreement with Ahidjo, the British or, indeed, anybody, of the action necessary if the plebiscite went the other way. They did, however, put the cat amongst the pigeons when they told John Field on 20th July 1960 that Ahidjo had made it clear to them in their recent talks that the republic of Cameroun would not be able to assume responsibility for the security of southern Cameroons if the plebiscite went that way, Ahidjo apparently said that the internal and external security of the Cameroons in such an eventuality would have to be a matter for local provision.[389]

This was an awful betrayal of trust, and clearly indicated that the KNDP had no reason to trust the Commissioner at all. In short, what had taken place was unmitigated treachery, that instead, JO Field the Commissioner of Southern Cameroons used this inside information to rush the withdrawal of the British and Nigerian defence forces from the territory on the eve of independence despite the pleas and protests

---

[388]Ibid., Milne, *No Telephone*, p. 413, see also p.401.
[389]Ibid., p. 414.

of Southern Cameroonians and even of British expatriates in the territory. Rather, the British Government decided at this very vulnerable point in their history to abandon the defence of the territory they had administered for over forty years. Actually, Malcolm Milne openly declared that the British expatriates had withdrawn their loyalty from the Foncha government but no one could have guessed that they would sink so low. Nothing could be worse than this.[390] The British protectors had become predators; in other words, the chickens were turned over for safe keeping to the fox.

Deadly Traps: Withdrawal of British Troops

Malcolm Milne recounts with an air of solemnity how the British Government issued an ultimatum to Foncha and Ahidjo:

> On 23rd June 1961, the UK Foreign Office sent a joint telegram to Foncha and Ahidjo conveying HMG'S final views to both gentlemen regarding the matters raised between 15th and 17th May. HMG considered that the UNO resolution required the termination of UK trusteeship on 1st October 1961 and consequently after that date HMG would cease to have any responsibility for the affairs of the southern Cameroons.[391]

By these decisions, HMG empowered JO Field to slam the hardest measures possible on Foncha forcing him to the tightest corner. It should also be recalled that 15-17 May was precisely when the Tripartite Conference was holding at Buea, characterised by open collusion between the British and Cameroon Republic delegations at the expense of the Southern Cameroons delegation headed by Foncha. To make matters worse, all this happened with JO Field in the chair. Hence Malcolm Milne continues clearly with an air of sadistic humour and satisfaction to describe the unpreventable trap that the British Government had set for Foncha and his Government; a quotation that cannot be over emphasized[392]

---

[390]Ibid. p. 414, The Ebubu massacre occurred at about this time.
[391]*Southern Cameroons Press Release no. 434.*
[392]Idem.

It is inconceivable that the British Government, the Administering Authority, caretaker and protector could have been carrying out these nefarious plots against unsuspecting Southern Cameroonians placed in their charge by the UNO. No doubt Foley Newns dispatched by Sir James Robertson, the Governor General of Nigeria earlier in 1959, to assess the situation had noted: "that it was attempting the impossible to expect a top-heavy complicated ministerial system with a rapidly changing constitution to work with ministers lacking formal education," furthermore, unlike Malcolm Milne:

> He judged Foncha to be 'a nice little man in his own lights quite sincere.' He understood that Foncha and his ministers were much more honest than many of the more sophisticated ministers in West Africa but he feared most of them were 'incapable of appreciating the complications of the present situation. 'They were living in a dream world'.[393]

Foley Newn thought 'the people of the Republic of Cameroon were more sophisticated and will swallow these people up'. In this wise he pre-empted the scourging questioning which Sir Fraser was soon to undergo in the House of Commons and ultimately, remorsefully confessed to by Malcolm Milne himself .Consequently, in the report, Newn cautioned:

> It is quite contrary to all British ideas of organizing constitutional development in colonial territories to leave the future of a country entirely to the representatives of one political party which had only a bare majority and whose leaders are incompetent to appreciate the issues involved.[394]

True enough the KNDP had won by a thin majority the January1959 election and at one point the parties in parliament were stalemated at 13:13. Both Malcolm and Field advised a coalition government. But the issue was not that simple. The number of ballots

---

[393]Ibid. Milne, *No Telephone..435*.
[394]Ibid., p. 435.

cast in the 1959 election was: KNDP: 73.304; KNC: 35.327 KPP 16.027. The totals of 73.304 for the KNDP and KNC/KPP alliance: 51.354 far exceeded the number of seats won by that party as was to be exemplified in the plebiscite results and the immediate election, following. Above all, the KNDP had requested for an election which the administering authority refused insisting instead on a coalition government between parties with ideologies that were as far apart as water is from fire.

Remarkably, when all the parties finally agreed to annul the plebiscite and undertook a trip to London to get the approval of the British Government, surprisingly they were referred back to the UN as the ultimate authority. In the meantime, instructions were dispatched to the British representatives there to ensure that any requests from Southern Cameroons for the cancellation of the plebiscite be rejected out of hand sticking to the UN resolution which sanctioned the plebiscite. Attitudes like this totally forfeited the right of the British to be trusted and considered as arbiters of any worth. The same inside information was used to block the "third choice" or question, as:

> Sir James Robertson, (Governor General of Nigeria) and his close advisers in Lagos feared that propaganda based on such conceptions might produce if unchecked, a plebiscite result that would prove unwelcome or dangerous to Nigeria since many Cameroonians in favour of a third choice might vote for unification with the R of C ... or Foncha might seek assistance which, in the event of Britain being unwilling to provide it, might well be from a country inimical to Nigeria, such as China.[395]

This is one of the most awful revelations which confirms the declarations in the declassified secret British papers and clearly indicates how they blocked the choice of Southern Cameroons standing alone: the most popular option for the plebiscite of 11 February 1961 by which they would have achieved independence pure and simple. This choice, the British deliberately blocked for obscure, selfish reasons. This is incredible, deplorable and unpardonable and is

---

[395]Ibid., p. 414.

one of those bitter pills that will remain stuck in the throats of former Southern Cameroonians seeking rectification in the knowledge that history does not forgive those who do not learn its lessons.

Milne and Foncha: "No Love Lost"

In the literature available in which Malcolm Milne makes reference to John Ngu Foncha almost without exception, not a single one of them is made in a positive light. Malcolm Milne and ST Muna easily struck a bond of lifelong friendship, which he could trace precisely to: the day, date, spot and occasion, perhaps also because it was when Buea Mountain erupted in 1959. Malcolm Milne could some forty years later in 1999 recall very vividly that they had:

> By driving the commissioner's Land Rover to the station, and then walking, Muna and 1 could watch the lava emerging from the depths between lunch and tea. … Muna certainly did his share of cutting a path through the thick vegetation. I have one very Mau Mau photograph of him at work with a machete. There was no nonsense about his dignity as a minister preventing him doing labourer's work. We formed a bond at the time which has lasted for over forty years.[396]

Interestingly, when on a similar occasion, he had to close the door of Foncha's official car, as Prime Minister after a party at the Lodge, eye brows were raised and history made, simply because Malcolm Milne was Acting Deputy Commissioner of Her Majesty's Government and what he did was below his dignity.[397] It is generally held that love and hate, like and dislike, are matters of the heart and emotions that do not necessarily have to be justified or rationalized. However, it can be reiterated in this circumstance that neither Malcolm Milne nor his boss, JO Field remotely saw the political platform of Foncha and his KNDP as likely to win in the forthcoming plebiscite. To them, 'Little John' had backed the losing horse or as a matter of

---

[396]Ibid., p. 386. Muna was the Chief Scout of Southern Cameroons.
[397]Ibid., p. 415

feeling, anything, "Foncha" simply put Malcolm Milne off although it did not permit him to make unnecessary pejorative reports about him. A few instances would suffice to illustrate this trend of bad blood between them. During their joint trip to London in 1960, in an attempt to obviate the plebiscite, Malcolm Milne had the "pleasure" of reporting how:

> Lennox-Boyd very kindly gave a splendid luncheon party in Foncha's honour in the penthouse …it was a glorious September day and Foncha turned up wearing Bamenda robes topped by a small, highly decorated, Bamenda cap. The effect was spoiled somewhat by a t-shirt he was wearing below the Bamenda robes, the armholes of which were distinctly grubby. Lennox – Boyd, even sitting at table, towered above Foncha. I recall Foncha, in his confident manner looking up at him and saying you know something, Secretary of State?" 'No, what do 1 know?' said Lennox-Boyd, politely, looking down at his guest. 'We have pigeons in our own country too'; said Foncha sawing at his half partridge. Muna scowled; nobody laughed.[398]

This description of an isolated, pre-selected guest almost to the exclusion of the invitees at the party entirely concentrated on Foncha was excessively derogatory, unnecessary and negative for no obvious reason than to denigrate Foncha. Rather, on the contrary it speaks volumes not of Foncha but of the character of his self-appointed assailant. He had of a sudden become an expert in matters of Bamenda traditional dress code, table etiquette and further assigned himself the role of a critic and reporter. In one of his numerous confessions Malcolm Milne owns that what he has written in here is reinforced by "documents that were subsequently released under the thirty years' rule for examination at the Public Records Office" and that there was no secret agenda. However, all of this must be taken with a heavy pinch of salt. He admits that in Southern Cameroons, the test of the loyalty of expatriate staff became extremely severe as:

---

[398]Ibid., p. 397.

The gap between the over confident forecasts of the members of the KNDP Government and the likely flow of events widened, so much so that a conflict arose between the role of expatriate staff as loyal servants of the Cameroons Government and their duty as representatives of the trusteeship authority. [399]

Although he does not indicate it here, he, Malcolm Milne was one of the leading expatriates who found it difficult to remain loyal to the KNDP Government or much less to Foncha as a person, because the expatriate staff deliberately and consistently took sides with the KNC/KPP alliance.[400] He equally admits that Southern Cameroonian researchers have asked 'what was the true intention of the HM Government at any one time?[401] So far and from his own mouth no one who has followed this account can be left in doubt as to what Malcolm Milne's attitude was towards Mr. John Ngu Foncha, the Prime Minster of Southern Cameroons. This could be described as anything ranging from the outrageous through the ridiculous to the treacherous. By Malcolm Milne, Foncha never did anything right. As they say, the eye sees not itself.

Certainly, there must have been security reports about him. As he puts it in his own way and in his own words: when his boss, JO Field was on leave, it devolved on him, and he had the task of explaining the weakness of Foncha's position to him. This can be deduced to have been that he, Foncha was backing the wrong horse, namely reunification. Then unexpectedly the axe fell and Malcolm Milne in his own words recounts how:

> On 8th December 1 received a letter from Foncha which he requested I should forward to the United Nations and to the HMG. This letter demanded my immediate removal from office on the grounds that my attitude and my criticism of the documents they had jointly produced with Ahidjo were non-constitutional on

---

[399] Ibid., p. 405.
[400] Ibid., p. 401.
[401] Ibid., p. 405; Discussion with Prof. V Fanso.

my part and a major source of opposition to him and his ministers.⁴⁰²

Clearly, therefore, it can be deduced that Malcolm Milne's reports on Foncha, his cabinet and party had overstepped their bounds becoming excessively and unduly negative and Foncha could not stand it anymore. This was even without knowing what finally came to the open in the declassified British secret papers. In any case, as a consequence, Malcolm Milne was declared persona non grata, directly by Foncha himself. However, the fences were soon patched up between them and the letter Foncha had written was withdrawn but the doddering poor as Malcolm only intensified his negative confidential reporting about Foncha to HMG. Nevertheless, that the KNDP finally won overwhelmingly in the plebiscite largely indicates who was wrong since all along the colonial service filed in bias reports. Malcolm's repeated confessions and apologies bear final testimony.

Furthermore, that his spite for Foncha was almost pathological is demonstrated by the fact that he could not stand the fact of Foncha's widespread popularity following his triumph in the plebiscite and the enactment of independence with ensuing euphoric celebrations with Foncha at the centre of it all. Malcolm's morbid animosity was amply demonstrated when he openly declared his feelings on the evening of 30 September 1961 as he drove with an exuberant President Ahidjo in the Commissioner's car from Tiko to Buea after the declaration of independence. Malcolm was not ashamed to note: "If the primary objective of his visit was to divert limelight from Foncha this was successfully achieved".⁴⁰³

Malcolm Milne Takes Seriously ill

Malcolm Milne had not remotely expected that the KNDP and reunification could carry the day in the plebiscite although he bravely maintains, when finally it happened: "The result was not unexpected, 97.741 in favour of joining Nigeria and 233, 571 for union with the Republic of Cameroon." But then he continues "my mind was

---

⁴⁰²NAB., *Press Release No. 416.*, also *No Telephone*, p.406.
⁴⁰³Ibid., pp. 426-7.

full of last minute difficulties concerning the plebiscite".[404]This was even though there was serious illness and eventual death of a close family member. Proof that Malcolm Milne was barely putting on a brave face is illustrated in what followed next. With the plebiscite results declared in early February, by month end his family were on leave and "went to Austria to get some skiing" but within six days he was taken seriously ill. He had to be taken to Britain, where he was hospitalised for three weeks. During this time: "I was in bed or sitting in an arm chair. Any sort of activity and the aches, pains and nausea returned".[405]He had been diagnosed with jaundice. From February ending it was only at the end of May 1961, that he was able to return to Southern Cameroons although still very weak. Malcolm Milne however, does not in any way directly link his illness to the devastating effect of the plebiscite results that had gone massively in favour of reunification with the Republic of Cameroon, which he had predicted was impossible,[406]but by insinuation it is obvious.

Wrapping Up

History seeks answers to questions and does not permit gaps and emptiness. By applying the parameters of: logic, cause, course and effect and asking the traditional insatiable questions: who, what, when, why, where and how, it becomes necessary to find out why Malcolm Milne made the terse observation juxtaposing Foncha and Ahidjo. This was his last day (actually 30 September – 1 October 1961) in Cameroon, Ahidjo's visit was brief, while Foncha generally identified with his flowing Bamenda gown ever afterwards continued to bathe in massive probations during his public appearances. Malcolm Milne had already confessed and apologized repeatedly and profusely though not

---

[404]Idem.

[405]Idem.

[406]Robert Louis Stevenson's enigmatic and challenging novel, *Dr. Jekyll and Mr. Hyde,* Two Diametrically Opposite Persona in One Person. However, Malcom Milne continued to apologise profusely and expressed his remorse about the dismal British administrative record in Southern Cameroons during public manifestations he chaired or attended in Britain while on retirement to individuals like Professors: Verkijika Fanso and Mathew Gwanfogbe, who encountered him during the 1990s in London.

directly to Foncha (at least not on record);*the plebiscite, reunification and independence were now fait accompli and part of history, so why would Malcolm Milne persist in consciously harbouring such bitter feelings against a man he was unlikely to meet formally. Was Malcolm Milne alone in this strange feeling, and for that matter, why had JO Field whose responsibility it was, though still in Cameroon to delegate Malcolm Milne, a man who had not come to terms with the disbanding of the British Empire, to deputize for him? That Malcolm ostensibly was still harbouring this painful self-inflicted bitter memory till 1999, the year of Foncha's demise marked by a memorable, resounding and oversubscribed state burial, which he surely must have learnt about only adds to Malcolm Milne's enigmatic behaviour.

Malcolm Milne Sets Final Seal on Conspiracy Theories

Malcolm Milne's mind-set underwent a complete 360 revolution, a situation that converted him from a zealous advocate and loyal executor of instructions from Whitehall, which until then he had considered infallible, to a rabid critic of the entire British colonial system. However, the theatrical manner in which this happened would call for psychiatric explanation to say the least. This is because these dramatic changes in his thought pattern all happened as if in a trance, within the wee hours of First October 1961, as he settled to write his ultimate report to the Colonial Office about the ceremony in which he had discharged his primordial role of declaring the nationhood of Southern Cameroons after over forty years of British tutelage.[407] Apparently, in carrying out that crucial exercise, the scales of deceit were suddenly cast off and he henceforth saw things in a completely different light in revocation of all that he had stood for. There are those who would consider him a typical split personality; a sort of Dr. Jekyll and Mr. Hyde.[408]

---

[407]Ibid., *No Telephone*, p. 21.
[408]Ibid., See John Percival, *the Southern Cameroons Plebiscite*, p. 103.

Malcolm Milne Receives President Ahidjo

Tiko International Airport 30 August 1961

However, Malcolm Milne himself disclosed that his attitudes and objectives of his work had kept on changing at different stages in the service. Expressly, he declared; "l joined the service with what l believed was a job for life eventually to find that the same service was being used to disband the empire, no longer to continue to maintain it".[409] Most strikingly, Kirk Green, his colleague, who wrote the preface to his autobiography already, disagreed with Malcolm Milne's observations and expectations of life in the British Colonial Service. Without mincing words he pointed out that: Malcolm belonged to the 'old school' and was out of step with the evolving times". Thus it could be concluded that owing to his idiosyncratic attitude, Malcolm Milne was a late convert to what was so obvious and logical, the decline and dissolution of the British Empire as all the others before it.

To this could be added the question he personally raised for research, what really the British objectives were in Southern Cameroons and the fact that they would rue for mishandling the nice little people of that territory one day. Amazingly, John Percival, his compatriot who had a Southern Cameroons experience from a vastly different angle as a UN Plebiscite Officer, like in a mathematical equation arrived at the same conclusion with Malcolm Milne; that the British Government had done the nice people of Southern Cameroons a great disservice, would rue it, and should right that grave wrong.[410] However, until Malcolm Milne wrote this report in which he underwent the miraculous transformation: when he drove with President Ahidjo from Tiko in the Commissioners' land rover, it was his most pleasant and fulfilling moment that for once, Foncha was placed out of the lime light and President Ahidjo had taken central stage.[411]

Milne and Ahidjo: Accomplices over Southern Cameroons

Putting Malcolm Milne and Ahmadou Ahidjo together may seem odd at first, nevertheless, interestingly; they were perfect bedfellows, acting as conspirators and accomplices, when it concerned their spite for Southern Cameroons and its political leadership epitomised especially by Foncha and Jua. The facts speak for themselves. This was clearly demonstrated on the floor of the meeting at the Buea Tripartite Conference when as a member of the British team; they colluded with the Republic of Cameroon Delegation led by President Ahidjo and nailed the Foncha cabinet over issues of defence, economic support, the repository of power and in short, the political isolation of the Foncha regime. The correspondence by Malcolm Milne and his boss, JO Field on Foncha with the Colonial Office in London bore massive testimony of this collusion and hate. Above all, it was Malcolm Milne, who, deputising for JO Field presided over the handing-over ceremony of Southern Cameroons to Ahidjo instead of Foncha, first at the Tiko International Airport and finally at Buea Mountain Hotel. As he declared when he drove President Ahidjo from Tiko in the Commissioner's land rover to Buea, out of unmitigated spite for Foncha, it was his most pleasant and fulfilling moment that for once, Foncha was placed out of the lime light.[412]

410
[411]Ibid., *No telephone*, p.147.
[412]Ibid., No telephone p.447.

In conclusion, taking a tall, holistic look at the man; Malcolm Milne acquits himself honourably. Ironically and astonishingly; finally, rather unexpectedly, but most equitably the entire mess is put to rest by no other person than Malcolm Milne himself. This is doubtlessly an act of great fortitude. He had duty-bound, ignited the smear campaigns against Foncha and the KNDP Government but finally in acknowledgment paid generous, glowing tribute to the Foncha cabinet. It is clear that his attitude all along had been conditioned by his unflinching patriotism and dedication to the service of his "Fatherland" and the firm conviction that whatever he did was in its best interest, until he was undeceived at the very last critical moment.

When that instant came, like Saint Paul of old, he was forthright, courageous and bold, keeping nothing back. Seen in this perspective, Malcolm Milne emerges as a typical British diplomat with a single track mind dedicated specifically to the service of his homeland, "My country right or wrong". But, he had the superb courage to denounce it when he got convinced that a grave wrong had been done to the "nice little people of Southern Cameroons". No mortal could ask for more, and no person could have balanced the equation better than Malcolm Milne did, thus distinctly marking him out as an embodiment of a sincere persona imbued with fortitude, deep introspection, a bountiful heart and readiness to admit error: the insignia of a soul at peace with itself in the ruthless, self-interested, faceless world of British colonial policy that was conceived by the "Whitehall Warriors" in his own words in London.

Certainly, in comparison this is far less than the brutal exploitation they visited on some of their erstwhile colonies such as Kenya, where they are making amends through apologies and huge financial compensations to the "Mau Mau" torture survivals at their hands. As well, the peace loving, loyal and hospitable people of Southern Cameroons did not deserve the dastardly manner in which they were denied autonomy and abandoned in the hands of a predator, whose apparent role was to ensure their perpetual subjugation. In this context, Malcolm Milne acquits himself honourably, especially, where he takes the stand that the British owe an obligation to right the wrongs done to these gentle people; he stands among the tallest he ranks amongst the best British diplomats, politicians or citizens as a great patriot of his time.

The Milnes and Munas Live Long Friendship

ST Muna, Mrs. Milne, Mrs. Muna and Malcolm Milne in 1980

Postscript

About History
"It is History and not the Historians that Society Requires" (Marwick)

A Brief Note on the Historian's Craft: Historiography

History is written following set principles defined by "historiography" and not merely the presentation of a catalogue of facts. Isolated facts in history make no sense. They must be seen in the context of place, time and circumstance. That is why similar facts and events occurring or happening in the same place, affecting the same or different persons at different times are characteristically different. History, therefore, cannot and does not repeat itself as it is impossible to re-enact past experiences, no second, no minute, nothing exactly repeats itself. This makes all historical comparisons at best, lame, and 'casual comparisons' dangerous. It is an "art" and "science" best handled by those trained in the craft. History is far more than just recounting the past, and credible history results from constructed solid facts and principles coded in historiography, the science of the craft of history. Otherwise, simply put, the craft of history is about the ceaseless search for the facts that bring to light the truth about our ancestral past; and since they are no longer there to answer our questions, this search is forever open. Consequently, no final full stop has ever been put to any topic in history. This requires stringent effort and as Ensor posits:

> The Historian must be determined to play the game, to deal in facts, not fiction. And as part of that he must strive to do his best to be impartial. I doubt if impartiality comes naturally to anybody; but it is possible to acquire a large measure of it by trying.[413]

---

[413] RCK Ensor, in: *Why We Study History* Manson Publishing Company, Oron 1990

In other words, few are born with these professional ethics, which comprise: distinguishing between facts, fiction and opinion, embellishments, propaganda, defence, denigration and self-projection. These have to be consciously cultivated through rigorous exposure to peer review and subjection to critical examination.

Levels of History

At the level of the primary school, history is defined simply as "the story of the past" children are taught basic facts based on people, place, time and circumstances which they retain by rote memory. This tends to make the study of history boring and discourages many. In the secondary school as they get older and their horizons widen children are taught to distinguish facts from opinion. They are introduced to causes or reasons course results and effects of historical events. They are equally taught to reason, analyse and categorize historical data. At the General Certificate of Education (GCE) A/L, they are more mature adults and history is no longer just a "story of the past"; its wider dimensions and ramifications are introduced. They are equally introduced to serious critical, logical thinking as they have to analyse, criticize, compare, and contrast and even to "compare and contrast" thereby being challenged to form objective opinions in concluding their essays or answering exam questions.

At the undergraduate or tertiary level in the university, they are introduced to still greater, critical, logical reasoning, as well as to historiography; the craft of history. History is far more than just recounting or narrating facts, dates and names at the tertiary level. Here critical analysis and interpretation is called for, reading, digging beyond the facts that catch the eye but sorting, classifying and presenting logical incontestable information that can stand the test of time. They are introduced to research methodology through writing reports, term essays and finally long essays. It takes a more solid formation and background by drawing from kindred disciplines in the humanities and social sciences (Archaeology, Anthropology, Sociology, Geography, Economics, Philosophy, Law and Logic). That is why history, described as the repository or "collective memory" of a community is classified as second only to the Bible (Koran) in providing wisdom from its rich store of common knowledge. In this connection, Richard TA Murphy articulates it: "History is a jewel with a thousand faces and Bible History is in a class by itself: clever, sophisticated, creative, often poetic, almost always entertaining and instructive." He further quotes Toynbee, who holds that, "History is a vision ... of God revealing Himself in action to souls that were sincerely seeking him".[414] However, unlike the Bible, History though abiding by eternal, universal values, is unyieldingly neutral and does not forgive those who do not learn from its lessons.

History Should be Logical, Chronological and Credible

"If the historian cannot say it then nobody else can." However this only applies when historical facts are based on thorough investigation with concrete supporting data as on his own the historian has no authority save that afforded by his sources. His credit is limited to his competence in collecting, analysing and interpreting his data.

It is for this reason that anything classified as history or as historical should of necessity be credible, a reference point for posterity, clarifying doubts and placing people and events in their correct and proper perspectives. To be factual, these must be based on scientific, statistical, concrete and verifiable sources. While historians may differ in their opinions and interpretation of facts of history, the facts themselves should never be in dispute because of their analytical, scientific, concrete, chronological and logical origins. No level of education or qualification can replace source material for the points of view presented by any historian of worth. The word "History" is derived from Greek and Latin, "Historia", and means, "I report on /after inquiry, investigation or research." Thus nobody speaks as a historian on his own authority. Nor are historical facts the preserve of any category of people - they should be available to the public or they are not historical. Arthur Marwick cautions on the historian and his work: "It is history rather than the historian which society requires: the

---

[414] Richard TA Murphy, *Background to the Bible, An Introduction To Scripture Study*, Servant Books, AN Arbor, Michigan, p.196. (By courtesy of Mr. Francis Nkwatoh).

historian who is too conscious of social needs may well produce bad history".[415]

Functional History

Another important point to note in this connection is that history and historical facts are not about perfect human beings; 'saints, sinners or devils' living in some ethereal world. No, it is about ordinary human beings with their short comings, strengths and weaknesses. These Southern Cameroons leaders like political leaders the world over, were naturally products of their time, place and circumstances. In other words, they were the best that their society could offer and any comparisons made outside this context are lame and in historical terms "anachronistic". The bulk of them were patriots, dedicated and selfless with great visions for their "beloved motherland".[416] They burnt out their lives and made enormous sacrifices in the service of their people and their community and in so doing, made their mistakes and learnt by them. It cannot be over emphasized that all comparisons in history are made within context; juxtaposed with similar examples and never in isolation.

Pseudo-History

This is slanted and inadmissible history. Writing history based on prejudice "Conspiracy Theories", gossips, skewed or biased information such as in Nazi Germany under Hitler, Fascist Italy under Mussolini, Communist Russia under Stalin, Communist North Korea. This type of history has led whole countries like China and Japan into serious conflicts or even threats of war and some of them have had to be officially re-written. Talk about Nazi Germany's genocide of the Jews, Armenian genocide or Rwandan genocide have entered the realm of legality punishable by law, when denounced by any individual. Other qualities of pseudo-history include work that uncritically accepts myths and anecdotal evidence without scepticism or work with political, racial, religious or other ideological agenda. Pseudo History includes:

---

[415] Arthur Marwick, *The Nature of History*, Macmillan Publishers Ltd.1985, p. 16
[416] Ibid., P M Kale.

selecting or ignoring evidence contrary to healthy views or work that is speculative, controversial, facts without foundation, unjustified interpretations; facts taken out of context; giving undue weight, distorted either innocently, accidentally or fraudulently playing on ignorance of the masses. History has a way of auto –correcting itself and pseudo-history sooner or later gets caught up with the truth either after further research or simply with time, after the dust settles and the facts are laid bare. Currently, we are witnesses to the fact that George Bush and Tony Blair have been tried for their policies in the Iraqi and Afghanistan wars in the "court of popular opinion".

This background commentary arises from the need to place the issues surrounding the Reunification regarded as a Gamble raised in the Summit Magazine interview in their accurate historical perspective. Basic knowledge of History as can be observed is imperative for all citizens, who desire and deserve to understand the background to the daily events touching not only Cameroon but Africa and the world. For this reason history is not the preserve of any special category of people. It should be read for pleasure, as well as for information or above all, as a profession for those opting to teach or to engage in diplomacy or other liberal professions. In some cases it is basic for survival; Fanso aptly captures this sense when he says:

> History is an interesting but delicate subject because the past we are writing about is never dead to the present and also because it is written and rewritten. Whoever thinks that the dead do not bite and that the past is gone for good does not think history.[417]

It is also known that history has a way of auto-correction arising from the fact that every generation is challenged to rewrite its history in the light of new discoveries such as those in the declassified British secret papers, memoirs, debates, archaeological findings or simply through peer review processes. Consequently, like in all intellectual

---

[417] See open letter: Professor Fanso on Professor VJ Ngoh's Reaction to his Valediction Address of Friday 23 September 2011, p.3. The real subject which should have emerged at the in3te2r4view should have focused on why these issues so widely and wildly reported by officials of the British Colonial Office did not feature at the Bamenda All Party Conference or at the Foumban Constitutional Conference

pursuits, no one has ever put a final full stop to any topic in history since it is dynamic and forever under regeneration and research. Though it deals with the past, history is continuous, alive, and dynamic; everything that "exists" is a subject of history and actually nothing exists outside history, whether active, passive or indifferent. As historians writing the history of our fatherland or any other history we owe it in trust to our venerable ancestors and, as an obligation to posterity to render nothing but what is credible, factual and balanced. Perfect history as such may remain elusive but this objective remains inalienable to the discipline. Knowledge of basic history is every citizen's right. All said and done, history is art and, carefully researched history should be inspiring and capable of being read for pleasure, entertainment, relaxation and ultimately for self-actualisation.

Epilogue

Below is the Summit Magazine No. 16 April –June 2011 interview with Professor, Victor Julius Ngoh anchored by Kange Williams Wasaloko (Publisher, Acting Editor-in-Chief) reproduced in full.

"Fifty Years after Reunification: Southern Cameroons Had a Raw Deal Because of the Greed of KNDP Politicians.

Foreword - The Reunification Gamble: Setting the Records Straight (sic)

Professor Victor Ngoh epitomizes history, history of Cameroon, and especially the history of sentiments that are goading Cameroon's English population. In featuring an exclusive interview with this unassuming but well-versed intellectual, we would be attempting to find answers to the numerous "why" that has cast doubts on the honesty of those we have referred to as the fathers of Reunification.

In accepting the deals that were struck between Foncha and Ahidjo how much of the people's interest was considered? Fifty years after Reunification, can anyone say that there was a balance in the negotiation leading to this union?

There doesn't seem to be any turning back now; but were you to bring back to life the Fonchas, Munas, Endeleys, Egbe Tabis, Fonlons, Mbiles and others, what account will they give to their people? Will they regret their selfish attitudes to the detriment of the people who heartedly hailed them? Or are they rolling in their tombs in total disarray for leaving their people in a disparaging mood? Why were the negotiations for the independence of Southern Cameroons as a separate and sovereign state torpedoed? Why were the constitutional talks in Foumban so one-sided as though the Southern Cameroons had no legal or constitutional experts?

Why were our leaders so blind-folded as to say "yes" to everything that was proposed to them?

Why did they seem to have been so ignorant and exposed their fool-hardiness because of a larger morsel of bread?

Why did they not listen to the counsel of some British experts who warned that they will be "swallowed" by the "locust-like" invasion from the East?.

Why were negotiations not based on equal partnership?

Why was the house of the negotiation so divided thus opening large loopholes for the other negotiator to manipulate their intelligence?

Why did the name of the country have to change at every bat of the eye? Fifty years down the line these questions have continued to haunt us.

The eventuality as is the case now is to "let the sleeping dogs lie"

Those who could have given us a clarification have bowed out of the scene. All we can do today is to speculate. However, we feel blessed to be endowed with historians despite some controversies in relating the sequence of events leading to Reunification; give us some food for thought.

Professor Victor Ngoh is one of them and we should benefit from his intellectual largesse. Peter Esoka (Editorial Adviser)

50yrs after Reunification - Southern Cameroons Had a Raw Deal Because of the Greed of KNDP Politicians

Prof Victor Julius Ngoh is one of the few authoritative researchers in Cameroon history. At the time when Cameroon history is polluted by some writers who have used their cultural background to distort facts about our history, Professor Victor Julius Ngoh has always stood firm on the truth about the process towards reunification, laying emphasis on the role of southern Cameroons politicians at the time. His stand that the KNDP politicians placed their personal interest ahead of their followers did not auger well to some people who tainted his public image tagging him a persona non-grata in his own country.

However today his position is being amplified by even those who black mailed him. Professor Victor Ngoh still maintains today that the greed of the southern Cameroons politicians was responsible for the raw deal in the process towards reunification coupled with the fact that John Ngu Foncha the southern Cameroons leader in the reunification struggle had struck a deal with Ahidjo that should the reunification process go through, he will be made vice president. Professor Victor Ngoh who is currently deputy vice-chancellor/research, corporation and relations with the business world, has written over twenty research publications on Cameroon Africa and the World. He is currently writing an essay titled" The hidden facts about the reunification of Cameroon. When we sat down to chat with him in his office at UB, the learned professor took time to release certain revelations amongst them was the fact that Foncha received material and financial support from Douala based billionaire, late Soppo Priso. He also revealed that ghost voters were imported from the Republic of Cameroon to vote in favour of reunification. This is just the tip of the interview we conducted for your documentation. Excepts.(sic)

Summit Magazine: The Venue for the celebration of the 50th anniversary Cameroon's reunification is up in the air pending the announcement of the Head of State, Paul Biya. Some people talk of Buea, others say Kumba, Bamenda and Foumban. As a historian where should the celebrations take place?

Professor Victor Julius Ngoh: Well I think it should be made absolutely clear, the reunification event was between British Southern Cameroons and the Republic of Cameroon. The centre of the power in British Southern Cameroon was in Buea. All negotiations between Ahidjo and Foncha in British Southern Cameroons were held in Buea. So there is absolutely no reason to say Kumba, Bamenda or Foumban should host the event. It should be made clear that even in in the days of the German colonial administration in 1904, the capital of German Cameroon was transferred from Douala to Buea. So nobody should think of another place except Buea. As a historian, I will say Buea is the natural host for the celebrations. It is now left for the politicians, elites, traditional leaders and opinion leaders to lobby the Head of State to announce the choice of Buea as the venue early enough.

As someone who has written extensively on Cameroon, what briefly are the reasons that were advanced by politicians at the time in favour of reunification?

For the purpose of clarification, I wish to mention that reunification was the least popular option. The most popular option was secession and independence of Southern Cameroons as a separate entity, followed by independence in association with Nigeria. The problem with reunification was that, the KNDP led by Dr. John Ngu Foncha was very smart and it tailored its messages according to the audience it was addressing at the time. This was enhanced by the confusion that emerged after the London Conference of November 1960, when Foncha and a good number of Southern Cameroonians went to London to impress on the Her Majesty's Government to reverse the United Nations' decision of 1959 and grant Southern Cameroons independence as a separate state. That request was rejected but the population though that the request was granted and this was also compounded by the fact that the KNDP made the population believe that there was a transitional period of five years, during which should reunification fail, Southern Cameroons will walk out from the union. The politicians, however, failed to understand that section 47 of the Federal Constitution ruled out the possibility of secession. So, on the day of election, most Southern Cameroons' voters thought they were voting for Southern Cameroons as a separate state or that they had five-year- trial period. You have to also bear in mind that the very popular area in favour of reunification was the Northwest or Grassfield population. The plebiscite options were twisted to be a struggle between the Grassfield led by Foncha and the Forest Zone led by Dr. E.M. L. Endeley. It is important to note that at that time, a good proportion of the workers in the plantation in the Forest zone came from the Grassfield and this tilted the population.

Unfortunately, the Cameroon peoples National Congress Party, the CPNC, led by Dr. EML Endeley did a very poor job as far as the campaigning was concerned. They relied a lot on the insecurity in the Republic of Cameroon and they felt that the intense insecurity in the Republic of Cameroon will naturally influence the voters to vote against reunification whereas Foncha and the KNDP whipped up the anti-Ibo scare and most of the electorate voted for reunification partly because of the fear of the Ibos at the time.

One other argument the politicians put forward factor for reunification was that the salary scale in Southern Cameroons was lower than what obtained in La Republique du Cameroun. How much did this influence the move towards reunification?

That was absolutely no factor because there wasn't any contact between the civil servants in British Southern Cameroons and the civil servants of La Republique du Cameroun to the extent that they were able to discuss their salary scales. So, the issues of salary scale between the two entities had no part to play in the reunification exercise.

Contemporary politicians increasingly blame the architects of reunification. It is that they lacked negotiation skills or that personal interest was put before that of the region?

All the issues were put on the table. Unfortunately, the KNDP decided to do the negotiation alone. The KNDP even refused to take along the British experts whom the Colonial Office had put at their disposal. You also have to understand that the KNDP government

lacked sufficient qualified personnel and therefore their negotiation skills were weak, and for one reason or the other which is difficult to understand, is that the KNDP did not follow the advice of the colonial master to take along the Southern Cameroons Bar Association. This was very detrimental to the KNDP at the Yaoundé Tripartite Conference Talks of 2-7 August 1961 because this conference, which came after the Foumban Conference of 17-21 July 1961, was meant to put the proposals from the Foumban Conference into legal form. The delegation that the KNDP took to the Tripartite Conference did not include the Southern Cameroons Bar Association in spite of the fact that the KNDP was advised to take along legal/constitutional experts from the Bar Association. This was enough proof that a deal had been concluded between Ahidjo and Foncha to the effect that should the Federal system succeed, Foncha would be Vice President and Muna the Federal Minister, and if Foncha stepped down as Prime Minister of West Cameroon, A.N.Jua would become Prime Minister.

Apart from Foncha and Muna who were not well educated there were other figures like E. T Egbe, Engo and Gorgi Dinka who were lawyers. Were their views not consulted?

In fact, Southern Cameroons had quite a handful of lawyers at the time. Why was the Southern Cameroons Bar Association not invited? Surprisingly, Emmanuel Tabi Egbe was an influential member of the pro-KNDP think tank. He was not invited, and if you do recall, during the All Anglophone Conference in Buea in 1993, Foncha and Muna told participants that they had a poor deal because they lacked the lawyers. That is not true. The lawyers were there but they were not consulted. They did not even invite the Attorney General, E. K Mensah.

According to you, as a historian, where did the error really come from?

The error was that at the end of the day, the Southern Cameroons politicians were more interested in promoting their personal interest. There is something which is very tricky in the whole exercise. The draft Federal Constitution was discussed in the National Assembly of the Republic of Cameroon in August 1961 and President Ahmadou Ahidjo signed it into law on September 1st, 1961. So the Federal Constitution was signed into law on September 1, 1961. There was nothing as the Federal Republic of Cameroon then. So Ahidjo signed the Federal Constitution as the President of the Republic of Cameroon and when the Southern Cameroons House of Assembly discussed it, it was not to adopt or ratify it. Rather, S.T Muna tabled a motion on September18, 1961 calling on the House to approve the method and the brotherly co-operation which the governments of Southern Cameroons and the Republic of Cameroon displayed to have the Federal Constitution. That was a major problem.

Fifty years after reunification. Do you think that the Anglophones have had a fair share of this political marriage?

You see, we have to be very careful. If we take off by saying that former Southern Cameroons and the Republic of Cameroon reunited as equal partners, then we are deceiving ourselves. The harsh realities that most of us do not want to accept for one reason or the other is that the reunification did not take place between two equal partners. The Republic of Cameroon was independent, had a national anthem, a flag and a motto. It had all the attributes of sovereignty and was a member of the United Nations. It sent its ambassadors to other sovereign countries and also received theirs. Southern Cameroons had no flag, no national anthem nor motto; in fact, no attributes of sovereignty. It was still a UN Trust Territory. So for public consumption, Ahmadou Ahidjo said the two would come together as equal partners. But the hard and unpleasant reality was that one was independent and the other was not. Let me tell you a sad story, in 1959, the British Secretary of State for Colonies asked one of his officials to undertake a study trip to the Southern Cameroons. After his five – day stay in Southern Cameroons, he wrote a report in which he said the Republic of Cameroon might swallow Southern Cameroons and that the people of the Republic of Cameroon were more sophisticated that those in Southern Cameroons. He used the word "swallow' and referred to Southern Cameroonians as these nice little people. And 50 years later, you can draw your own conclusion on the above prophetic words. It should be pointed out that Foncha was not really in favour of Southern Cameroons attaining independence as a separate state. In March 1956, Foncha told Eastwood of the Colonial Office, in confidence, that he did not see Southern Cameroons as being an independent separate political entity as a permanent solution. This is what Cameroonians do not know.

Where did Ahidjo draw his strength in terms of negotiation? Was it only with the support of French advisor. Some people go as far as saying that, French businessmen bribed Southern Cameroon's politicians?

First of all, it should be understood that Ahidjo was not very interested in reunification. What he wanted was reunification with British Northern Cameroons only because of the Moslem population. If that option was not accepted, he would reluctantly accept reunification with both British Southern and Northern Cameroons. Reunification with Southern Cameroons only was a last resort to Ahidjo. This came out very clearly on January 1, 1960 during the independence anniversary when Foncha led a 12-man delegation to Yaoundé. During the celebration, Foncha talked about the virtues of reunification unlike Ahidjo whose address hadn't a single sentence on reunification. So to answer your question as to where Ahidjo got his strength, he was very much aware that Foncha was in a desperate position. As far back as October 1956, Foncha had written a confidential letter to Soppo Priso begging for financial and material assistance to be used against the KNC and the KPP which wanted independence with Nigeria unlike the KNDP which wanted independence with their brothers of Eastern Cameroon. Soppo Priso and the Pro-reunificationist groups in the Republic of Cameroon provided material and financial support to the KNDP.

Why was the idea of Southern Cameroon gaining independence with Nigeria not very popular amongst people of the Grassfield region?

The idea was not very popular due to the harsh treatment Southern Cameroonians received from Nigerians especially the Ibos at the time. Secondly, the battle was seen as being between the Grassfield led by Foncha and the Forest Zone led by Dr. E.M.L Endeley. Those who were from the Grassfield naturally supported their own person and since they had the numerical strength, they normally won the day. It is important to mention that in some areas like in Nso where you had Vincent Lainjo of the KNC, for several years, he had the support of the KNC in that area.

Let's talk about the London Conference of November 1960 and the role in the reunification process?

You see, in October 1959, the KNDP, KNC and KPP accepted that the plebiscite question should be reunification with French Cameroon or association with Nigeria. The KNDP militants felt that Foncha had betrayed them because Foncha had promised that the question would not be reunification versus association with Nigeria. Foncha had told them that he would get a trusteeship extended for two to three years. When he went to London and it was nailed down that the question would be reunification with the Republic of Cameroon or association with Nigeria, it got to a point where Augustine Ngom Jua sent him a telegram saying what he had done was very unpopular. In fact, things got to a stage where moves to force Foncha to resign as President of the KNDP but he was able to weather the storm. So that option of reunification with the Republic of Cameroon was very unpopular. It got to a point where the CPNC and KNDP convinced Foncha and the Southern Cameroons Commissioner J O Field that it would be better that they should go back to London and revisit the UN compromise. Precisely at this time, you had the Kamerun United Party, KUP, of PM Kale who came out strongly for independence as a separate state. So these politicians with J O Field went to London to request the British government to revisit the plebiscite option. At one time it was thought that the Southern Cameroons delegation would get their request accepted but things changed because the British government found out from its representatives at the UN that the plebiscite option would not be reviewed. In addition, the Afro-Asian bloc was very much against small African countries having independence since the Afro-Asian bloc was against the balkanization of Africa. So then they came back from the London Conference they did not really explain to the population that what they went for, had failed. Immediately after their return, Foncha went to Yaoundé and met Ahidjo; and they signed the two Alternatives reaffirming the October 1959 plebiscite compromise.

Let's talk about the plebiscite. How did it go?

The Plebiscite was well conducted. In September 1960, the Southern Cameroons Order-in-Council was signed; dividing British Southern Cameroons into 26 constituencies or electoral districts and the campaign went on smoothly. As I said earlier, the CPNC had a very poor campaign strategy. Their whole message was that blood was flowing in the Republic of Cameroon, "the UPC terrorists are killing people there – is that where you want to go?" etc… Such as Campaign was not very convincing at the time. The KNDP was more aggressive in the field especially as they had financial and material support from the Republic of Cameroon. What is not well known is that some people came from the Republic of Cameroon and voted for KNDP. These voters were, for instance, transported from Loum, Nkongsamba, and Mbanga.

Let's look at the heart of the negotiation process. Is it true that Foncha refused to present the draft constitution to his Anglophone peers before the Foumban conference?

In fact, I do recall when I first wrote that in 1990, it created a whole lot of problems to the extent that in certain areas, I was declared persona non grata. I have a copy of the threatening letter in my library. How the writer declared me a persona non grata in my own country beats my imagination. But today, everybody is saying that it is true. Yes, it is true. In Dr. E. M. L. Endeley's opening speech at the Foumban conference of July 17-21, 1961, he said "some of us are seeing this document" here for the first time. I had the privilege of interviewing S. T. Muna, N. N. Mbile and Moussa Yaya. They all confirmed that. There is a confidential note that the British Commissioner at the time, J O Field, sent to London also confirming that. It is important to note that J O Field's confidential note goes further to say that based on reliable information, Foncha and Ahidjo had struck a deal.

The first point is that no actual discussion of substance took place because the southern Cameroons delegates. They were shocked to discover that after preparing their position in the Bamenda "All-

Constitutional Conference" of June 1961 with the understanding that then they got to Foumban, they would place their document on the table together with that of the Republic of Cameroon and both sides would debate and reach a consensus. But they were shocked when Ahidjo told them that "this is what you have to work on. I gave this document to Foncha a long time ago." What makes it worse was that the document presented to them in Foumban was in French. So they had to take time to work on the translation. While that was being done, the delegates from La Republique were bored and were walking about. Confirmed reports say the delegates from Southern Cameroons were well treated. They were given all what they wanted and I use the words all what they wanted. So they felt at ease and believed that these were really our brothers who would take care of us.

To whom was the sovereignty of the Southern Cameroons given?

This is an issue which the SCNC has been playing about a lot. Some books say the sovereignty of the Southern Cameroons was handed over to Ahmadou Ahidjo or to the Republic of Cameroon. This is not true. I am working on an essay that will soon be published. It is titled: "The Untold Story of Cameroon's Reunification". Let me say that the issue of sovereignty was one of the burning issues that were discussed at the Yaoundé Tripartite Conference of the August 2 - 7 1961. at one time, Foncha proposed that the sovereignty should be transferred to Southern Cameroons while Ahidjo was held that the sovereignty should be given to him. It got to a point where Foncha asked the Attorney- General of Southern Cameroons to prepare a legal brief on that subject. The brief was prepared in which it was stated that sovereignty should be transferred to the body representing the two territories. That was rejected by Ahidjo. Ahidjo was able to do that because Southern Cameroons politicians were divided. Following the disagreement, it was agreed that an exchange of notes be done on September 27th 1961 to settle the issue. The exchange of notes in summary was thus: "The British Ambassador in London at the time, C.E. King wrote to Ahidjo saying that at mid-night on September 30, 1961, Southern Cameroons would become independent and Ahidjo replied, "Yes I acknowledge receipt of your Note. On the 1st of October 1961, Southern Cameroons will become independent."

A lot has been written about reunification to the extent that some historians have been accused of distortion of facts. What are some of the issues that you as a senior historian will like to address so as to help clarify public opinion?

The first is that sovereignty of the Southern Cameroons was not transferred to Ahidjo. Secondly, Foncha was given a draft constitution and it was meant for him to discuss it with his colleagues in Bamenda which he never did. Thirdly, there wasn't an over whelming support for reunification per se even within the KNDP. In fact, the KNDP was able to get votes because it played on the fears of Southern Cameroonians and also exploited the numerical superiority of the Grass Field population where most of the people voted KNDP. I will give you a simple example: in 1957, Fon Galega II wrote and told his people that Dr. E. M. L Endeley used him as a house boy in London by asking him to carry his bag. That story is false. It never took place but it spread like wild fire and if you do understand what it meant in those days, to humiliate a Fon then you can understand. This is an issue that was not true but worked against the KNC, KPP and in favour of KNDP. The KNDP fellows also said Dr. E.M. L Endeley never respected the Chiefs. This is not true. When the Prime Minister or President goes to an event, he is not the one to choose where to sit. To say that he sat on chairs reserved for chiefs, where and when? Finally, it should also be made clear that southern Cameroons had a raw deal because of the greedy approach of the KNDP politicians. The KNDP never wanted to share power in spite of the fact that they had agreed in New York in April 1961 to work together with the CPNC to ensure that reunification would take place smoothly. But immediately they came back, of course, everything fell apart.

It was alleged that the Bamenda Conference was intended to prepare the constitutional talks in Foumban. What happened at the conference that the delegates still went ill-prepared to Foumban?

It was not that it was not an allegation. The essence of the Bamenda Conference in June, 1961 was to prepare the Southern Cameroons delegation for the Foumban Constitutional Conference. It meant that the Southern Cameroons delegation would come with their own proposals. So the conference was meant for the Southern Cameroons delegation; CPNC, KNDP and the rest to come with their draft, with the understanding that in Foumban, they would present the draft and the Republic of Cameroon, led by Ahmadou Ahidjo would also present theirs and the two delegations would arrive at a consensus. The Bamenda Conference provided the unique opportunity for the Southern Cameroons delegation to say exactly what they wanted. They asked for a Senate and a House amongst others. They deliberately gave powers to the West Cameroon State and the East Cameroon State. The Federal government was not supposed to be strongly centralized. Unfortunately, while they were discussing all of these lofty ideas, Foncha did not tell them that what they were discussing was completely a sharp contrast to what Ahidjo had handed to him. The Federal draft constitution was a slightly modified constitution of the Republic of Cameroon. Foncha decided to hide this draft constitution from Southern Cameroonian politicians because he had already made a deal with Ahidjo to the effect that should the Federal constitution go through, he would be made Vice President. While they were discussing all of these, he sat quiet and allowed them to discuss and adopted the draft. So when they got to Foumban, they were surprised when they wanted to present their own draft for discussion. Ahmadou Ahidjo said no! I have already given a draft to Foncha and that is what, we are going to discuss now.

After the entire hullabaloo about re-unification, the Anglophones met in Buea in 1993 for the All Anglophone Conference, AAC1 and moved over to Bamenda for AAC2. From the discussions, was the Anglophone problem addressed?

The sad part of AAC, I belief very strongly, is that it was an opportunity that the Fonchas and the Munas wanted to polish up the mistakes they made in 1959, 1960, 1961.Surprisingly, in that same hall in Buea, there were politicians as well as civil servants and civil society members, who knew exactly what the situation was in 1959 and the 1960s. I am still surprised that when they were told that they had a poor deal with Ahidjo because they did not have lawyers, none of them raised a finger. [Whereas] there were seasoned lawyers like Egbe Tabi, Gorji Dinka and Engo whose services were not solicited. It was argued very strongly that the Southern Cameroons delegation should make use of the Southern Cameroons Bar Association. They never did. This became very important when they met in Yaoundé for the Yaoundé tripartite Conference, which comprised; the Southern Cameroons, the Republic of Cameroon and the UK. The principal goal of the Yaoundé Tripartite Conference, from 2-7 August 1961 was to put into legal form the Foumban constitutional proposals. So, how could they be putting proposals into a legal form, when the Southern Cameroons delegation did not have a lawyer?

After that came the birth of the Southern Cameroon National Council, SCNC launched by Barrister Ekontang Elad. What are they preaching?

I have great respect for almost all the members of the SCNC, as Cameroonian patriots. But my problem is that either deliberately or out of ignorance, some of them distort the history. And secondly, one is tempted to conclude that the SCNC is a collection of a mixed bag of politicians, and disgruntled civil servants, who somehow thought that they did not get that they wanted. It is interesting to ask why most of those who are strong in the SCNC are retired civil servants. I am not saying all, I say most. Why did they not complain when the going was good? I think this is a where I may be reluctant to go along with them. Some of their ideas are good. You may have a good idea, but the way you go about it, will spoil it. It is strange that for quite some time, they were able to convince some Anglophones that they went to the UN and the UN gave them a flag, promising that the UN would reopen discussions on the Southern Cameroons' problem. That was not true. You can go to the UN shop in New York and buy all what you find there. I have been there and bought all those things. The idea of saying that the UN will reopen Southern Cameroons' question is deceitful. Southern Cameroons achieved independence following the UN Resolution 1514 and UN resolution 1541 of December 1960 which clarified UN Article76B of the UN Charter.

The view of SCNC notwithstanding, Is there an Anglophone Problem in Cameroon?

You have to understand who is an Anglophone before you move along. In Cameroon there are three definitions of who an Anglophone is. One group holds that an Anglophone is somebody whose parents, both mother and father, are either from the present – day South west or Northwest Regions. Another school of thought holds that an Anglophone is someone, although born somewhere in former East Cameroon, has developed the Anglo-Saxon culture. Another group holds that some of the parents should be of either from the Northwest or Southwest Region. There is even a third group of those whose grandparents migrated from East Cameroon, even before German Cameroon was split into two. I am referring to the Doualas, the Bamilekes, the Ewondos, the Bassas, the Bamouns. They came as far back as 1916 to work in the German plantations. They got married here, they had their kids here. That is another group. This group feels and believes that they are Anglophones. It depends on how you look at it.

Let's narrow the definition to those from the Southwest and Northwest Regions of Cameroon, is there any bias on them?

If we look at the fact that they form a totality of one group and Cameroon was split in 1916 into two parts; the French took one part and the English the other. It was believed that this provisional partition was not supposed to be permanent. The League of Nations, the UN, administered their respective parts of former German Cameroon as equal parts. It was not said that the French part was superior to the English part. The fact that the French took a larger portion and therefore a greater population doesn't mean that the English part of former German Cameroon was inferior. When they united in 1961, it was believed that they were coming as equal partners. And coming as equal partners, meant they had had to be treated equally. Unfortunately, the realities on the ground did not promote that so called equality. That is where we have this problem. It has been reinforced and compounded by the lack of the political will on the part of some Anglophone and Francophone politicians to the extent that you find and hear some prominent Anglophone politicians say that there is no Anglophone Problem. If you look at it from the standpoint that the Northwest and Southwest Regions are just like the other region in Cameroon, then you will be tempted to say there is no Anglophone problem. We should bear in mind that the Northwest and Southwest Regions are not just like any other region in Cameroon. The other regions; North, Far North, Adamawa, West, Centre and South were never administered as a separate entity by the League of Nations or the UN. So, you cannot equate the Northwest and Southwest as being equal to the West or East Regions. They came in as a separate group, joining another separate group.

50 years after re-unification, what are we celebrating?

Cameroonians, both French and English are celebrating the 50th anniversary of the coming together of the two territories, which were provisionally partitioned in February 1916 and re-united on October1st, 1961. It is that which is to be celebrated, the 50thanniversary of reunification.

As a Historian, how will you react if someone says reunification has been a marriage of convenience?

It is not correct to say it was a marriage of convenience. If you say it was a marriage of convenience, it gives the false impression that either former British Southern Cameroon's or former French had no choice. So, to make things move smoothly they just accepted. It should be made clear that the British Southern Cameroons had a choice; either joining Nigeria or joining former French Cameroon. Before the UN decision in October 1959, Southern Cameroons had three options; independence as a separate state, independence by joining Nigeria or independence by joining French Cameroon. Finally, Southern Cameroon politicians decided on the two options: independence by joining Nigeria or independence by joining French Cameroon. So, one cannot say re- unification was a marriage of convenience. No it was not.

Interviewed by Kange Williams Wasaloko

Appendix I

Declassified British Secret Documents (Excerpts on Foncha and Southern Cameroons these made compelling reading)

Note: The numbering is basically intended for easy reference and convenience and has no bearing to the original arrangement.

1. "Our policy remains strongly against a separate Southern Cameroons state ...if Cameroons political parties combine to take action to establish an independent state, this would place us in a very embarrassing position. With support of moderate Afro-Asians and others, we have always argued that separate independence would produce an entirely unviable state." (Sir Andrew Cohen in a secret Brief of 11 October, 1960 to the secretary of state at the Foreign office).

2. "What would worry me is if a sequel to the Southern Cameroons' try for independence was that the Northern Cameroons went the same way. That would really, I think, upset our relationship with Nigeria as a whole and for which we must, at all costs, avoid. The Southern Cameroons and its inhabitants are undoubtedly expendable in relation to this" (Lord Perth, British Minister of state at the colonial office in a minute of 12thOctober 1960 to Sir John Marten of the same office.)

3. One question was always asked. This was "why have we not had a third choice?....Why can we not stand alone? Why should a poor man sell his independence to join with bigger and richer men? ..... There was widespread ignorance of what exactly the Republic of Cameroon was; particularly in the remote area". Mr. K. Lees, Plebiscite Supervisory Officer, Bamenda, in a Report on the first plebiscite Enlightenment Campaign dated 28th October, 1960, to the Deputy Plebiscite Administrator, Buea.)

4. "We are as anxious as the French that the Southern Cameroons should join the Cameroun Republic effectively on 1stOctober 1961 ... the French may be right that we should not give the Southern Cameroons authorities too much reign." (Mr. E.B. Booth by, in a confidential Memo of 4th July 1961, to the British Permanent Under-Secretary.)

5. In particular we must be very careful about independence and temporary sovereignty lest Northern Cameroons is likely influenced not to join Nigeria. This, I believe is the overriding consideration so we must be more or less tough with Foncha that joining Cameroun Republic does not allow sovereignty for a term (sic) of years and then a Federation,"

6 "Mr. Hammarskjold was afraid lest a difficult security situation should arise and was anxious to avoid any thing in the nature of a "contest between two independent states" (Nigeria and Cameroun Republic) he was wondering therefore whether it would not be a good thing for him to summon about March a "round table discussion" between Ahidjo, Foncha, Endeley and representatives of Nigeria. It might then be possible to work out a formula, which would avoid the necessity for any plebiscite. The formula could however be tested by a plebiscite if the United Nations so wanted. We criticized this idea rather sharply."

7. "First of all I take it that objections hitherto seen as establishment of a separate Southern Cameroons state remain as strong as ever." .... I am therefore assuming in what follows that our policy remains strongly against such a solution. If Southern Cameroons political parties did combine to take action envisaged in paragraph 2 of telegram under reference, this would place us in a very embarrassing position. With support of moderate Afro-Asians and others, we have always argued that separate independence would produce an entire unviable state. We have supported a unanimous resolution prescribing plebiscite which involves choice between Nigeria and Cameroon Republic."

8."There is an increasing movement in the Southern Cameroons in favour of a third choice in the plebiscite. Total independence with United Kingdom aid or continued United Kingdom Trusteeship. We have not supported this proposition."

9."I realize of course that the Cameroons question is of such a nature that whatever line we take, we must make enemies. This is recognized in paragraphs 10 and 11 of brief for Colonial Secretary enclosed in Greenhill's letter of 17th November. This being so instead of trying to please everyone and failing might it not be worth while trying to please one side viz Nigeria? If we try to be impartial, both Nigeria and Afro-Asian bloc will believe that our real aim is to keep Southern Cameroons as a colony and military base. By coming down firmly against the "third question" we will keep Nigeria as a friend and blunt any teeth of our enemies."

10. "When I wrote my letter 1519/166/60 of June 7 about the Southern Cameroons, I had not seen Halls letter1847/s.6/112 of May 25 to Kale about the third question. The terms of the last sentence of that letter cause me some concern. It seems to me that they amount to a statement that the United Nations, may well be prepared to reconsider its decision on the choices if a majority of the Southern Cameroons assembly wishes to do so. This seems to me likely to encourage Foncha, if he wants to ask for the questions to be changed, to come to the United Nations and do so. It is impossible to predict what reception he would in fact get there if he did any such thing. I think it quite likely that he would fail to secure the necessary two thirds majority but in the process, United Kingdom and the United Nations generally would be placed in an exceedingly difficult position, and need not elaborate on the possible complications for our relations with both Nigeria and the Cameroun. I must reiterate therefore what I said in my letter of June 7, that I think we ought now to use all our influence to prevent this third question idea being raised at the United Nations. This may mean saying publicly that we can see no likelihood of United Nations agreeing to changing its position on this matter."

11. I think it is important that we should not allow this matter to slide as may happen if we are not sufficiently firm with Foncha and perhaps also with Field about the "third question" matter movement. I believe a firm attitude on this now may save us a great deal of trouble later and think that H.M.G's position should be made abundantly clear to Foncha in an effort to scotch tendencies towards the third question."

12. "Can one argue the terms of the question; "Do you wish to attain independence by joining the Republic?" allow for an interim period during which the Southern Cameroons will virtually have its own separate and independent existence while, the terms of reunification with the Republic are being worked out? The words "by joining the Republic" taken literally appear to rule this out. But it may be that Foncha will seek to argue that if his solution having been argued to by Ahidjo is not opposed by the U.K, the U.N may be induced to wear it. Then would be the better grounds for this if Endeley were prepared also to agree to this interpretation of the question. We do not like this at all. But we kike the alternatives even less. To go for complete independence or to seek to insert a third choice in the plebiscite would create major difficulties."

13. But from the point of view of our relations with Nigerian delegation and of getting the most satisfactory result, it seems to us essential that, when we discuss tactics with them, they should be left in no doubt not only that we disagree with Foncha's interpretation of the second question but that whatever tactics we adopt, our objective in Assembly discussion will be to secure that question is not redefined as Foncha proposes, or changed, or supplemented by a third question. That does not mean of course that we would not accept Assembly decision to redefine the second question. It would mean that we should pursue tactics to prevent this."

14. "Our trusteeship over the Southern Cameroons is due to terminate on October 21(sic) upon the Southern Cameroons joining the Cameroon Republic." These last words are taken from the UN General Assembly resolution and are read by the Cameroon

Government as implying that sovereignty over the Southern Cameroon Republic on October I, and that a federal constitution should be worked out after wards. The Southern Cameroons view is that it has always been recognized that the association between the two territories would be a federal one and that it was on this basic that the people of the Southern Cameroons elected to join Cameroun. They think that, on October 1, they should transfer their sovereign powers to an organization representing the federation rather than to the Cameroun Government itself.

15. The problem is quite a complicated one, from a legal point of view and no doubt it is possible to hold different views about it. But from preliminary examination the Deputy legal Adviser thinks that the Southern Cameroons has quite a strong case. At the end of 1960 President Ahidjo of Cameroun and Prime Minister Foncha of the Southern Cameroons, subscribed to communiqués which emphasized that a federal state would be created and requested that "immediately after the plebiscite and in the event of the people voting for unification with the Cameroun Republic, a conference should be held attended by representatives of the Cameroun Republic and the Southern and Northern Cameroons ... which ...would have as its aim for the transfer of sovereign powers to an organization representing the future federation." We are as anxious as the French, that the Southern Cameroons should join the Cameroun Republic effectively on that date. But it could be argued that we have a responsibility to the Southern Cameroons to that before we relinquish our trusteeship there is a provision for carrying out our engagement to which the two leaders subscribed before the plebiscite.

16. We very much hope that Foncha and Ahidjo will eventually reach an agreement on the question and save us the, embarrassment of taking a definite line on it ourselves. We have no intention of making things difficult for the Cameroons Government, so long as they can carry the Southern Cameroons authorities with them. But it would be difficult for us to approach the matter in the same black and white way as the French and the Cameroonians. Apart from legal difficulties, there is the question of what sort of tactics are likely to have the best

effects on Foncha. We are afraid if he is pressed too hard, opposition from certain circles in the Southern Cameroons might prevent the federation from taking place at all. This is a matter of guess work and the French may be right that we should not give the Southern Cameroons authorities too much rein".

17. Independence for the Southern Cameroons would face us with considerable problems. They would expect financial support from us up to the tune of perhaps one million pounds a year and also that we should leave our troops in the country to defend them. If we met these requests it would be expensive for us financially and militarily and we would be accused of "neo- colonialism." If we refused the requests, Ghana, Guinea or the Russians would, no doubt, be only too pleased to help. In short this is not a course which we should at all encourage Foncha to adopt.

18. The department is strongly of the opinion that we should not encourage Foncha to go to the U.N. at all. In the telegram authorized by the African Committee, we have in fact said that "H.M.G. considers that this (ending of Trusteeship on 1stOctober.) must be regarded as final decision by the U.N. and will not be able to support any proposal for extension of U.K Trusteeship or any other arrangement other than that the Southern Cameroon joins the Cameroun Republic on October 1st. The French would be most strongly opposed to any approach to the U.N. M. Gorse repeated this to our Ambassador on Saturday and we should antagonize them if they thought that we were supporting it.

19. The Cameroon Government appear seriously worried about the possibility that Foncha or Jua may appeal to the United Nations for a ruling that reunification should come about on the terms set out in the joint communiqué and declarations issued on December 10th and used in the pre-plebiscite enlightenment campaign. At a farewell luncheon given for me by Mr. Okala, two members of the ministry of foreign Affairs, one of them in charge of U.N. Affairs pressed a member of my staff to indicate the line that would be taken by the United Kingdom delegation if the matter came up for debate in the United Nations. This impression has been confirmed by the American

Embassy who have told us that the Secretary General of the ministry of foreign Affairs agrees with the view expressed in paragraph 2 of your telegram to Paris No. 2472 saying that the Southern Cameroons would have quite a respectable legal case for opposing an unconditional transfer of sovereignty. In accordance with your telegram No. 197, we have been stressing that as far as we are concerned sovereignty will be transferred to the Republic on October 1 and that it is up to the Cameroonians to reach an agreement among themselves".

20. "Foncha is due to see Ahidjo again this week. The main purpose of the visit this time is to get Ahidjo's support for an economic mission to tour the capitals of Europe between now and October to get aid for various development projects after independence. I can't see Ahidjo being very enthusiastic about such a jaunt on the eve of unification but one never can tell and if he doesn't shoot it down, I suppose I shall be writing to you about it before long. I have naturally thrown what cold water I can on the idea at this stage."
" I agree generally with paragraphs 5 and 6 of your letter to the effect that if the southern Cameroons so chooses, sovereignty will have to be handed over to the United Kamerun when Trusteeship Agreement is terminated, and that this will involve the new federal Government having from the outset the necessary powers in foreign affairs. Otherwise Foncha might apply for U.N; membership? In other words Foncha will have to be told that the point in paragraph
6(4) of Milne's dispatch personal No.6 of October 18 is not possible. This is in accordance what I said in my telegram Brief 154 to John Martin. I of course, appreciate the need to drive Foncha back to no plebiscite and separate independence.

21."You asked me to discuss with Field the possibility of requiring the woman member to resign so that Foncha would no longer have a majority I find the situation here has changed. There now seems a distinct possibility that Government and Opposition may combine together to urge H.M.G to use their influence with the U.N to cut out plebiscite, and secure immediate independence for the Southern Cameroons on its own leaving the question of union with either of their neighbour over for settlement later. Field will be writing dispatch explaining background to this."

Reasons are:

• Realization by Endeley and co the vote is most likely for Nigeria.

• Doubts by all parties as to capacity of Republic to replace Nigeria Federal services and provide financial and economic support."

22. "I referred to the possibility of some positive and success full action to sway Cameroons to choose other than to re-join Nigeria."

23. "Most people in the Southern Cameroons do not want to be administered by the Republic; they do not want to have anything to do with French army or police (which they fear.) They do not want a French system of law, they do not the French language, they do not want to risk being pushed around by French officials and they do not want policy dictated to them by Republic politicians. Least of all they do not want the British connection to be completely severed or to be cut off from British help ... They fear being pushed into Nigeria as much as they fear being pushed into the Republic."

24. "Her majesty's Government position should be made abundantly clear to Foncha in an effort to scotch tendencies towards the third question. The policy of Her Majesty's Government is to discourage any tendency towards a "third question" very strongly".

25. "The Southern Cameroons is a frontier exposed....to communism– inspired influence which can become a danger of serious magnitude. This reason not to speak of its great potentialities makes the Southern Cameroons an area of serious concern for the United States. The present government in the Southern Cameroons made up of almost totally inexperienced and naïve ex-primary school teachers with good intentions is incapable of grappling with the tremendous problems which face it. Leadership in the Southern Cameroons is inexperienced, untrained and naïve .... The logical conclusion would

seem to be that the Southern Cameroons with its remoteness from Lagos, its complexities and its vulnerability, deserves increased attention on the part of the United States."

Appendix II

Outline Proposals for a Draft Constitution

(Now, at their third meeting holding in Yaoundé between the 10th and 14thOctober, 1960 resolved that the outline draft proposals for a constitution in the event of unification be adopted).

Reunification of Southern Cameroons with Republic Of Cameroun

RESOLUTION

Whereas by a resolution of the 14th Session of the United Nations a plebiscite will be held in February, 1961 to decide whether Northern and Southern British Cameroons will gain independence by joining the Federation of Nigeria or the Cameroun Republic;

And whereas in the event of the vote favouring the joining of the Cameroun Republic, the implementation of reunification on a Federal basis adaptable to conditions peculiar to all sections of Cameroon cannot be automatic but gradual;

And whereas the delegations of the Government of Cameroun Republic and the Government Party in the Southern Cameroons reaffirm their peoples' strong desire to reunite as a nation, and the same leaders having held two previous discussions to initiate the constitutional nature of the Union;

Now, at their third meeting holding in Yaoundé between the 10th and 14thOctober, 1960 resolved that the outline draft proposals for a constitution in the event of unification be adopted.

OUTLINE PROPOSALS FOR A DRAFT CONSTITUTION FOR A FEDERAL UNITED KAMEROUN REPUBLIC.

At the third meeting of the Representatives of the Government of the Republic of Cameroun and the Government Party in the Southern Cameroon to continue their discussions on a draft constitution for the Unification of the Republic of Cameroons and Northern and Southern British Cameroons the following declarations were made by Premier Foncha, President Ahidjo Head of the Cameroun Republic, and Mr. G. Assale Prime Minister of Cameroun Republic.

1. (a) That they intend to do everything possible (in their power) to implement the country-wide desire for Unification to which they have dedicated themselves.

(b) Reaffirmed that the territories shall be unified as a federal, sovereign state outside the British Common-wealth and the French Community. And agreed on the following draft Constitution:-

2. Federation shall compose of the Republic of Cameroun and the Southern Cameroons. The two parties hope that Northern British Cameroons will join the Federation whether as a separate State or as a unit with the Southern Cameroons.

3. The main features of the constitution of the Federation of Kamerun States:

The Federation of Kamerun states shall be democratic, and freedom of worship, of speech of the press and movement shall be guaranteed in so far as these rights are exercised within the law of the Federation. The Federation shall have a common motto, national anthem and a national flag. All indigenous people in all the states shall have Cameroonian Citizenship.

4. Minimum Federal Subjects:

Citizenship Civil rights National defence Foreign Affairs Higher Education

Immigration and Emigration

Federal Budget

Posts and Telegraphs.

The remaining subjects which are likely to fall within the power of the Federal Government will for the time being be legislated upon by the States.

5. The Legislature of the Federation:

There shall be two legislative Houses for the Federation: The National Assembly and the Senate.

The Federal Authority: The Supreme Authority of the Federal State shall be composed of – the Federal Executive with the President who is also Head of the Federation, and the National Assembly.

Constitutional Safe-Guards: Certain Federal Acts shall be enacted in such a way that the majority shall not impose on any state a measure which would be contrary to its interests. In case of a conflict between a Federal law and a law of one state the Federal law shall supersede- The states can legislate only on matters which do not fall within the Federal list.

A Federal Tribunal shall arbitrate on conflicts arising between the states.

Federal Judicial System: A Federal Court of Justice shall coordinate the two judicial systems and to create a Federal Supreme Court of Appeal.

State Organs: The governmental organs of the states as at present will have to continue until the Federal organ is created.

Signed by:
President Ahidjo: For and on behalf of the Government of the Cameroun Republic
Mr. Assale: Prime Minister, of Cameroun Republic
J.N. Foncha: Premier for and on behalf of the Government of the Southern Cameroons

Appendix III

Attendance at the Buea Tripartite Conference: 15-17 May 1961

Republic of Cameroon (08)

HE M, Ahmadou Ahidjo, President of the Republic HE M. Charles Okala, Minister of Foreign Affairs M, Krob (?)Secretary General to the Presidency

M, Betayene, Secretary General, Ministry Of Foreign Affairs

HE M, Oyono, Ambassador to Liberia

M. Missomba, Surete Nationale

M. Domissy, Conseiller Economique to the Presidency

Colonel Blanc, Conseiller Technique Government of Southern Cameroons: (05) Hon. J N Foncha, Premier

Hon. A N Jua, Minister of Social Services

Hon. S T Muna, Minister of Commerce and Industry Hon. P M Kemcha, Minister OF Natural Resources United Kingdom: (08)

Sir Roger Stevens, Foreign Office

Mr. C G Eastwood, Colonial Office

Mr. A G H Gardner-Brown, Colonial Office Mr. P M Johnston, Ambassador to Yaoundé Mr. P M I-Her H M Embassy, Yaoundé

Also present:
The Deputy Commissioner
The Attorney General The Financial Secretary
Total: 20

Appendix IV

The Constitution of the Federal Republic of Cameroon

Part I
The federal republic of Cameroon

1.

(1) With effect from the 1st October 1961, the federal republic of Cameroon shall be constituted from the territory of the Republic of Cameroon, hereafter to be styled East Cameroon, and the territory of the Southern Cameroon, formerly under British trusteeship, hereafter to be styled West Cameroon.

(2) The Federal Republic of Cameroon shall be democratic, secular and dedicated to social service.

It shall ensure the equality before law of all its citizens; and it proclaims its adherence to the fundamental freedoms written into the universal Declaration of Human Rights and the Charter of the United Nations.

(3) The official languages of the Federal Republic of Cameroon shall

be French and English.

(4) The motto shall be "Peace Work Fatherland"

(5) The flag shall be of three equal vertical stripes of green, red and yellow, charged with two gold stars on the green stripe. (6) The capital shall be Yaoundé

(7) The national anthem of the Federation shall be: O Cameroon, cradle of our forefathers."

(8) The seal of the Federal Republic of Cameroon shall be a circular on the reverse and in the centre the head of a girl in profile turned to the Dexter towards a coffee branch and flanked on the sinister by five cocoa pods, encircled beneath the upper edge by the words "Federal Republic of Cameroon" and above the lower edge by the national motto "Peace - Work - Fatherland".

(9) The subjects of the federal states shall be citizens of the Federal Republic with Cameroonian Nationality.

(1) National sovereignty shall be vested in the people of Cameroon who shall exercise it either through the members returned by it to the Federal Assembly or by way of referendum;

Nor may any section of the people or any individual arrogate to itself or to himself the exercise thereof.

(2) The Vote shall be equal and secret, and every citizen aged twenty- one years or over shall be entitled to it.

(3) The authorities responsible for the direction of the State shall hold their powers of the people by way of election by universal suffrage, direct or indirect.

(1) Political parties and groups may take part in elections;

And within the limits laid down by law and regulation their formation and their activities shall be free.

(2) Such parties shall be bound to respect the principles of democracy and of the national sovereignty.

4. Federal authority shall be exercised by

a) The President of the Federal Republic, and b) The Federal National Assembly.

Part II
Federal Jurisdiction

5. The following subjects shall be of Federal jurisdiction

(a) Nationality
(b) Status of Alien
(c) Rules governing the conflict of Laws
(d) National Defence
(e) Foreign Affairs
(f) Internal and External Security of the Federal State, and Immigration and Emigration.

(7) Planning, Guidance of the Economy, Statistical Services, Supervision and Regulation of Credit, Foreign Economic Relations, in particular Trade Agreements.

(8) Currency, the Federal Budget, Taxation and other Revenue to meet federal expenditure

(9) Higher Education and Scientific Research.

(10) Press and Broadcasting

(11) Foreign Technical and Financial Assistance

(12) Aviation and Meteorology, Mines and Geological Research, Geographical Survey

(13) Conditions of Service of Federal Civil Servants, Members of the Bench and Legal Officers

(14) Regulation as to procedure and otherwise of the Federal Court of Justice

(15) Border between the Federal States.

(16) Regulation of services dealing with the above subjects 6.

(1) The following subjects shall also be of federal jurisdiction.
a) Human Rights
b) Law of Persons and of Property
c) Law of Civil and Commercial Obligation and contracts.
d) Administration of Justice, including rules of Procedure in and Jurisdiction of all Courts (but not the Customary Courts of West Cameroon except for appeals from their decisions).
e) Criminal Law
f) Means of Transport of Federal concern (roads, railways, inland, waterways, sea and air ports
g) Prison Administration
h) Law of Public Property
i) Labour Law
j) Public Health
k) Secondary and Technical Education
l) Regulation of Territorial Administration
m) Weights and Measures

(2) The Federated States may continue to legislate on the subjects listed in this Article and to run the corresponding administrative services until the Federal National Assembly or the President of the Federal Republic in its or his field shall have determined to exercise the jurisdiction by this Article conferred.

(3) The executive or legislative authorities as the case may be of the Federated Starts shall cease to have jurisdiction over any such subject of which the Federal authorities shall have taken charge.

(1) Wherever under the last preceding Article the authorities of the Federated States shall have been temporarily enabled to deal with a federal subject, they may legislate on such subject only after consultation with the Federal Co-ordination Committee.

(2) The chairman of the said Committee shall be a Federal Minister, and the members shall be nominated by the President of the Federal Republic in view of their special knowledge.

Part III
The president of the Federal Republic

(1) The President of the Federal Republic of Cameroon, as head of the Federal State and head of the Federal Government, shall ensure respect for the Federal Constitution and integrity of the Federal, and shall be responsible for the conduct of the affairs of the Federal Republic.

(2) He shall be assisted in his task by the Vice President of the Federal Republic.

9.

(1) The President and the Vice President of the Federal Republic shall be elected together on the same list, both candidates on which may not come from the same Federated State, by universal suffrage and direct and secret ballot.

(2) Candidates for the offices of President and Vice President of the Federal Republic must be in possession of their civic and political rights, and have attained the age of thirty-five years by the date of the election, the nomination of candidate, the supervision of elections and the proclamation of the result being regulated by a federal law.

(3) The offices of President and Vice-President of the Republic may not be held together with any other office.

10.

(1) The President of the Federal Republic shall be elected for five years and may be re-elected.

(2) Election shall be by majority of votes cast, and shall be held not less than twenty or more than fifty days before the expiry of the term of the President in office.

(3) In the event of vacancy of the Presidency for whatever cause the powers of the President of the Federal Republic shall without more devolve upon the Vice President until election of a new President.

(4) Voting to elect a new President shall take place not less than twenty or more than fifty days after the vacancy.

(5) The President shall take oath in manner to be laid down by a Federal Law.

11.

(1) Ministers and Deputy Ministers shall be appointed by the President of the Federal Republic from each Federated state at his choice, to be responsible to him and liable to be dismissed by him.

(2) The office of Minister or Deputy Minister may not be held together with elective office in either Federated State, office as member of a body representing nationally and occupation or any public post or gainful activity.

12. The President of the Federal Republic shall

(1) Represent the Federal Republic in all public activity and be head of the armed forces.

(2) Accredit ambassadors and envoys extraordinary to foreign powers

(3) Receive letters of credence of ambassadors and envoys extraordinary from foreign power.

(4) Negotiate agreement and treaties

Provided that treaties dealing with sphere reserved by Article 24 to the Federal legislature shall be submitted before ratification for approval in the form of law by the Federal Assembly.

(5) Exercise the prerogative of clemency after consultation with the Federal Judicial Council.

(6) Confer the decorations of the Federal Republic

(7) Promulgate federal laws as provided by Article 31

(8) Be responsible for the enforcement of Federal Laws and also of such laws as may be passed by a federated State under the last paragraph of Article 6.

(9) Have the power to issue statutory rules and orders. (10) Appoint to federal civil and military posts

(11) Ensure the internal and external security of the federal republic. (12) Set up regulate and direct all administrative services necessary for the fulfilment of his task.

Provided that where he considers it advisable he may after consultation with the heads of the Government of the Federal States assume authority over such of their services as exercise federal jurisdiction as defined by Article 5 or 6 and may by Decree delegate any part of his functions to the Vice President of the Federal Republic

13. The Governments of the Federal States shall be bound before adopting any measure which may impinge upon the Federation as a whole, to consult the President of the Federal Republic who shall refer the matter to the Committee provided by Article 7 for its opinion.

14. The President of the Federal Republic shall refer to the Federal Court of Justice under Article 34 any federal law which he considers to be contrary to this Constitution, or any law passed by a Federated State which he considers to be in violation of the constitution or of a federal law.

15. The President of the Federal Republic may where circumstances require proclaim by Decree a State of Emergency, which will confer upon him such special powers as may be provided by federal law.

(2) In the event of gave peril threatening the nation's territorial integrity or its existence independence or institutions, the President of the Federal Republic may after consultation with the Prime Minister of the Federated States proclaim by Decree a State of Siege.

(3) He shall inform the nation by message of his decision

(4) The Federal National Assembly shall without more be in session throughout the state of siege.

Part IV
The Federal Legislature

16. The Federal National Assembly shall be renewed every five years, and shall be composed of members elected by universal suffrage and direct and secret ballot in each federated State in the proportion of one member to every eighty thousands of the population

17. Federal Laws shall be passed by simple majority of the members

18. Before promulgating any bill the President of the Federal Republic either State request a second reading, at which the law may not be passed unless the majority required by the last preceding Article shall include a majority of the votes of the members from each Federated State.

19. (1) The Federal National Assembly shall meet twice a year, the duration of each session being limited to thirty days and the opening date of each session being fixed by the Assembly's steering committee after consultation with the President of the Federal Republic

(2) In the course of one such session the Assembly shall approve the Federal Budget. Provided that in the event of the Budget not being approved before the end of the current financial year the President of the Federal Republic shall have power to act according to the old Budget at the rate of one twelfth for each month until the new budget is approved.

(3) On request of the President of the Federal Republic or of two thirds of its membership the Assembly shall be recalled to an extraordinary session, limited to fifteen days, to consider a specific programme of business.

20. The Federal National Assembly shall adopt its own standing orders, and at the opening of the first session of each year shall elect its Speaker and steering committee.

- The sittings of the Federal National Assembly shall be open to the public.
- Provided that in exceptional circumstances and on the request of the Federal Government or of a majority of its members strangers may be excluded.

21. Federal election shall be regulated by a federal law.

22. Parliamentary immunity, disqualification of candidates or of sitting members, and the allowances and privileges of members shall be governed by a federal law.

Part V
Relations between the federal executive and legislature

23. Bills may be introduced either by the President of the Federal Republic or by any member of the Federal Assembly

24. Or the subjects of federal jurisdiction under articles 5 and 6, the following shall be reserved to the legislature.
- (1) The fundamental rights and duties of the citizen, including. a) Protection of the liberty of the subject.
- b) Human rights
- c) Labour and trade union law
- d) Duties and obligations of the citizens in face of the necessities of national defence.

(2) The law of persons and property, including
- a) Nationality and personal status.
- b) Law of moveable and immoveable property
- c) Law of civil and commercial obligations

(3) The political, administrative and judicial system in respect of.
- a) Election to the Federal Assembly
- b) General regulation of national defence
- c) The definition of criminal offences not triable summarily and the authorization of penalties of any kind, criminal procedure, civil procedure, execution procure, amnesty, the creation of new classes of courts.

(4) The following matters of finance and public property
- a) Currency
- b) Federal budget.
- c) Imposition, assessment and rate of all federal dues and taxes
- d) Legislation on public property

(5) Long term commitments to economic and social policy, together with the general aims of such policy.

(6) The educational system appropriate committee before debate on the floor of the House.

26. The text laid before the House shall be that proposed by the President of the Federal Republic when the proposal comes from him and otherwise the text as a mended in committee but in either case amendment may be move in the course of the debate.

27. The President of the Federal Republic may at his request address the Assembly in person, and may send messages to it, but no such address or message may be debated in his presence.

28. Federal Ministers and Deputy Ministers shall have access to the Assembly and may take part in debate.

29.(1) The programme of business in the Assembly shall be appointed by the chairman's conference, composed of party leaders, chairmen of committees and members of the steering committee of the Federal National Assembly, together with a Federal Minister or Deputy Minister.

(2) The programme of business may not include bills beyond the jurisdiction of the Assembly as defined by Articles 5, 6, and 24, nor may any bill introduced by a member or any amendment be included which if passed would result in a burden on public funds or an increase in public charges without a corresponding reduction in other expenditure or the grant of equivalent new supply.

(3) Any doubt or dispute on the admissibility of a bill or amendment shall be referred for decision by the Speaker or by the President of the Federal Republic to the Federal Court of Justice.

(4) The programme of business shall give priority, and in the order decided by the Government, to bills introduced or accepted by it.

(5) Any business shall on request by the Government be treated as urgent.

30. (1) The President of the Federal Republic shall promulgate laws passed by the Federal National Assembly within fifteen days of their being forwarded to him, unless he receive a request for a second reading, and at the expiry of such period the Speaker may record his failure to promulgate and do so himself.

(2) Laws shall be published in both official languages of the Federal Republic.

Part VI
The Judiciary

31. (1) Justice shall be administered in the Federation in the name of the people of Cameroon by the competent Courts of each State.

(2) The President of the Federal Republic shall ensure the independence of the judiciary and shall appoint to the bench and to the legal service of the Federated States.

(3) He shall be assisted in his task by the Federal Judicial council, which shall give him its opinion on all proposed appointments to the bench and shall have over member of the bench the powers of a

Disciplinary Council; and which shall be regulated as to procedure and otherwise by a federal law.

32. (1) The Federal Court of Justice shall have jurisdiction

(a) to decide conflicts of jurisdiction between the highest Courts of the federated States;

(b) to give final judgment on such appeals as may be granted by federal law from the judgments of the superior Courts of the Federated Stated wherever the application, whether claiming federal law is in issue;

(c) to decide complaints against administrative acts of the federal authorities, whether claiming damages or on grounds of ultra vires;

(d) to decide disputes between the Federated States, or between either of them and the Federal Republic.

(2) The composition of, the taking of cognizance by and the procedure of the Federal Court of Justice shall be laid down by a federal law.

33. Where the Federal Court of Justice is called upon to give an opinion in the cases contemplated by Articles 14 or 29, its numbers shall be doubled by the addition of personalities nominated for one year by the President of the Federal Republic in view of their special knowledge or experience.

34. Warrants, orders and judgments of any Court of Justice in either Federated State shall be enforceable throughout the Federation.

PART VII IMPEACHMENT

35. (1) There shall be a Federal Court of Impeachment which shall be regulated as to composition and taking of cognizance and in other respects by a federal law.

(2) The Federal Court of Impeachment shall have jurisdiction, in respect of acts performed in the exercise of their offices, to try the President of the Federal Republic for high treason, and the vice President of the Republic and Federal Minister, Prime Ministers and Secretaries of State of the Federated States for conspiracy against the security of the State.

PART VIII
FEDERAL ECONOMIC AND SOCIAL COUNCIL

36. There shall be a Federal Economic and Social Council which shall be regulated as to powers and in other respects by a federal law.

PART IX
THE FEDERATED STATES

37. (1) Any subject not listed in Articles 5 and 6, and whose regulation is not specifically entrusted by this Constitution to a federal law shall be of exclusive jurisdiction of the Federated States, which within those limits, may adopt their own Constitution.

THE FEDERATED STATES

(3) The House of Chiefs of the Southern Cameroon shall be preserved

38. (1) The Prime Minister of each Federated State shall be nominated by the President of the Federal Republic and invested by a simple majority of the Legislative Assembly of that State.

(2) Secretaries of State shall be appointed to the Government by the dismissed.

39. (1) Legislative power shall be exercised in the Federated States by a Legislative Assembly, elected for five years by universal suffrage and direct and secret ballot in such manner as to ensure to each administrative unit representation in proportion to its population:

Provided that in West Cameroon the House of Chiefs may exercise specified legislative powers to by defined together with the manner of their exercise by a law of the Federated State in conformity with this Constitution

(3) There shall be one hundred representatives in the Legislative Assembly of East Cameroon and thirty seven representatives in the Legislative of West Cameroon

(4) The electoral system qualifications for candidates and disqualification of sitting members, parliamentary immunity and the allowances of representatives shall be regulated by a federal law

40. (1) Each Legislative Assembly shall adopt its own standing orders and shall annually elect its steering committee.

(2) It shall meet twice a year, the duration of each session being limited to thirty days, on dates to be fixed by the steering committee after consultation with the Prime Minister of the Federated State and so that the opening date of the budgetary session shall be later than the approval or the federal budget

(3) On request of the Prime Minister, of the President of the Federal Republic or of two thirds of its membership, it shall be recalled to an extraordinary session limited to fifteen days to consider a specific programme of business.

41. The sittings of each Legislative Assembly shall be open to the public provided that in exceptional circumstances on the request of the Government or of a majority of its members strangers may be excluded.

42. Bills may be introduced either by the Government of each Federated States or by any representative in the Legislative Assembly, and shall be passed by a simple majority.

43 (1) A motion of no confidence passed by a simple majority, or a vote of censure passed by an absolute majority shall oblige the Prime Minister to Place his resignation in the hands of the President of the Federal Republic or be declared to have forfeited his office; and the President may then dissolve the Legislative Assembly.

(2) President discord between the Government and the Legislative Assembly shall enable the President of the Federal Republic to dissolve the latter of his own accord or on the proposal of the Prime Minister.

(3) New elections shall be held within two months of dissolution

AMENDMENT OF THE CONSTITUTION – TRANSITION AND SPECIAL

(4) Until investiture of a new Prime Minister the outgoing Government shall be responsible for the dispatch of current business

44. (1) The Speaker of each Federated State shall within twenty- one days forward bills passed for the President of the Federal Republic, who shall within a further fifteen days promulgate them.

(2) Within the said period the President of the Federal Republic may either request a second reading by the Legislative Assembly or act under Article 14.

(3) At the expiry of such period the Speaker of the Legislative Assembly in question may record the President's failure to promulgate and do so himself.

45. In so far as they do not conflict with the provisions of this constitution the existing laws of the Federated States shall remain in force.

PART X
AMENDMENT OF THE CONSTITUTION

46. (1) No bill to amend the constitution may be introduced if it tend to impair the unity and integrity of the Federation.

(2) Bills to amend the Constitution may be introduced either by the President of the Federal Republic after consultation with the Prime Ministers of the Federated States, or by any member of the Federal Assembly

Provided that any bill introduced by a member of the Assembly shall bear the signature of at least one third of its membership

(2) The amendment may be passed by a simple majority of the membership of the Federal Assembly

Provided that such majority include a majority of the membership elected from each Federated States

(3) The President of the Federal Republic may request a second reading of a bill to amend the constitution as of any other federal bill and in like manner.

PART XI TRANSITION AND SPECIAL

47. The jurisdiction defined in Article 5 shall pass without more to the federal authorities as soon as they are set up

48. The Government of each Federated State shall forward to the Federal Government all papers and records necessary for the performance of its task, and shall place at the disposal of the Federal Government the service destined to exercise federal jurisdiction under the authority of the latter.

49. Notwithstanding anything in this Constitution, the President of the Federal Republic shall have power, within the six months beginning from the 1st October 1961, to legislate by way of Ordinance having the force of law for the setting up of constitution organs, and

pending their setting up for governmental procedure and the carrying on of the federal government.

TRANSTION AND SPECIAL

50. The President of the Republic of Cameroon shall be for the duration of his existing term the President of the Federal Republic

51. For the duration of the term of the first President of the Federal Republic; and the disqualifications prescribed by Article 9 for the Vice President of the Federal Republic shall during that period be inapplicable

52. With effect from the 1st October 1961 the National Assembly of the Republic of Cameroon and the House of Assembly of the Southern Cameroon shall become the first Legislative Assembly of East Cameroon and of West Cameroon respectively

53. Until the 1st April 1964 the Federal Assembly shall be composed of members elected from among themselves by the Legislative Assemblies of the Federated States according to the population of each State in the proportion of one member to every eighty thousands of the population

54 notwithstanding the provisions of Article 11 and until the election of a Federal Assembly under Article 16 the offices of Federal Minister and Deputy Minister may be held together with parliamentary office in either Federated State

55. Government of the Republic of Cameroon and the Government of the Southern Cameroons under British trusteeship respectively shall become on the 1st October 1961 the Governments of the two Federated States

56. Pending the setting up of the Federal Economic and Social Council, the Economic and Social Council of the Republic of Cameroon shall be preserved.

57. Pending approval of a definitive federal budget a provisional federal budget shall be drawn up an shall be financed by contributions from each Federated State to be settled after agreement with the Government of each such state

58. This Constitution shall replace the Constitution of the Republic approved on the 21st February 1960 by the people of Cameroon ; shall

come into force on the 1st October 1961; and shall be public in its new form in French and in English, the French text being authentic

59. (1) For the purposes of this Constitution the population of each Federated State shall on the Faith of statistics of the United Nations Organization, be taken to be as follows

East Cameroon 3 200,000
West Cameroon 800 000

2) Such figures may be amended by a federal law in the light of significant variation established by census

Yaoundé, the 1st September, 1961 Ahmadou Ahidjo

Select Bibliography

A. Books

Aka, Emmanuel A., The British Southern Cameroons, 1922-61: A Study in Colonialism and Underdevelopment, Madison, Platteville, Nkemnji Global Tech, 2002.

Ardener, Edwin, *Coastal Bantu of the Cameroons*, London International African Institute, 1956.

Bongfen, Chem.-Langhee, *The Paradoxes of Self Determination in the Cameroons under United Kingdom Administration*, Maryland, University Press of America Inc., 1975.

Bory, Paul (ed.), *As Told by Ahidjo, 1958-68*, Publishing Monaco, February1968.

Fonlon, Bernard, *A Simple Story Simply Told or The Rise of Dr. Pavel Verkovsky, First Archbishop of Bamenda.* Yaoundé, CEPER, 1983.

Johnson, Willard R, *The Cameroon Federation, Political Integration in a Fragmentary Society*, New Jersey, Princeton University Press, 1970.

Joseph, Richard (ed.), *Gaullist Africa: Cameroon under Ahmadou Ahidjo*, Fourth Dimension Publishers, 1976.

_____, *Radical Nationalism in Cameroun*, Oxford, Clarendon Press, 1977.

Kingah, David and Tazifor John, "Introducing Cameroon History," in Pius Soh, and Sylvester Ngemasong, *Crises within the KNDP,1959-66:An Historical Analysis*, University of Buea,2004.

Lantum, Daniel N (ed.), *Tribute to Dr. John Ngu Foncha, by Southwest and Northwest Elite*, eulogy by E T Egbe.

Lugard, Frederick, *The Dual Mandate in British Tropical Africa, 1926.*

Mbile, NN, *Cameroon Political Story: Memories of An Eye- Witness*, Presbyterian Printing Press, Limbe, 1999.

Milne, Malcolm , *No Telephone to Heaven - from Apex to Nadir – Colonial Service in Nigeria, Aden, the Cameroons and the Gold Coast-1961*, Meon Hill Press, 1999.

Ndi, Anthony, in *Africa Between The Wars*, London, Longmans, 1986.

Ngoh, V J, *Constitutional Developments in Southern Cameroons 1946-1961*, Buea CEPER, 1990.

Nyamndi, Ndifontah B, *The Bali Chamba of Cameroon: a Political History*, Paris, Editions Cape, 1988.

Soh, Pius, *Dr. John Ngu Foncha: The Cameroonian Statesman*, Centre For Social Sciences, n.d.

B. Articles

Abwa, Daniel "Contributions of Francophone Cameroonians to the Reunification of the Cameroons," in *Eden Xtra* No. 001 October2011.

Ardener, Edwin, "The Kamerun Idea" *West Africa*, June 7 and 14, 1958. Atem, George, "The Celebration of the 50th Anniversary of the Cameroon Unification" *Cameroons Panorama*, No. 657 of December 2012.

Awasom, Nicodemus Fru, "The Reunification Question in Cameroon History: Was The Bride An Enthusiastic or Reluctant One?" in, *Africa Today*, Volume 47. No. 2.

Herbert, Boh and Ntemfac Ofege, "The Story of Cameroon Calling: Prison Graduate", in Albert Mukong, *Prisoner without a Crime*, Calabar, Nigeria, 1991.

Kah, Henry Kam, "The Anglophone Problem in Cameroon: The Northwest/Southwest Dichotomy from 1961-1996," in the *Cameroon Journal on Democracy and Human Rights, CJDHR*, Vol.6 No. 1 – June 2012.

LeVine, Victor T., "Political Integration and the United Republic Of Cameroon", in David R. Smock and Kwamena Bentsi – Enchill, *The Search For National Integration in Africa*, London, Free Press, Collier Macmillan Publishers, 1976.

--------, Victor T., "Ahmadou Ahidjo Revisited," in Jean Germain-Gros (ed.), *Cameroon Politics and Society in Critical Perspectives*, Oxford, University of America, 2003.

"Locally and Western Trained Intellectuals Facing Decolonisation in Cameroon, 1946-1961," in *Annals of The Faculty of Arts, Letters and*

Social Sciences, The University of Ngaoundere, Editions CLE, Yaoundé, 2011.

Ngwane, George, "The Anglophone File (Or, The Story of the Gulf Between the 'Coastal' and 'Graffi' in Anglophone Cameroon)", *The Messenger*, 1994.

Ngwane, George, "There Was West Cameroon", in *Cameroon Panorama*, No. 655 of October 2012.

Sakwe, Kevin and Javlon, Frankline, "The influence of Machiavelli on Contemporary African Politics," in *Searchlight Magazine* published by the St. Thomas Aquinas Major Seminary, Bambui, No. 101, June2011.

C. Reports

CO554/2258 XC 4122 of 15 June 1961. CO554/2252 Xc4478 of 2 May 1961.

CO554/2258 XC 3911 Burr to Emmanuel of 11 July 1961. CO554/2249 XC 3406 of 19 July 1960.

PRO CO554/2252 XC 6478 of 2 May 1961. PRO CO 554/2260 XC of 11 August 1961.

CO554/2258 XC 3911 Burr to Emmanuel of 11 July 1961. CO554/2249 XC 3406 of 19 July 1960.

Conference CO554/2188 XC 3406.

Johnston, Patrick, Report on Tripartite Conference in Buea, PRO, Ref.CO554/ XC 3406 Yaoundé, July 191960.

CO554/2249 XC 3406 of 19 July1960.

PRO No. CO554/2249 XC 3406, "Proposals for the Federal Constitution," of July 19 1960.

PRO CO554/2188 XC 3406 of 26 June 1961. PRO CO554/2247 XC 3343 of 1 July 1961.

PRO CO5542247/2247 XC 3343 Milne to Geoffrey of 1 July 1962.

PRO COS54/2247XC3343 JO Field to Christopher Eastwood of 9 June1961. PRO CO5S4/2188 XC CPC61 (19), paras, 11-14 of June 1961.

PRO CO554/2252 XC 6478 of 2 May 1961

PRO CO 554/2260 XC of 11 August 1961

PRO CO 553/2265 XC C34O6 of 21 July 1961.

PRO COS54/2412 XC 3343: John Marten of 7 October 1960. PRO COS54/2412 XC3343 of 12 October 1960.

Patrick Johnston to Commissioner of CO554/2249 XC 3406 of 19 July 1960.

Report by Her Majesty's Government in UK to the General Assembly of the UN for 1959, London, 1960.

D. Dissertations

Fonsah, Nug Eliana, "The Ngyenmbo – Bali Nyonga Land Conflict: 1905-2003," MA Dissertation in History, University of Yaoundé I, 2005.

Ngemasong, Sylvester, "Crises within the KNDP, 1959-66: An Historical Analysis," MA Dissertation, University of Buea, 2004.

E. Archival Material

NAB Vb(6 1962)2 *Press Release* No.1498, "Southern Cameroons discussed in British Parliament,"1962.

NAB *Press Release* No. 485, "Plebiscite Questions, Premier and Opposition Leader Disagree at UN," 29/09/59.

NAB *Press Release* No. 1498 "Southern Cameroons Discussed In House of Commons."

NABRef. 0.36/31/35 the "Muanë Ngoe" of Bakossi, under Ajebe Sone Francis, the Bakweri "Molongo" under Motomby Woleta and Dr.EML Endeley together with the Balundu "Monkanya" led by NN Mbile.

NAB, Southern Cameroons Information Service Press Release no. 911 of 19July, 1960.

NAB Press release no 485 of 29/09/59 "Plebiscite Questions- Premier and Opposition Leader Disagree at UN,"

NAB V6 (b1962)4 Press Release no.485 of 29/09/59; "Premier and Opposition Leader Disagree at UN."

NAB Ref. O.36/31/35 "Bakossi Secret Society" of 25August 1962.

Ebolowa Congress of UC, 4-8 July 1962. NAB *Press Release* no.1465.

NAB Press Release no.1462 Southern Cameroons. NAB *Press Release* no.1467 of 20 July 1961.

NAB *Press Release* no. 1467: All Party Conference Opens on 20 July1961.
NAB *Press Release* no 1468 of 24 July 1961. NAB Press Release no. 906 of 16 July 1960.

F. Newspapers

Cameroon Champion of 4 July 1961. Cameroon Star vol. 1 Monday 30 May 1966. Cameroon Times, Monday, 28 April 1962.
Cameroon Panorama
Eden Xtra Magazine, 'Setting the Record Straight,' No. 001 October 2011.
Frontier Telegraph, Vol. II no. 0007 of 16 January 2008.
Les Cahiers de Mutations, Vol. 018 of January 2004.
Kimeng Hilton Ndukong, "Northern Cameroons in *Cameroon," TribuneHors Serie,* Octobre 2011.
Summit Magazine no. 16, "Fifty Years after Reunification: Southern Cameroons Had a Raw Deal Because of the Greed of KNDP Politicians".
The Post Newsmagazine, October 2007.
The Post Newspaper No, 01266of Friday , 22 July 2011

G. Miscellaneous

Danto, Arthur C Humanism, Microsoft @ student 2009, (DVD), WA: Microsoft Cooperation 2008.
Kamerun National Democratic Party (KNDP) Tenth Annual Convention Working Papers, Kumba, November 1964.
KNDP, 10th Annual Convention, Kumba, November 1964. Presidential Decree no. 52 of 7 May, 1969.

The Anglophone File (or, the story of the gulf between the "coastal "and "graffi" in Anglophone Cameroon), Serialised in *the Messenger* and published in 1994.
The All Anglophone Conference, The Bamenda Declaration April 29th - May1st.1994.

Resolution 1350(XIII), para 6 of the General Assembly on the Future of Northern Cameroons.

Sendze, My Reflections on Mr. John Ngu Foncha in Cameroon Politics, 7

INDEX

A

Abdoh, Djalal Dr. 84, 94
Absolute truth, 14
Abwa, Daniel, 316
Achirimbi II Fon, 59, 86, 87
Ade, Nicholas Ngwa, 107
African American Institute (AAI), 77
Afro-Asian bloc, 91, 206, 232, 241, 243, 273, 285
Agreed "Federal body"5
Ahidjo, 'Bad faith' ix, Totalitarian Adventurer, vii, Regime, 3, Ahidjo President, Southern Cameroons, viii, Factor, 9, 23; "Bloody Dictator"24, 54; and John Ngu Foncha, 30,- Factor
54, 38, 55, Royal Presidency of
Alhadjj Ahmadou Ahidjo, 44
Opens the Conference, 127
Magnanimity 30, 142, 144; Foncha and Assale Co-Signed Constitutions, 250;
Ajebe Sone FN, 89, 242, 318
Alan Lennox Boyd, 85
All Anglophone Conference, 76, 157, 270, 278, 319
Andre- Marie Mbida, 56
Anglophone Cameroon, 7, 16, 42, 169, 317, 319; Delegates 16, 35, 85, 86, 89, 108, 115, 117, 120, 123-125, 130, 132-134, 136-139, 141, 148, 152, 154, 159, 161-165, 169
Cameroonians, 30; Problem 38, Delegates Opportunely Undeceived! 163.
Anglo-Saxon Minority, "Needs Protection" 10
Anglo-Southern Cameroons, 224, talks 224
Asonganyi of Fontem, 59
Assale, Charles, 41, 130, 152, 154, 177
Atem, George, 63
Auberge de Foumban, 162
Azikiwe, Nnamdi, NCNC of, 61, 105, 219

B

Bamenda All Party Conference 29, 40, 88, 112- 115, 117, 118, 120, 121, 124, 134, 137, 138, 145, 172, 176, 177, 179-181, 197, 198, 213-215, 263; and Foumban Conferences; 63; xxvi-xxviii June 1961; 112, 113, 115, 176, 182, 183, 186, 187, 193, 201, 246, 275, 277, 317; Unanimous 120

Endorsement at Bamenda, 148, 172, 194, 276, 278;

Bag, 174, 180; and the Secret Deals 234; Secret Deals and the "Bamenda Bag": Origins, 103, 106;

Benevolent Neutrality Bloc, 31; Benevolent Neutrality, 107

Best Decision Everything Being Equal, 158

Solution Obstructed by Britain, 52

Beyond the "Glamour and Glitter of Foumban, 199

Biya, President Paul, 3, 91

Brash Unsubstantiated Accusations, 257

Britain and France, 15

British Blatant Disloyalty to the Foncha Government, 8

British, Man O' War Ship 4; Northern Cameroons 15; Southern Cameroons 15; tutelage 2, 254; intrigues, 3; Colonial Secretary, 85

Support: Remarkable Suggestive Trends 103; Masters, 103

Brooks, Angela Miss, 242

Buea, Tripartite conferenc, 29, 34, 40, 64, 144-146, 171, 172, 176, 179, 182-185, 188, 189, 191, 192, 194, 197, 209, 243, 256, 297, 317

'Secret Deal' So-Called: Sources, 204;

Lamentable Failure 194;

Embarrassing Disagreements, 186;

Bilingual Grammar School (BGS) 225;

Proceedings and Impact 182; Mountain Hotel, 189, 256;

"Uncouth Republic of Cameroun forces", 4

C

Cameroon Anglophone Movement (CAM), 6, 116, 157;

West of the Mungo or Anglophone, 62; Times, 39, 63, 171, 172, 319;

United Congress (CUC), 242
Cameroon, Federal, Republic of, 27, 47, 54,61, 165, 290;
National Assembly, 116, 145, 183, 270, 295, 300, 301, 304, 305, 307, 312; Assembly, 169
Cameroonisation, 76-78
Cannibals and "Frenchy people", 18
Capitalist Western Europe, 1; West, 112
Case of Sheer 'Bad Faith', 37
Champion Newspaper, 124, 134, 162
Chilling revelations of British deeds and misdeeds, 2, 4
Choice of Foumban: A Contrary View, 160
Co-Conspirators, Search for, 244
Cold War politics, 241
Collusion between British and Cameroun Republic, 214
Commandeur de l'ordre de la valeur" 156
Communist Eastern Europe, 34; East, 91
Concerted Determination to Teach Foncha a Lesson, 175
Conclusion Malcolm Milne Acquits Himself Honorably 254
Consistent Voting Patterns in favour of Secession 101
Conspiracy, theories 13, 110, 134, 135, 171, 172, 175, 198, 201, 210, 217, 254, 262; and treachery, 3;
Constitutional Marathon Bamenda to Foumban, 115
Contemporary Observations on Foumban Accord, 143
Counting the Votes, 93, 99
CPNC, 9, 29, 32, 39, 41, 50, 51, 53, 63, 70, 83, 84, 92, 97-99, 110, 112, 118, 120, 123-125, 133-135, 143, 149, 162, 171, 175, 179, 213, 217, 220, 242, 244, 268, 273, 274, 276, 277
Critical Omissions(Two) and a Flawed Target, 40

D

Dag Hammarskjöld, 108, 187
Deadly Traps Withdrawal of British Troops 246.
Derogatory Statements about the Plebiscite 97
Devolution in Point of Law 145
DingaA. 297

Distinct Southern Cameroons Political Culture 57
Distinction of the Summit Magazine interview 25
Double British Standards 3, 208
Draft Constitution for the "Federal Republic of Cameroon, 294
Dual Mandate, 60, 61, 71, 315

E

Eastwood, Christopher, 188, 200, 201, 317
Ebubu Massacre, 185, 215, 246
Ecole Supérieure, 56
Economic non-viability, 242
Eden Xtra Magazine No. 001 of October 2001, 18, 319
Egbe Tabi Emmanuel, 151;
Reflections on Foumban, 151
Endeley, Dr. EML, and Kale, PM. Jua, AN,Muna, ST 43,47, 55, 78, 84, 107;
Refrained from Attending Bamenda All Party Conference 118;
Reconciliation 33, 133, 192,
"Endeley Exclusions" 134.
Endeley, Gladys Silo Ramatou,134;
Fueling Conspiracy Theories: Equality Clause: Reunification a Political Decision, 169
Every generation rewrites its own history, 10
Evolved Political Culture; 39, 49

F

Father Samson Foundation for Underprivileged Children (FASAF), 221
FCWU, KUNC, 30
Field, Johnson O, Commissioner, 13, 15, 238; and
Malcolm Milne 13-15, 73, 157, 175, 180, 186, 198, 213, 217, 228, 229, 235, 240, 251, 258.
First School Leaving Certificate (FSLC), 51, 54, 217

Foncha, JN, and Ahidjo, A. xvi; Alleged Secret Deals, xvi ; Indictments: Opposed Southern Cameroons Independence, 257; Inescapable traps, xvi, 2, 9; Administration, 8, 26, 32,

37, 43, 69, 70, 84, 102, 145; Welcome to Premier Foncha, 125

Speaks for Southern Cameroons Delegation 131;

Star of Foumban, Awards and Decorations, 152

Civil and Municipal Decorations 154; "Alleged" Secret Deals and Hidden Constitution; 197;

"Star of Foumban", 180; Waterloo: Withdrawal of British Defence 221; Suspected of Communist Sympathies; 190

Sketch Biography 217; as observed in His Nkwen Home Town, 223; Tribalistic, 224; Traps, 3, 41, 169, 184, 212, 246; Launching into Political Life, 218

Fonlon, Bernard Nsokika Prof, 222;

Facilitates Serene Procedure, 142

Forging A Unique Identity, 33

Former German Kamerun colony, 3

Foumban Conference in Complete Agreement, 141; 16-21 July 1961; 115, 121, 158; Reception at, 12, Opening the Conference: President Ahidjo, 181; Constitutional Conference 3, 157, 173, 177, 183, 195;

Beyond the Foumban Constitutional Conference, 16, 20, 29, 32, 33, 35, 37, 40, 85, 111, 115, 118, 120, 123-125, 134; (Sous Prefect) of, 3

Francophone brothers, and Protagonists, 38

Franco-Prussian War, 203

Fraser, Hugh, 188

French Cameroon, 294

Functional History, 262

G

Gbagbo, Laurent, 52, 71

German Kamerun, by Article 76(b); 36

Golden Age, 49, 51, 70, 73, 77, 79, 82, 209, 238; of Southern – West Cameroon, 39, 49, 79

Golden Jubilee, 1, 2, 25; Celebrations Whet Appetites, 23

Gorji Dinka, xxiii, 87, 278
Governor of Nigeria, 175

H

High Calibre Political Leaders, 61
Hippocratic Oath, 14
Historian's Craft, Brief Note on Historiography, 259
Historical Panorama, 2, 26, 259, 260
Historiography, 1
History Should be Original, Logical, Chronological, 321
Hosni Mubarak, 89

I

Idi Amin Dada, 71
Independence (and Reunification)of Southern Cameroons, 1, 13; for Southern Cameroons 19, 36, 90, 107, 110, 120, 145, 188, 199-209, 212;

Foncha's Passion 201; Excluded as Plebiscite Option 242.

Integration with Nigeria, 3, 4, 10, 32, 55, 89, 97, 99-101, 104, 107, 112, 176, 197, 200, 202, 204, 234

Inverted kindness and hospitality, 7
Invisible Hand of British Colonial Administration, 100
Levels of History, 260
LeVine,Victor T., 5, 97, 316
Loi Cadre, 34
London Constitutional Conferences, 101

J

Johnson, Willard, 117, 159, 172
'Jocular' Not Bloody Fights, 70
Jua, Augustine Ngom, 55, 220, 273.

K

K" [Kamerun]: KNDP, KNC, KPP, OK, KUP, xxv
Kale, Paul M, 55, 64, 219
Kamerun idea, 5, 23, 227, 316
Kemncha, Peter M, 64, 112, 123, 131, 204
King, CE, 13, 189, 328, 197
Kirk Green, Anthony, 229-231, 234, 255

KNC/KPP alliance 57, 58, 62, 74, 89, 102, 111, 112, 150, 207, 220, 244, 245, 248, 251; turncoat politics 103; Spree of Resignations from Endeley's KNC, 105; platform 129; Support for KNC/KPP Alliance, 244.

KNDP, 23, lacked sufficient qualified personnel, 49, 269, leadership 12, 17, 19, 20, 24, 25, 28, 29, 40, 41, 48, 50, 51-53, 55, 57, 61, 63, 68, 73-75, 101, 103, 105, 112, 120, 130, 134, 136, 156, 158, 174, 175, 197, 211, 219, 225, 233, 242, 244, 256, 290; Opposition 58, 203; Ideology: "Independence before Reunification" 265; and CPNC, OK Party 213; UC Joint Committee 174; and KNC/KPP alliance 248;

Koutaba Military Airport, Foumban Town, 123, 125
KUNC, 30, 35, 36, 64
Kwame, President Nkrumah, 191

L

Landscape, 9
Leader of Government Business (LGB), 34, 103, 105, 200
Long live the Premier of Southern Cameroons, 125
Long pens, 54
Lugard, Lord, 71
Lumumba, Patrice, 191, 192

M

Macleod, Iain, 17, 183, 189, 244
Macmillan, Harold, 231, 232;

"Winds of Change Address" 231

Macpherson Constitution, 61

Malcolm Milne in his own words 204, 251; denunciation of the entire British Colonial Policy, 13; Revelations Revolutionize Cameroon History 15;

Pays Glowing Tribute to Foncha Cabinet, 74; and CE King 197; and Prof. Ngoh, 277-246, 248, 249, 250; Seal Set to Conspiracy Theories by 253; 255, 274; 280;

Nadir: Malcolm Milne "Awful Disclosures" 227; Dread of Destitution, 230, and Field Innately Idiosyncratic 233;

Milne Pays Generous Tributes to Civil Servants 235;

Takes Seriously Ill, 252; Sets Final Seal on Conspiracy Theories, 254; Fox among the chickens, 242; and Foncha: "No Love Lost" in

Mamfe Plebiscite Conference 10-11 August 1959, 106, 260, 272, 305; All Party Conference, 85, 202, 212, 243.

Mandela, Nelson, 85, 88, 212, 243

Mandla Nkomfe, 29, 33, 40, 88, 112, 113, 115, 117, 118, 120, 121, 124, 134, 137, 138, 140, 145, 165, 172, 176, 177, 179, 180, 181, 197, 198, 213-215, 263, 319

Maqizzards, 232; Rebels, Nationalists, or Freedom Fighters, 53.

Marten, John, 32

Masquerade, 65

Mau mau, 210, 283, 318

Mazrui, Ali , 19, 162

Mbile, Nerius N, 19, 249, 257; Favours Centralisation , 53

McCarthy, 64, 121, 123, 149, 219

Mengueme, Jean-Marcel, 149

Methodology: the nature of history, 91, 92, 216

Missionaries, 159

Mobutu Sassa Seko Wazabanga, 90

Mokam, David, 7, 18, 49, 72

Moor Plantation, Ibadan, 71

Moumie, Felix Roland, 53

Muambo, Wem, 56

Mukong Albert Womah, 56, 67, 68, 91, 159, 191

and George Mbarga to represent OK, 124, 134;

Critical of Britain and the UN, 124; Pertinent View, 143,

Muna, Solomon T, 55, 64

N

Nangah, Daniel A, 221-223
National Union of Kamerun Students (NUKS), 86
Native Authorities, (NA), 60
Nature, Reason and shape of Reaction, 12
Ndi, Ni John Fru, 11
Ndu Tea Estate and Santa Coffee Estate, 242
Ngoh, Victor Julius Dr., Professor of History and Deputy Vice Chancellor 1, 12, 26, 265-267
Nigeria, Federal Republic of, 9
Nigerian Federal Elections, 4
Ninyem Kamdem, 193
Njoya Emmanuel, 3, 7, 73, 225 193
Nkondengui, 163
North/South West Anglophone Cameroonians, 42
Northern Cameroons Democratic Party (NKDP), 4
Northern Elements Progressive Union (NEPU), 4
Northern People's Congress (NPC), 4
Ntumazah Ndeh, 128 142; Opponent and Critic, 118
Nyo'Wakai, Justice ,xxiii, 162

O

OK party, 5, 68, 100, 124, 133, 143, 148, 206, 213
Okala, Charles, 187, 297
One Kamerun (OK), 5, 68, 118, 120, 123, 124, 130, 143, 148
One-party rule, xxiv
Open collusion, 191, 246, between British and Republic of Cameroon, 191, 246, Support for KNC/KPP alliance; 244
Opportunism, 30, 73, 112, 185
Ordinance No. 062/OF/18 of 19 March 1962,xxiii
Origins of the Plebiscite, 84

Other Awards, Tributes and Decorations, 156
Otto von Bismarck, Prussian Chancellor 203

P

Padmore, George, 240, 241
Paradox, 8, 9, 20, 87, 112
Peaceful, Harmonious Transfer of Power in 1959, 58
Penultimate Conclusion, 157
Pertinent, Sober Reflections with Hindsight, 147
Phillipson, Sydney, Appointment: Seals Fate of Southern Cameroons, 301; Constitutional and Economic, 243.
Plebiscite Litmus Test of Political Maturity, 81; in Context: Statistical Analysis, 99; Questions: Reasons and Genesis, 95; Basic Irreconcilable Positions, 89
Political Leaders: Past, Present and Global, 71
Professional Teacher, 218
Pseudo-History, 262, 263
Public Records Office", 250

Q

Qaddaffi, Muammar, 71, 72
Qualifications and Political Leadership, 52, 57
Quan, ED, 75, 236
Quasi Federal status, Southern Cameroons, 33, 103

R

Ramified Conclusion, 168; Wrapping Up, 253
Remorse and Regret, 237
Republic of Cameroon using law N° 84-1 of February, 26, 1, 294
Response: Inherent Limitations, 27
Reunification Account 23; Gamble, 29, 33, 37, 263, 265;

Fifty years After 40; Certainly, Not a "Gamble"44, Richard Joseph, 38, 46, 68, 69, 186, 226

Robertson, James, 73, 85, 108, 204, 235, 241, 247, 248;

Role of Kamerun Students Unions, 87

S

Sacred Heart School, 217
Saoudou Daoudou, 186
Sendze, Omer BB, 75, 203, 216
Sengat Kuo, François, 117
Setting Basic Records Straight, 23;
Significance, 11, 31, 32, 76, 121, 133, 134, 149, 150, 153-156, 202
Skewed Circumstantial Evidence, 235
Smear Campaigns and Conspiracy Theories, 171
Smith, BG, 230, 247
Socio-Cultural Spiritual Life: House Arrest, Trapped, 281
Sous Prefect, 159, 161, 326
Southern Cameroons, xx; Political leadership 05; Delegates 6, 34, 9; Fifty Years after Independence 10; 18 Years after Reunification 19; Refused Independence, 8; Political Maturity 23, 34, 35, 49, 51, 81, 99, 145, Recruitment Committee 77; Intellectuals, 1, 53-57, 77, 78, 316; House of Assembly (SCHA), 106, 107;

Special UNTC Status and Privileges, 35
St. Anthony's Primary School, 218
St. Charles' College, 217
St. Francis' Teachers' Training College, Fiango, Kumba, 55
St. John the Baptist Mission Station Church, 221
St. Joseph's College, Sasse 55, 216; Mission 279
St. Michael's Roman Catholic School, 217
St. Peter's Teachers Training College, Bambui, 55
Sultan Ibrahim Njoya, 125, 154
Sultan Njoya Seidou Njimouluh 148, 179,177
Summit Magazine interview xx- xxiii, xxvii, 1, 2, 9, 13, 19, 23-25, 29, 41, 48, 57, 75, 84, 117, 135, 157, 172, 199, 263

T

Tabi Egbe Emmanuel, Reflections on Foumban, 151
Tataw Obenson, 47, 135
Taylor, Charles, 71
Telemachus, xix
Third, Option, 82, 87, 89, 91, 105, 109, 120; Question, 138
Thoroughness and Harmony, 174, 228, 239, 255, 256
Tiko International Airport, 318
Time, Scape Magazine, 137; Extended for Anglophone Delegates, 125;
Together we shall build Cameroon, 148
Top secret, 247
Touré, Shanda, 11
Towards Provoking Civil Strife, 212
Traditional Rulers, Sagacity of, 59
Tragic story of "woes", 7
Traumatizing experience, 9, 13
Tripartite Conference, 29, 34, 35, 40, 44, 63, 64, 138, 144-146, 171, 172, 176, 179, 182-185, 188, 189, 191
Trust Territory of Southern Cameroons?" 9; of British Southern Cameroons 15
Truth and Justice to Our People, 173
Tumi, Christian Cardinal, 10, 11

U

Um Nyobe, Reuben, 56, 66-68
UNESCO, 59
Union Camerounaise (UC), 136
Unions des Populations du Cameroun (UPC), 5
Unique Southern Cameroons Civil Service, 75
United Nation (UN), Trust Territories torn apart 20; Southern Cameroons 51,122; Debate: "A Catch 22" Scenario 112; Visiting Mission, 30, 36, 100; General Assembly; 36, 38, 82, 95, 202, 211, 242,

286, 318; Trust Territories, 8, 15; Visiting Mission (UNVM) 5; Trusteeship Council 4, 36, 89, 96, 144, 198, 208, 211
Unity Group, 174
UNO, 63, 246, 247
Unpredictability of Mbile, 237
Unveiling Inescapable Traps, xx

V

"Veranda Boys", 80, 310; and Ahidjo: Accomplices over Southern Cameroons, 256.
Victim of international conspiracy by default, 9, 36; Predators and Oppressors 23, 41
Victoria Harbour, 4
Visionary Leaders: simple, austere, honest and realistic, 73
Voluntary Agencies, 55

W

West Cameroon's Anglo-Saxon Westminster Parliamentary System, xxv
Westminster Parliamentary Democratic Principles and Procedure, 35
Woleta, Motomby Ndembo, 55, 56, 162

X

X-ray, 23

Y

Yaoundé Tripartite Conference, 35, 40, 138, 269, 275, 278

Post script: the bibliography and indices are far from exhaustive.

www.ingramcontent.com/pod-product-compliance
Lightning Source LLC
Chambersburg PA
CBHW032149010526
44111CB00035B/1253